Previous Books by Rabbi Berel Wein:

TRIUMPH OF SURVIVAL
The Story of the Jews in the Modern Era 1648–2000

HERALDS OF DESTINY
The Story of the Jews in the Medieval Era 750–1648

ECHOES OF GLORY
The Story of the Jews in the Classical Era 350 BCE–750 CE

FAITH AND FATE
The Story of the Jews in the Twentieth Century

PESACH HAGADAH
Notes and Comments on the Seder Night

PIRKEI AVOS – The Ethics of the Fathers
Notes and Comments to the Book of Jewish Values

SECOND THOUGHTS

BUY GREEN BANANAS

TENDING THE VINEYARD
The Life and Vicissitudes of Being a Rabbi

LIVING JEWISH
A Guide to Jewish Life

THE ORAL LAW OF SINAI
An Illustrated History of the Mishnah

RABBI BEREL WEIN

An Illustrated History
of the Talmud

מגיד

MAGGID

Vision & Valor
An Illustrated History of the Talmud
First Edition 2010

Maggid Books
An imprint of Koren Publishers Jerusalem Ltd.

POB 8531, New Milford, CT 06676-8531 USA
POB 2455, London W1A 5WY, England
&POB 4044, Jerusalem 91040, Israel

www.korenpub.com

Graphic Design: Ben Gasner Studio

ISBN 978 159 264 286 1, *hardcover*

A CIP catalogue record for this title is available from the British Library

Printed and bound in Israel

Table of Contents

Acknowledgments   XIII
In the Beginning   1
Introduction   9

The First Generation of Amoraim in Babylonia
c. 210 – 250 CE

The Era of Rav and his Colleagues   21
Mar Shmuel   40

The First and Second Generations of Amoraim in The Land of Israel *c. 250 – 300 CE*

Rabi Yochanan   55
Rabi Shimon Ben Lakish   66
The Scholars of Caesarea   76

III The Second Generations of Amoraim in Babylonia *c. 250 – 300 CE*

Rav Huna   85
Rav Chisda   89
Rav Yehudah Bar Yechezkel   95

IV The Third Generation of Amoraim in Babylonia *c.300 – 330 CE*

Rabah bar Nachmani   105
Rav Yosef   110
Rav (Rabi) Zeira I   114
Other Amoraim of the Third Generation   118

V The Third Generation of Amoraim in the Land of Israel *c.300 – 330 CE*

Rav Ami and Rav Assi   125

VI The Fourth Generation of Amoraim in Babylonia *c.330 – 375 CE*

Abayei   135
Rava   142
Other Amoraim of the Fourth Generation   148

VII The Fifth Generation of Amoraim in Babylonia *c.360 – 400 CE*

Rav Papa and Rav Huna breih d'Rav Yehoshua 153

VIII The Sixth Generation of Amoraim in Babylonia
c.390 – 430 CE

Rav Ashi   *161*
Ravina (The First)   *165*

IX The Seventh and Final Generation of Amoraim in Babylonia *c.390 – 430 CE*

The Completed Talmud   *171*

Appendices

Epilogue   *181*
Amoraim Timeline   *184*
Notes   *186*
Glossary   *239*
Index   *245*
About the Author   *252*
Photo Credits   *254*

In memory of
my dear and beloved friends,
Lillian and Leslie Hirtz,
whose exemplary lives and behavior
made every moment of their lives
and the lives of their children and
grandchildren – in the words
of the Mishnah – "A Time for God."

Acknowledgments

I am indebted to many for their helping me in being able to see this book come to print and distribution. I thank my dear friends, Rabbi Yehonosan and Rochelle Hirtz, Dr. Henry and Susie Zupnick and Menachem and Marjorie Adler for their moral and financial support that enabled this book to be designed and set. It was their help that provided the impetus for the book project to become real. My gratitude to the Green family in all of its generations and their Darchei Noam Foundation is as unlimited as their friendship and support of me has been over the years. Without their generosity and encouragement, this book would probably have remained merely a good idea whose time somehow had not come. They helped raise me from a moment of personal despair and challenged me to keep on going. And they did so in the classy, gentle and firm way that is the hallmark of their relationships with others. My colleagues at Destiny Foundation, Elaine Gilbert and Miriam Cubac, were also of inestimable help to me in seeing this book through to its final completion.

On the technical end of whipping this book into shape my thanks and deepest gratitude go to Charlotte Friedland, the editor par supreme. Her painstaking review of the manuscript uncovered many weaknesses and prevented much slipshod language or undocumented research to enter the book. Ben Gasner is one of the world's great book designers and graphic artists. The layout, illustrations and appearance of this book testify to his genius and talent in this area. His entire staff in his Jerusalem workshop excelled in every facet of skill and professionalism. Special thanks go to Simone Dahan for her diligence and talents. Dr. Allison Kupietzky researched and obtained the photographs and illustrations that are such an important part of the book. Her expertise and skill in so doing is to me amazing. My thanks also go to Joslynne Halibard, Nechama Margulies and to Rabbi Eitan Kupietzky for their help and contributions to this book. I appreciate all of their fine efforts.

My thanks go to Matthew Miller of Toby Press/Koren Publishing of Jerusalem who has successfully shepherded this book project to completion and publication. The book is being published under the Magid imprint of Toby/Koren. Matthew's understanding, encouragement and quiet competence have added a great deal to this work. I am delighted to have him as a friend and grateful to have him as a publisher. It has been a joy to work with the staff of Toby/Koren on this book.

Finally my thanks go to my wife, Mira and to my family and the members of my Beit Kenesset Hanassi congregation here in Jerusalem who stood by me while this book was being written and produced. There are no adequate words to convey my appreciation to them and my love for them. May the Lord of Israel and of all of humanity bless them and may the merit of the great people of the Mishnah and the Talmud who appear in this book stand us all in good stead accompanied by faith and blessings.

To my beloved friends,
Pinky and Libby
and all of their family
with deep appreciation
and affection.

Rehov Synagogue mosaic floor, 6th–7th century CE
This mosaic provides important archaeological evidence for the textual history of rabbinic literature and halacha. The inscriptions explain how classical rabbinic texts were applied to life in the Beit Shean region during the final years of the Mishnaic and Talmudic periods
See below for enlargement
(Israel Antiquities Authority Collection)

In the Beginning

his book is a companion volume to my previously published book on the Mishna, The Oral Law of Sinai. Originally I thought that the books on the Mishna and the Talmud should be combined in one volume. However, for various technical and publishing reasons the books on the Mishna and the Talmud are now published as two stand alone volumes though they are really one conceptual entity. Because of this I am taking the liberty to reprint in this volume on the Talmud much of this opening section of the book that appeared in the earlier volume on the Mishna, The Oral Law of Sinai. I feel that the words of background that this section contains are of great importance in understanding the Talmud. In fact I have taken the liberty of even repeating many of these ideas once more in the actual following introduction to this book and I do not feel that this seeming repetitiveness is superfluous. The basic rule in studying Talmud is to always review what has been learned. And so I am humbly following the methods of my teachers of Talmud over the years – review, review, review. Anyway, my friends, practice makes perfect and every author strives for the elusive and unfortunately unattainable goal of perfection in his works. This volume is therefore an imperfect but truly heartfelt attempt to explain and elucidate the times and the lives of the great creators of the Talmud. Thank you for reading on.

There is no intellectual work known to the human world that is even similar to the Mishnah and its companion work, the Talmud.

The Talmud is a law book, a faithful transmission of the Oral Law of Sinai to all later generations of Jews. It is a book of ethical principles and moral values. It is a book of legends and stories, and also of psychological and historical observations. It discusses medicine, pharmacology, dreams, botany, astronomy and mathematics, as well as human and animal biology. It is a detailed, painstaking commentary to the Written Law of the Torah, based on rigorous logic, scrupulous scrutiny of the biblical texts, and an unremitting search for truth.

It does not debate matters of faith – it is faith itself. It discovers God and His Torah in every nook and cranny of human existence and there is nothing about life, humans, nature, spirituality or physicality that is a taboo subject. All is Torah; all is holiness.

Replete with humor, irony, pathos, soaring optimism and cold-hearted realism, its mode – and drama – emerge from the give-and-take of intensive scholarly debate and unending questioning, probing and hypothesizing.

It is a joy to study, but it is not entertaining. The Talmud is maddeningly difficult and sometimes determinedly abstruse. It makes no concessions, not in language nor intellect, to its students. Its reasoning and methods are rigorous. Every word, every sentence and phrase is a new challenge. The text has very little punctuation, and its long and complicated run-on sentences can go for pages on end. It demands a seriousness of purpose, a willingness to commit time and sweat to its study, before it will give up its secrets and insights.

In reality, the Talmud is two separate books comprising the Oral Law. The first is the Mishnah, the subject of a previous book of mine. Written circa third century BCE, its language is

Jerusalem Talmud Shabbat, Oriental, 12th century (The Library of the Jewish Theological Seminary)

classical, post-biblical Hebrew. It is studied as a subject in and of itself. However, the Talmud, also known as Gemara, is written in the Aramaic of third to sixth century Babylonian Jewry. Every page of the Talmud includes the passage of Mishnah upon which its discussion is based, as well as later teachings and commentary.

A key feature of both the Mishnah and the Talmud is that they can never be understood from the outside. As a unique work with its own method of reasoning, it can be known only from the inside – from the Talmud itself! So, the obvious question is, where does one begin? One must struggle to get into the heart of the Talmud, for only by reaching its heart can one hope to penetrate the intricacies of its mental processes and appreciate the magic of its logic. Since the Talmud can only be known from inside, intellect alone (though certainly necessary) is insufficient to master it. Minds can speak to minds, but only hearts can speak to hearts.

The Talmud is a book of godly personalities and deep insight into the human condition and the world. It is a book of love, of compassion, of striving spirituality and also of withering candor. It is a book for the masses, but it is again a book only for the few. It has simple wisdom on its surface and majestic mystery in its depth. It is the book of love between Jews and Jews, between generations and generations, between the people and the God of Israel. Therefore, one who measures the Talmud by the yardstick of facts, laws, and discussions alone makes a fundamental error, for that is a very narrow, and even unjust, view of this monumental work.

For the triumph of the Talmud and its personalities against its enemies, both within and without the Jewish people, was based upon its hidden greatness and human warmth, not only on its soaring intellect and wise interpretations of Jewish law. The creators of the Mishnah and Talmud are the worthy successors to the prophets of Israel in their vision, their fire and passion, their unsparing honesty, their love for the people and God of Israel; and most of all, in their almost unrealistic yet unquenchable optimism. Theirs is the unshakable faith in the Torah and mission of Israel that sustained generations of Jews for centuries.

But perhaps the greatest contribution of the Oral Law – and of the Mishnah and Talmud that now represents that Oral Law – is found in the words of Midrash itself:

> *"I [the Lord] do not wish to grant them the Oral Law in writing because I know that the nations of the world will rule over the Jews and take it away from them. Thus, the written Bible I give them [now] in writing, while the Mishnah, Talmud and Aggadah I grant to them orally, for when the nations of the world will in the future subjugate Israel, the Jews will still be able to be separate from them ... for they [the words of the Oral Law] are what will separate the Jewish people from being assimilated and lost into the general society"* (Midrash Rabah Shmos, chapter 47, section one).

Thus, even though the entire Torah, both Written and Oral, is from Sinai, the portion of Torah that is the Oral Law remains solely in Jewish possession, unlike the written Bible that has been co-opted by other faiths. In this way, the Oral Law has contributed significantly to the survival of the Jews as a unique and vital people. The Oral Law can be seen as the dividing line between Israel and the nations of the world. The Written Law, the Bible, can be characterized as universal: the Oral Law, as represented in the Mishnah and Talmud, as particular. The genius of incorporating both of these ideas and balancing them harmoniously within Judaism is testimony to the strength and truth of the Jewish faith.

The Oral Law is built upon the Written Torah. Though it was a product of centuries of study, writing, editing and endless review, Judaism posits that the Oral Law – its structure, mechanisms, and its interpretations of the Written Torah – stems from the Divinity of the Revelation at Sinai. Every subject in the Talmud begins with the question: "Where in the Written Torah [in the text itself] do we find the basis for this discussion?"

However, the development, scholarship and popularization of the Oral Law were accomplished by people. And it is these people who lie at the heart of the Mishnah and Talmud. These great human beings accelerated this process of developing the Oral Law after the end of the period of prophecy in Jewish history, during the era of Ezra and the Men of the Great Assembly (approximately 350-300 BCE). In fact, the development of the Oral Law as the main spiritual and intellectual basis of Judaism from the time of Ezra onwards should be seen as the replacement for the now absent gift of prophecy which had previously sustained the nation of Israel from the time of Moses till Ezra. Until the final redaction of the Babylonian Talmud (approximately 500 CE), this process of interpretation and decision-making, stretching over almost a millennia in time, continued unabated.

Neither the destruction of the Second Temple (70 CE) nor the failure of the later Bar Kochba rebellion (c.132 CE) stopped the process of refining and studying the Oral Law. Through Greek and Roman persecution and the challenges of pagan culture, even through the later rise of Christianity and its open hostility towards Jews and Judaism, the work of the noble scholars of the Mishnah and Talmud continued. Their academies of learning flourished, first in the Land of Israel and then in Babylonia.

Who were these great men? What do we know of their lives and fortunes? How were they able to ignore the damaging winds that swirled around

Babylonian Talmud Bava Kama, Oriental, 12th century (The Library of the Jewish Theological Seminary)

them and remain focused on the development of the Oral Law? Like the Talmud itself, their life stories are not found in outside sources. They are found only in the Mishnah, the Talmud and in attendant works of Torah scholarship – Midrash, Tosefta, Targum, etc. As stated above, the only way to understand the Talmud is through its heart, and these transcendent individuals are its very heart. It is therefore through the lives of these people that the story of the development of the Mishnah and Talmud will be told. That is why I believe that this book can be a boon to all students of the Mishnah and Talmud, veteran and novice, skilled and struggling.

The study of Mishnah and Talmud has been enhanced and popularized by its relatively recent availability in English. Special commendation is due to the Mesorah Heritage Foundation that has supported the publication of the monumental Artscroll edition of the Talmud with its English and Hebrew elucidations. However, to the best of my knowledge, a popular review of the lives and personalities of the creators of the Mishnah and Talmud has not yet been made available to the wider English-speaking public. There are some wonderful works on this subject in Hebrew. Chief among them are those of Eliezer Shteinman, Avraham Naftal, Aharon Heiman, Yisrael Konovitz, Chaim Koolitz, Yitzchak Isaac Halevi, Reuven Margoliyus and Zev Yavetz. Mosad Harav Kook in Jerusalem has published a multi-volume series in Hebrew anthologizing the sayings and teachings of many of the individual scholars of the Mishnah and Talmud. I have availed myself liberally of these works in my endeavor to portray the lives of the masters of the Talmud for the English-speaking public. I humbly acknowledge my debt to the scholarship and intellectual prowess of these above named scholars, and to other unnamed ones as well. But as this book will continually show, primarily I have allowed the Mishnah and Talmud itself to speak about its creators and authors. Therefore, this book is more a work of organization and compilation than of original creative scholarship.

Babylonian Talmud Bava Metzia, Spain, 13th century (The Library of the Jewish Theological Seminary)

The chapters of this book are arranged in an approximate chronological order. Naturally, the story of some of the people discussed will cover pages, while others will only fill a few sentences. This distinction is not a judgment as to the relative importance of the subjects involved, but rather a reflection of the amount of material present in the pages of the Mishnah and Talmud regarding that particular personage. Many remarkable people preferred to remain hidden in the history of that time (and of later times as well) and the Mishnah and Talmud apparently were willing to accommodate those wishes. In any event, this work is not an encyclopedia nor is it meant to be all encompassing in its scope. My goal is to reveal the heart of the Oral Law and illuminate the lives of the creators of these great books upon which the Jewish nation has built its society and lifestyle for the past fifteen centuries.

The volume hopefully will detail the lives and times of the Amoraim, the people who, in studying and analyzing the Mishnah, created the Babylonian and Jerusalem Talmud, which absorbed the Mishnah into its corpus. The period of time involved in completing this endeavor was approximately 250 years, ending in the middle decades of the fifth century CE. The final editing of the Talmud, in the form that we have it today was accomplished by the Savoraim – the "explainers" – who completed their redaction of the Talmud by the beginning of the seventh century CE.

Of course, this book is unable to detail the lives of the many hundreds, if not thousands, of people involved in producing this massive and monumental work of holy scholarship. In fact, as I have mentioned earlier, many of these extraordinary people have successfully retained their anonymity through-out time. I have therefore chosen the key people, as the Talmud itself lists them, as the subjects of this book.

Babylonian Talmud Avodah Zarah, Ubeda, Spain, 1290, Scribe: Shelomo ben Shaul ben-Albagli (The Library of the Jewish Theological Seminary)

I pray that in some way I do justice to their lives and achievements. I am ever mindful of the assessment of the rabbis of the Talmud: "If the people of the previous generations were angels, then we may consider ourselves to be humans. But if they were only humans, then we are only as donkeys…" (Shabbos 112b). I have therefore stayed away from character judgments and any personal opinions of mine. I am satisfied to let the Talmud itself tell the story of those who fashioned it so carefully and lovingly.

Map of Babylonian
Captivity: Jews in Exile

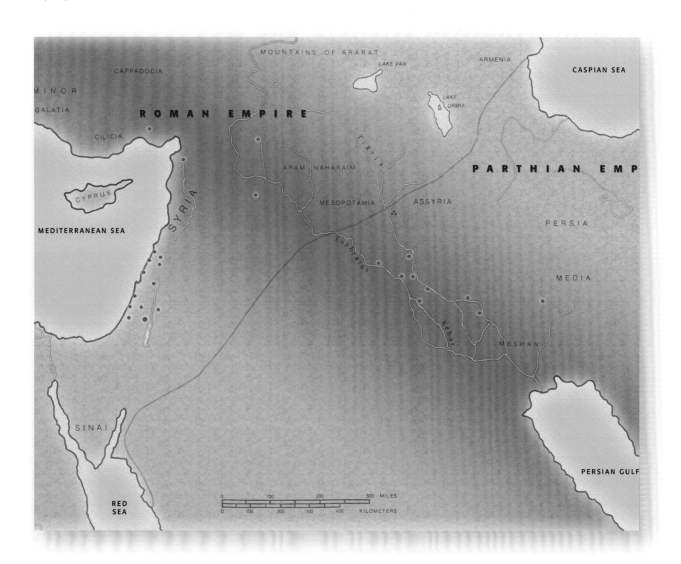

Introduction

The Talmud characterizes itself as a book that was written "in darkness."[1] While it may have been written in darkness, it is a book of light and magic – and it has preserved the Jewish people through the long night of its exile and persecution.

The Talmud has been compared to a mighty sea with roaring waves, but it is also the shores of serenity and inner peace. It is at once a book of law, and a guidebook in life. Yet it is also comforting and uplifting, for it is not only the product of great minds, but of deep spirituality and expansive hearts. As the Spanish Jewish poet, Moshe ibn Ezra, wrote: "Words emanating from the heart are able to enter the hearts of others."[2] Every word of the Talmud is from the heart.

The people of the Talmud – the *Amoraim* – are the worthy successors to the great men of the Mishnah – the *Tannaim* – who in turn were the successors to the prophets of Israel in their unconditional love for the people and God of Israel; in their almost unrealistic yet unquenchable optimism, and unshakable faith in the Torah and eternal mission of Israel. The sea of the Talmud is formed not only by waves of inquiry and words; it is also an ocean of fire and passion.

Of course, the Talmud is not one "book," but is comprised of tractate after tractate of soaring intellect as well as brutally honest conscience and moral standards.[3] The deep analysis of legal matters that characterizes the Talmud and its study is no less deep and

Words emanating from the heart are able to enter the hearts of others.
Moshe ibn Ezra

9

diligent when it comes to judging and analyzing people, moral values, spirituality and the true meaning of Torah and its rituals.

As mentioned in the introduction to the companion volume to this book, my work on the Mishnah, perhaps the greatest contribution of the Oral Law and the Talmud to Jewish survival is its very particularism. I reiterate the point here because it is key, one of the "secrets" of living Judaism. The Midrash[4] states that the Lord gave the Jewish people the Written Torah, The Five Books of Moses, knowing that the other faiths and cultures of the world will eventually co-opt it. Yet He reserved the Oral Law (what later came to be crystallized as the Mishnah, Talmud and Aggadah) for oral transmission from generation to generation. This form of personal transmission of a particular body of knowledge will itself separate the Jews from general society and prevent them from becoming lost. Thus, even though the entire Torah – both Written and Oral – is from Sinai, the portion of the Torah that is the Oral Law remained and yet remains exclusively in Jewish possession. King David wrote in Psalms 147 that "the laws of the Torah (the oral explanation of the written Torah) were not made to be known to the nations of the world." In this way, the exclusivity of the Oral Law has significantly contributed to the ability of the Jewish people to survive as a unique and vital people. The Talmud is therefore pretty much the dividing line between Israel and the nations of the world.

Even though it is now a written work, the Talmud sees itself as basically an oral presentation.[5] And indeed, anyone who has tried to plumb the depths of Talmud without a mentor has discovered the difficulty of that effort. It is written in such a way that it still requires explanation, most effectively oral, by one who has learned it previously from the mouth of his own teacher, usually a member of a previous generation. It is more vitally alive than any other written work of its type, and it sparkles with personality and character. Its "lips drip with myrrh and honey."[6] As an eternal, living entity, the Oral Law is never ending and unlimited. "There is no study hall of Torah that does not develop new ideas in the study of Torah."[7] This is the secret of the written Oral Law, of the Talmud. It constantly rejuvenates itself and is always alive, fresh, and challenging. It speaks to us and leaps off the printed page.

We are assured that God, so to speak, loves to hear the discussions of the students of the Talmud.[8] In fact, the rabbis of the Talmud stated that God had no place in the world, so to speak, where He could find Himself comfortable except within the "four ells of halachah" – the study halls of the Talmud.[9]

Moreover, the Talmud provides the student with a panorama of Jewish history and values. All of the illustrious individuals of the Bible pass in review in the Talmud, their characters and motives revealed and their actions and behavior carefully studied and critiqued. There is nothing in the Bible that escapes the eye of the Talmud. In reality, the student is soon aware that without the Talmud, the Bible itself – despite being written and preserved – is a sealed book. It is not by chance that non-Jewish understandings of the Bible are often radically different, even diametrically opposed, to the Jewish view. This is because the Jewish reading of the Bible is framed by the Oral Torah, the Talmud, which explains and enriches its meaning.

Jewish tradition is sacrosanct in the Talmud. Everything has a source, either written and explicit in the Bible, or oral and traditional. These sources are not subject to the usual methods of proof, yet they are holy and correct, because our teachers and ancestors were truthful people.[10] There are concepts and laws in the Talmud that are merely "hanging by a thread"[11] that are nevertheless essential to and derived from the basic body of Torah itself.[12] The Talmud is creative and innovative, but always within the framework of its history and tradition. It is almost as if the Talmud continually asks itself the question "What would Moshe say to this opinion and decision? Would he recognize it and approve of it?" Moshe and the Written Law are willing participants in the Talmudic debates. Many times the Talmud asserts that the source and justification for its decision or opinion is halachah l'Moshe mi'Sinai[13] – this is the law as explained to Moshe on Sinai. Even the "innovations" of all later scholars of the Talmud were already part of the tradition of Israel as received on Sinai by Moshe.[14]

Thus the Talmud is representative of the Jewish people itself – at one and the same time being old and new, traditional and ever innovative, reverent and respectful, yet fresh, sometimes brash and always vital. I would hazard to say that no book in the history of mankind has been studied, debated and discussed as much, and with such creativity, intensity and fervor, as the Talmud. This fact alone reveals the holy and eternal character of the Talmud and the Oral Law that it represents.

Jewish history has shown that those who departed from the Talmud, who subjected it to "scientific" analysis and superficial criticism, mocked its legends and attitudes, and denigrated its students, soon found themselves and their descendants outside of the pale of authentic Judaism altogether. The attempt to substitute "culture" for Torah and "literature" for the Talmud has only led to abject ignorance of Judaism, and boorishness and assimilation in those Jewish circles that opted for such programs.

The Talmud is eternally relevant and wise. As such, it is never on the cutting-edge of modernity. However, as I have grown older, and hopefully wiser, I remember the sayings of the Talmud that I studied in the yeshivah in my youth (and admittedly one may have been then – in the flush of youthful omniscience – somewhat more naive and less understanding about the Talmud's view of people and life.) Now, in my later years, I become ever more impressed with the deep psychological insights and truisms that the Talmud provides. It is no wonder that Ben Bahg Bahg, that holy convert to Judaism and thus someone with an outside perspective regarding the matter, stated: "Delve into it [the Torah and Oral Law] and continue to delve into it, for everything is within it."[15] The genuine student of Talmud is able to see that truly "everything" is within it.

A work of this magnitude required the intensive labor of many over a long period of time. Indeed, the Talmud is the product of three and a half centuries of study, writing, editing and constant review. And it is the story of the lives of these outstanding individuals that lies at the heart of the story of the Talmud itself.

While vociferous in regarding Jewish tradition as valid and

Delve into it [the Torah and Oral Law] and continue to delve into it, for everything is within it."

Avos

binding, the Talmud yet remains coolly logical and even skeptical until a point is proven. Its implied statement of methodology is, "If this is a valid tradition, we accept it; but if the matter is open for discussion, let us analyze and discuss it."[16] This process of de-

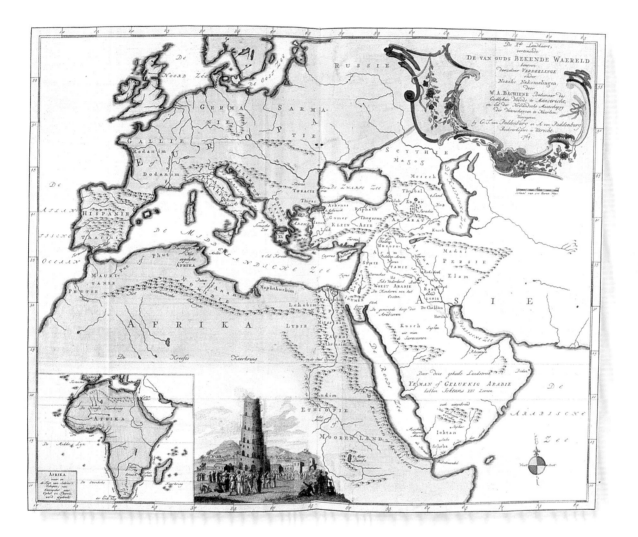

veloping and publicizing the Oral Law outside of the core circle of scholars began after the age of prophecy, with the beginning of the Second Commonwealth and its Temple, the era of Ezra and the Men of the Great Assembly, c.400-350 BCE. In fact, the development of the Oral Law as the main spiritual and intellectual basis of Judaism from the time of Ezra onwards should be seen as the replacement for the now absent presence of prophecy, which had previously sustained the nation of Israel.

The Tower of Babel and a "Map of the World Known to the Ancient", Bachiene, Willem Albert, Dutch, 1712-1753 (The Israel Museum, Jerusalem)

Until the final redaction of the Babylonian Talmud (approximately 550 CE), this process of continual interpreting and decision-making regarding the Oral Law, continued unabated for about a millennium. Nothing could stop the work from continuing: not the destruction of the Second Temple (70 CE) nor the bitter failure of the Bar Kochba rebellion (c.137 CE); not persecutions by the Greeks and Romans, nor the rise of Christianity. Despite everything, Torah study flourished, in the Land of Israel and in Babylonia.

As I stated in my introduction to an earlier volume of mine on the history of the Mishnah, the study of the development of the Talmud must also focus on the extraordinary sages who composed it. Their lives and fortunes give us a glimpse into the vitality of this great work. Understanding their challenges and enormous strength it took to overcome them helps us appreciate how the Talmud withstood the onslaughts of alien cultures and persecutions that have threatened it from its inception.

And their stories appear only in the Talmud itself and in its attendant works of scholarship – *Midrash*, *Tosefta*, *Targum*. Because these scholars are the heart of the Talmud, they speak to every student of the Talmud, veteran and novice alike. It is my hope that this book also will serve as an aid and guide to all who are interested in knowing more about Judaism and have never been exposed to the study of Talmud, as well as to those who have already spent time and effort in studying it. As I have consistently stated, there is no way to truly understand and appreciate the faith of Judaism without some understanding and knowledge of Talmud, and even secondary sources such as this book can be of value in acquiring that understanding and knowledge.

Again, as I have noted regularly, the study of Talmud in our time has been greatly advanced and its popularity increased by the fact that the Talmud is now available in English, Hebrew and French language editions. The original Soncino Press English translation of the Talmud, published in England in the 1930s, paved the way for an English language understanding of Talmud, though that work was hardly considered user-friendly. Special commendation is therefore due to the Mesorah Heritage Foundation that has supported the publication of the monumental Schottenstein Artscroll edition of the Talmud with its excellent, graphically enhanced, and superbly executed English elucidation. It has opened the Talmud to the entire English-speaking world in a fashion that was unimaginable even a few short decades ago.

Nevertheless, as stated earlier to the best of my current knowledge, a popular review of the lives and personalities of the creators of the Talmud has not yet been made available to the wider English-speaking public. There are some wonderful works on the subject written in Hebrew. Chief among them are those of scholars and rabbis such as Eliezer Shteinman, Avraham Naftul, Aharon Heiman, Yehuda Leib (Fishman) Maimon, Yisrael Konovitz, Chaim Koolitz, Yitzchak Isaac Halevi, Reuven Margoliyus, and Zev Yaavetz. In addition, Mosad Harav Kook in Jerusalem has published a multi-volume series in Hebrew anthologizing the sayings and teachings of many of the great men of the Talmud. I have availed myself most liberally from the contents of these works, especially those of Naftul, Halevi, and Shteinman. I am humbled by the breadth and depth of knowledge displayed by these scholars and I am indebted to them for much of the information, and even some of the organization, that will be found in this book. But in the main, I have allowed the Talmud itself to speak about its creators and authors. Therefore, this book is more a work of organization, classification, and compilation rather than of original research or creative scholarship.

The Talmud, which is based on principles of associative memory, does not easily lend itself to pinpoint dating or rigid chronological order. Nevertheless, I have attempted to adhere to some generally acceptable form of chronological order. Naturally, the story of the lives of some people of the Talmud will fill pages while other biographies may only be a paragraph or a few sentences in length. This is not a judgment on my part as to the relative importance of the subjects involved, but rather a reflection of the amount of information relating to each individual that is found in the Talmud. In addition, many great people preferred to remain hidden in the shadows of Jewish history, and the Talmud was willing to accommodate those wishes. In any event, this book is not meant to be an encyclopedia or an all-encompassing scholarly work in its scope. It is a popular review of the Talmud and its authors, designed to enlighten people of all educational levels.

This volume deals with Jewish life and history from c.210 CE to c.500 CE. It concentrates primarily on Babylonia, though a part of this text is concerned with life in the Land of Israel – especially as it relates to Talmud Yerushalmi, the Jerusalem Talmud. Scholars generally define periods of the Talmud's composition into seven generations of Amoraim,[17] corresponding roughly to the years mentioned above. Like the Talmud itself, there is no definite beginning or end to this time line, which therefore must remain only an approximation.

The lives of the people who authored the Talmud differed considerably. Some of the scholars were wealthy and healthy, while others were poor and chronically ill. Some gained great notoriety, while others remained humbly in the shadows. The Talmud recognizes and even exalts the differences between people, especially great people. It states: "Just as the facial features of humans differ, so too do their opinions and thoughts."[18] The Talmud revels in discussions, debates, contradictory opinions, and polarizing personalities. It abhors self-righteousness, conformity, hypocrisy and pomposity. However, all of the fashioners of the Talmud were alike in being people of mission and vision, hope and scholarship, piety and devotion to the God of Israel and His Torah. They were intensely "human," but their level of humanity defies our current comprehension of that term. Such people do not exist in our world of today. They are beyond our level of experience and acquaintance.

As stated previously, the Talmud is humor and pathos, shrewd psychological insight and soaring faith, hard realism and eternal optimism. After the Bible, it is certainly the book of books. It is with no small amount of trepidation therefore that I approach this subject and the lives of the people who appear on the Talmud's pages. I have attempted to avoid editorial comments of my own on the

Just as the facial features of humans differ, so too do their opinions and thoughts.
Midrash Rabah

lives and events described in this book, for I believe that it is more than sufficient to allow the Talmud to tell its own story in its own way and words. And in its inimitable way, it certainly does so.

I am indebted to the many people whose kindness to me has enabled me to write this book. My years at the yeshivah Beis Midrash L'Torah (then in Chicago, currently in Skokie, Illinois) and my wonderful teachers there opened for me the gates to the wonderland of the Talmud. My father, of blessed memory, taught me the rudiments of its study when I was yet a child. During my professional life as a congregational rabbi and as a yeshivah teacher, I have taught Talmud almost every day of my life for many decades. My students have in turn taught me to appreciate the beauty of the Talmud even more than I previously imagined.[19]

My wife and family were of great encouragement and infinite patience during the writing of this book, as they were and are in all of my other past and present endeavors. More than the words of books, one's family and generations are many the times the greatest accomplishments and satisfaction in life. I am blessed with such a family. I thank Ben Gassner and his wonderful staff for the production and artistic beauty of this book. He is the champion in his field. Dr. Allison Kupietzky was the photographic editor and her talents and creativity is evident throughout the pages of this book. Charlotte Friedland was and is my long time editor who has saved me from many errors of style, content and hubris. Matthew Miller of Toby/Koren Press has shepherded this book to completion and publication. He is a master of patience and production. I also must thank Arthur Kurzweil for his help, friendship and advice. And naturally any errors of omission and commission in this work are my sole responsibility.

I am grateful that the God of Israel has allowed me to write this book in His holy city of Jerusalem and has preserved me in health and years until now. "May the pleasantness of the Lord be upon us, and may the works of our hands be established upon us, and may He yet establish the work of our hands."[20]

SECTION I

THE FIRST GENERATION OF AMORAIM IN BABYLONIA

C. 210 - 250 CE

*Detail of an auroch, Ishtar
Gate, Babylon, c. 575 BCE*

The Era of Rav and his Colleagues

Rav Abba bar Ayvu was one of the main disciples of Rabi Yehudah HaNasi.[1] Just as his great mentor was known simply as Rabi, Rav Abba was also simply known as Rav. This name was both a title and a term of endearment bestowed upon him by his colleagues, by students and later by all of Israel. Rav was of most distinguished lineage, descended from Shimi, the son of the biblical Yishai and the brother of King David.[2] Rav's grandfather was Abba bar Acha Karsala from the village of Kafri in Babylonia,[3] which was near the great Jewish center of Sura.[4] Abba bar Acha Karsala had five sons of whom Ayvu, Rav's father, was the oldest and Rabi Chiya, Rabi's colleague, was the youngest.[5]

In fact, Rav was a nephew of Rabi Chiya through both his father and his mother.[6] This unusual family connection was due to the fact that Ayvu was the oldest son of Abba bar Acha Karsala from a first marriage. Rabi Chiya was the son of Abba bar Acha Karsala, born of a second marriage. Rav's mother, Ima, in turn, was a stepdaughter of Abba bar Acha Karsala, brought into that family from the second marriage; thus she was the half-sister of Rabi Chiya, both sharing a common mother.[7] The prominence of Rav's ancestral descent was recognized by all of his colleagues and he was called *ben pachsi* – the son of great leaders.[8] This was the affectionate name by which his uncle Rabi Chiya called him. But the name was itself

RAV
Rosh Yeshiva
of Sura
c. 210 CE

Teachers:
- Rabi
- Rabi Chiya (Rav's uncle)

Colleagues:
- Mar Shmuel
- Karna

Students:
- Rav Yehudah
- Rav Huna
- Rav Chisda
- Rav Gidel
- Rabah bar Avuha
- Rav Zutra bar Tuvia
- Rav Chanan bar Rava
- Rav Chiya Bar Ashi
- Rav Chananel
- Rav Yirmiya Bar Abba

Relatives:
- Father: Ayvu
- Uncle: Rabi Chiya
- Cousins: Yehudah and Chezkiyah, the sons of Rabi Chiya.
- Cousin: Rav Chanina bar Chama
- Son: Rav Chiya bar Rav.
- Son-in-law: Rav Chanan bar Rava
- Grandson: Rav Shimi bar Chiya
- Grandson: Raban (Ravna) Ukva and Raban Nechemiah

a challenge to Rav, indicating that significant achievements were expected of him. Rav did not disappoint.

He studied Torah with many teachers,[9] as described below, but his main teacher in life and Torah was his uncle, Rabi Chiya. Rav affectionately called him *chavivi* – my beloved one[10] – and he was very attached to Rabi Chiya and to his sons, Rav's cousins. When Rabi Chiya and his sons left Babylonia and settled in the Land of Israel to join Rabi Yehudah HaNasi (Rabi), his yeshivah and Sanhedrin in Beis Shearim and Tzipori, Rav accompanied them. This occurred in c. 175 CE,[11] when Rav was yet a very young man.

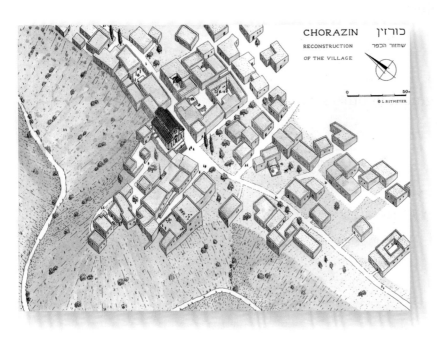

CHORAZIN כורזין
RECONSTRUCTION שחזור הכפר
OF THE VILLAGE

0   50m
© L. RITMEYER

Reconstruction drawing of the village of Chorazin, late 2nd century CE

Once in the Land of Israel, Rav studied under his uncle, Rabi Chiya, under Rabi Yehudah HaNasi[12] and also with Rabi Yitzchak ben Avdimi (Avudimi), the colleague of Rabi.[13] The arrival of Rav Chiya and his family had tremendous impact on the revival of Torah study in the Land of Israel during the time of Rabi.[14] It also brought blessing to the economy and agricultural development of the Land of Israel, as the Jews there were still suffering from the aftermath of the Roman persecutions and the devastation of their country.[15] Rabi Chiya was a person of wealth – a silk and flax merchant[16] and a field owner.[17] As such, he provided employment and support to scholars who were financially strained, making them sharecroppers on his fields.[18] Rav was active in the commercial ventures of his uncle, Rabi Chiya,[19] earning his keep while studying under his uncle and in the yeshivah of Rabi Yehudah HaNasi. He was mindful of the importance of being financially self-sufficient and valued the commercial blessings of the flax and linen business.[20]

Rav soon came to the attention of Rabi Yehudah HaNasi, and rose to prominence amongst the leading students of his household and yeshivah.[21] The fact that he was the nephew of Rabi Chiya also helped to bring him to Rabi's attention, for Rabi loved and respected Rabi Chiya greatly.[22] Thus, Rav had the opportunity to study and learn from the two greatest men of the generation. Rav adored Rabi and stated that the Messiah would surely resemble him.[23]

Rav patterned his own lifetime behavior after the characteristics and values of these two illustrious men. As they were physically and spiritually imposing, so was Rav. He was called *Abba Aricha* – "tall Abba" because of his great height.[24] Like his outstanding role models, he was generous with his wealth.[25] Rav was modest, careful and even fearful in judgment of others[26] and tolerant of others' foibles and contrarian natures.[27] He insisted on truthful behavior and words from his children, even at the cost of his own comfort.[28] Again, like his teachers, Rav was a person of delicate and fastidious behavior and demeanor.[29] He never ate from a public meal that was not a *seudas mitzvah* – a meal held in celebration of the fulfillment of a commandment such as a circumcision, wedding, redemption of a first-born male child, the completion of a section of Torah study, etc.[30]

Because of Rav's immense Torah knowledge and unusual piety, Rabi appointed him to his yeshivah court, even though he was far younger than the other members of that group. Because of his youth, Rav's opinion was requested first, as per the tradition of the Sanhedrin that the elders and leaders of the Sanhedrin expressed their opinions last, in order not to unduly influence the judgment of the younger and newer members of the court.[31]

Despite Rav's recognized greatness in Torah erudition and piety, Rabi refused to grant Rav the ultimate *semichah* ordination – *yatir bechoros* – which would have allowed him to become a member of the Sanhedrin.[32] However, Rabi did grant him the two lower forms of *semichah, yoreh yoreh* and *yadin yadin*.[33] Later in life, Rav attempted to receive this *semichah* ordination from Raban Gamliel III, Rabi's son, but was again rebuffed! Raban Gamliel III told him: "I cannot add to whatever ordinations my father previously gave to you."[34] Rav's cousin and colleague, Rabah bar Chana[35] was nevertheless granted that highest form of *semichah* at that time.

Rabi's reasons for not granting Rav that *semichah,* while granting it to Rabah bar Chana, are not explicitly clear. The matter remains somewhat of a mystery till this day. The Talmud[36] raises two possibilities for Rabi's refusal to ordain Rav: One is that Rabi wanted to honor Rabah bar Chana, so he thus differentiated him from Rav in the matter of the *semichah*; the second reason offered is that Rav was *so* great an expert in the matter of *yatir bechoros* (declaring a first-born animal unfit for Temple sacrifice or holy status because of a permanent physical blemish), that he would produce lenient rulings. While these rulings would be technically correct, others not as expert as Rav would then likely misinterpret and misuse them.[37]

Rav spent approximately fifteen to twenty years in the Land of Israel, studying with Rabi and Rabi Chiya. Circa 190-195 CE Rav left the Land of Israel and returned to Babylonia accompanied by his cousin, Rabah bar Chana.[38] Rav's reasons for returning to Babylonia are not known[39] and his stay there was a short one, for he soon returned to the Land of Israel. Apparently, while in Babylonia, Rav did not receive the recognition that he correctly thought was due him. He ruefully said about himself, "I am the Ben Azai here in Babylonia."[40] By that, he meant that he was the greatest scholar in Babylonia – as Ben Azai had been in Tiberias during Rabi Akiva's time – yet somehow true recognition and appreciation of his greatness eluded him as it had Ben Azai. As a result of Rav's assertive statement, an elderly Babylonian scholar posed a question in *halachah* to him and he was not able to answer it correctly.[41] That the elderly scholar had been correct was later confirmed to him by Rabi.[42] That experience undoubtedly left its mark on Rav.

After the death of his father and mother, (c. 196 CE), Rav immediately returned to the Land of Israel, there informing his uncle Rabi Chiya of the sad news of the passing of his parents (who, as mentioned, were Rabi Chiya's half-brother and sister).[43] Rav was received back warmly in the court and yeshivah of Rabi and many respectful distinctions were bestowed upon him. He was given a seat of honor in the yeshivah[44] and was permitted to sit while other scholars stood during the discourses of Rabi.[45]

When Rabi died in c. 210 CE,[46] his son, Raban Gamliel III, became the *Nasi*, while his other son, Rabi Shimon, became the head of the yeshivah.[47] Rabi Chiya passed away also, soon after the death of Rabi.[48] Rav was thus left without the two great teachers and role models who had guided him throughout his formative years. Rav continued in Rabi's yeshivah and studied with Raban Gamliel III.[49]

Raban Gamliel III did not have a long reign and after his early death, his son, Rabi Yehudah Nesiah I, served as the *Nasi*. Rav was present in the Land of Israel at the beginning of the reign of Rabi Yehudah Nesiah I, but little is known of his activities during that time. What we do know is that by then Rav had become well-known as a teacher and scholar, and he began to teach publicly as well.[50] Rav developed a close association with Rav Chanina bar Chama, who was appointed by Rabi to sit at the head of the yeshivah,[51] a position of great honor and prestige. Numerous halachic decisions are quoted in the Talmud as having been stated by Rav and Rav Chanina jointly.[52] But eventually tensions arose between the two.[53] In spite of Rav's attempts to reconcile, Rav Chanina hesitated to do so.[54] He was determined to see to it that Rav should leave the Land of Israel and move to Babylonia, there to spread Torah and found yeshivos.[55] Finally, in 219 CE (during the lifetime of Rabi Yehudah Nesiah I)[56] Rav left the Land of Israel and immigrated again to Babylonia.[57] He regretted having to leave.[58]

During the reigns of Raban Gamliel III and Rabi Yehudah Nesiah I, Rav served as one of the heads of the yeshivah in the land of Israel. Rav thus becomes the bridge between the generations of the *Tannaim*, the men of the Mishnah whose time ends with the death of Rabi, and the *Amoraim* – the men of the Talmud. Rav is seen as having stature in both generations, the last of the *Tannaim* and the first of the *Amoraim*. The Talmud often states that Rav "*Tanna hu upalig*"[59] i.e. "Rav is considered to be a *Tanna* and therefore may disagree with a Mishnah." Yet Rav is mainly seen as the founding father of the Babylonian Talmud. He is thus the living combination of the eminence of the ancient Jewish communities of the Land of Israel and of Babylonia, of the Mishnah and of the Talmud.

To lead a generation of change and of a new era, special talent, and greatness is required. Rav supplied that necessary greatness in full measure. Rav would respect the customs of Babylonian Jewry,[60] but would put his stamp on all future life of that community. His reappearance in Babylonia would mark a turning point in Jewish history.

When Rav returned to Babylonia, he found the center of Jewish life and learning was in the city of Nehardea. Nearby was a town called Hutzal, which contained a *sidra* – a house of Torah study, headed by Rav Assi I.[61] Even though there was excellent Torah scholarship in Babylonia throughout the ages in the generations preceding Rav's settling there, the Talmud states that "Rav found an open valley (Babylonian Jewish life) and he enclosed it with a fence."[62] Rav established the supremacy of Torah knowledge and scholarship in Babylonia on a permanent basis.

Relief depicting an emissary from Israel spending a Sabbath in Nehardea, Babylon, from the permanent collection of the Beth Hatefutsoth Museum

His stature and forceful personality made a deep impression upon his colleagues in Babylonia, but perhaps due to his very greatness, Rav's initial experiences in Babylonia were difficult ones. When he arrived, the Torah leaders of the community were Karna and Mar Shmuel. Karna was a member of the rabbinical court in Nehardea.[63] An established scholar with a yeshivah of his own, he was an expert in the laws of torts; a number of his decisions are quoted in the Talmud.[64] He was a close friend and colleague of Mar Shmuel and was reckoned as one of the great "judges living in the Exile."[65]

Karna and Mar Shmuel awaited the arrival of Rav, though they knew him only by reputation. Mar Shmuel was much younger than Rav.[66] As they stood on the riverbank, Mar Shmuel noticed that the waters of the river were polluted and rising. He sent Karna to greet Rav and to determine if Rav was truly a great Torah scholar. Rav, who was then ill from drinking the polluted waters, was disturbed by Karna's testing of him and spoke sharply to him in return. Mar Shmuel, who was a noted physician, treated Rav for his intestinal ailment. Sadly, that treatment was one that was most uncomfortable and painful, and Rav – in agony and not realizing Mar Shmuel's intention was not to cause him any discomfort but rather to cure him – cursed Mar Shmuel that he should never have sons.[67] And thus it occurred: Mar Shmuel had daughters and no sons. Rav would later reconcile himself with both Karna[68] and Mar Shmuel[69] and they formed a triumvirate of mutual respect and help to one another.

Aside from Karna and Mar Shmuel (to whom a detailed description and biography will be dedicated in the next chapter of this book) there were other prominent scholars leading Babylonian Jewry at the time of Rav's arrival there. These men, together with Rav, formed the generational transition in Babylonia from the period of the *Tannaim* to the time of the *Amoraim,* with the primacy of Torah authority shifting to Babylonia from the Land of Israel.

I have already mentioned Rav Assi I as being the head of the *sidra* in Hutzal. He is associated throughout the Talmud with that city, knowing its history and testifying that it was a walled city at the time of Yehoshua bin Nun.[70] In Hutzal, a certain Rav Achi maintained a yeshivah where Rav served as a teacher and advisor for a short period of time.[71] While in Hutzal, Rav became friendly with Rav Assi I, a companionship that remained strong throughout their lives. Rav Assi I is a mentor, student and colleague of Rav all at one and the same time. Rav is careful to take Rav Assi I's opinion into account when deciding the law.[72] We find in numerous places in the Talmud that Rav Assi I disagreed with Rav's decisions.[73] We also find that Rav himself attempted to explain and defend Rav Assi I's opinion, even when it did not concur with his own.[74] It is obvious from the Talmud's account that Rav, Mar Shmuel and Rav Assi I all respected and granted honor to each other.[75]

Rav Assi I was one of the main teachers and mentors of Rav

Rav found an open valley (Babylonian Jewish life) and he enclosed it with a fence.

Talmud

Huna and Rav Yehudah bar Yechezkel. Even though both of these scholars of the second generation of *Amoraim* in Babylonia were primarily students of Rav, they nevertheless considered themselves disciples of Rav Assi I as well.[76] It appears that many of the disciples of Rav and of Mar Shmuel also studied under Rav Assi I. This may have occurred mainly after the death of Rav in c. 246-7 CE, though Rav Assi I himself died soon after Rav's demise.[77] After Rav's death, a ruling of Sheila bar Avina (a student of Rav) who had based his ruling on an opinion that he had heard from Rav was disputed by Rav Assi I who claimed that Rav had later retracted that opinion. The two scholars engaged in a heated debate on the subject, a dispute that spread among the other scholars as well. Both Sheila and Rav Assi I died soon thereafter, with Sheila stating to his wife that he had to "hurry [to the World to Come] to defend himself there before Rav, against Rav Assi's assertions."[78]

A companion scholar to Rav Assi I was Rav Kahana I,[79] with whom he studied and debated Torah. Both Rav Kahana I and Rav Assi I were closely associated with Rav for a while.[80] However, shortly after Rav's arrival in Babylonia, Rav Kahana I settled in the Land of Israel, never to return to Babylonia.[81] There he was held in great esteem by the scholars of the Land of Israel, with Rabi Yochanan and Rabi Shimon ben Lakish (the leaders of the first generation of *Amoraim* in the Land of Israel, and the heads of the revered yeshivah in Tiberias) hailing him as a "great man" [in Torah knowledge.][82] In the Land of Israel, he studied with the sons of Rabi Chiya, Yehudah and Chezkiyah,[83] as well as with Rabi Shimon, the son of Rabi.[84] The Talmud teaches us that both Rav Assi I and Rav Kahana I were remarkable in Torah and knowledge and were, in fact equal, to Rav in explaining and deducing Torah principles and laws.[85] We find that Rav bowed to their halachic opinions in certain instances.[86] Nevertheless, Rav was greater than they were in knowing and explaining the traditions of Torah from previous generations.[87]

Another imposing Torah scholar who flourished in Babylonia at the time of Rav was Zeirei I.[88] He had been a disciple of Rabi Chiya before Rabi Chiya immigrated to the Land of Israel, and considered him his main teacher.[89] Zeirei I debated Rav,[90] Mar Shmuel, Rav Assi I and the other great scholars of the time on a number of halachic issues and is quoted widely in the Talmud.[91] His reputation as a scholar and as a teacher of Torah was extremely high, so much so that Rava, in a later generation, proclaimed that any *breisa* (a decision of law based on the Mishnah) "that Zeirei [I] did not explicitly quote and explain should not be considered as being authoritative."[92] In his expertise in *breisos*, Zeirei I followed in the footsteps of his great mentor, Rabi Chiya, who was also famed as the accurate transmitter of the *breisos* and their explanations. Zeirei I had many disciples, and many of the students of Rav and Mar Shmuel also studied with him and quoted his halachic opinions and teachings. Chief among these were Rabi Yehudah bar Yechezkel,[93] Rav Chiya bar Ashi,[94] Rav Gidel,[95] and Rav Chisda.[96] Even the great Rabi Yochanan of Tiberias in the Land of Israel – who was a contemporary of Rav and Mar Shmuel and thus of Zeirei I as well – quotes Zerei I in halachic matters.[97] Zeirei I was also known for possessing supernatural powers, apparently able to speak to the dead[98] and ward off black magic.[99] Unfortunately, little more is known of his personal life, his family or life experiences.

Also present in Babylonia when Rav returned was Abba bar Abba. He is better known throughout the Talmud as *Abuha d'Shmuel* – the father of Mar Shmuel. So great was the fame and reputation of Mar Shmuel, that his father's persona, and even his name, was subsumed in him. There are various legends about the circumstances and blessings that gave such a son to Abba bar Abba.[100] A great scholar and teacher of Torah, Abba bar Abba also was a wealthy silk merchant.[101] He communicated with Rabi in the Land of Israel[102] and apparently also met and studied with that great editor of the Mishnah.[103] Abba was especially known for his integrity and honesty; monies belonging to orphans were deposited with him for safekeeping.[104] He guarded these funds with a greater degree of care than even his own wealth.[105]

Abba bar Abba was one of the leading scholars of Nehardea, and during Rav's stay in that community he and Rav studied Torah together.[106] Abba's greatness was eclipsed by his son's fame and reputation, something which surely must have been of great satisfaction and joy to the father. We find matters of *halachah* in dispute between him and his son, Mar Shmuel.[107] Abba lived a very long life and was seen as the elder scholar and leader of the community. His forthcoming nature made him a most beloved person.[108] Aside from Shmuel, Abba had another son named Pinchas.[109] Among Abba bar Abba's students were Rav Masna and Mar Ukva, second generation *Amoraim*.[110] The great scholar Levi – Rav Levi ben Sissas – was Abba's fast friend and Abba's emotional eulogy over him is recorded for us in the Talmud Yerushalmi.[111]

Even though Rav and Mar Shmuel surpassed Abba bar Abba in Torah knowledge and education, Abba remained the titular head of the Babylonian Torah community centered in Nehardea until his death in 248 CE. After his death, he appeared to his son Mar Shmuel to inform him of how highly he was thought of in the heavenly court.[112] He also sadly informed him that he would soon join his father in the next world and so it was;[113] Mar Shmuel's demise occurred only one year after his father's passing.[114]

As mentioned above, Levi – Rav Levi ben Sissas – was a loyal friend and a colleague of Abba bar Abba as well as a colleague of Rav. He was originally a student and colleague of Rabi in the Land of Israel, and he only settled permanently in Babylonia some time after Rabi's death. Rav had already become the head of his yeshivah in Sura when Levi settled in Babylonia.[115] Rabi had held Levi in great esteem, stating that he was "my equal."[116] and indeed, Levi was a reliable transmitter of Rabi's teachings.[117] He was also one of the compilers of *breisos* that expanded and elucidated the words of the Mishnah. "Levi's *breisos*" is a phrase found a number of times in the Talmud.[118] Levi thus joined Rav Chiya, Rav Hoshiya, Bar Kapara and others of the generation of scholars who bridged the period of the *Tannaim* and the *Amoraim*, in creating the basic supplement to the Mishnah: the *breisos* that filled in the white spaces of the Mishnah itself.

Levi was the teacher of many of the great men of the first generation of *Amoraim*, including Mar Shmuel.[119] He was a well-known and gifted orator, and a person of great influence and charisma.

In celebrating the *Simchas Beis HaShoevah*[120] with Rabi, Levi performed extraordinary feats of juggling – keeping eight knives in the air at one time![121] However, when he demonstrated *kidah* – a form of worshipful prostration causing great muscle tension on the arms and thighs – in front of Rabi, he dislocated his hip and remained with a limp thereafter.[122] The Talmud tells us that one of the causes for Levi becoming a cripple was that he spoke harsh words against Heaven, so to speak, for not immediately responding to the prayers and fast days of Israel during a period of drought in the Land of Israel.[123] Nevertheless, Levi's demand for rain was answered.[124] Levi was recognizable because of his great height and his limp, and he was popularly called *"gavra rabah u'mitla"* – "the great tall man with a limp."[125]

Also as mentioned above, when Rabi died Rabi Chanina bar Chama was to be appointed the head of the yeshivah, as per Rabi's last will. However, Rabi Chanina deferred to Rabi Afeiss, who was two years older than he.[126] Ironically Rabi Chanina refused to accept Rabi Affeis as his halachic authority, feeling that his own erudition was far more profound than that of Rav Afeiss. Because of this, Rav Chanina remained "outside" of the yeshivah that was now headed by Rabi Afeiss, not entering its premises when Rav Afeiss delivered his lectures. In order to give honor to Rav Chanina, who was a great scholar, Levi decided to join him in remaining "outside" the yeshivah's premises.[127] Apparently this action was frowned upon in the Heavens, for Levi was forced to sit "outside" the heavenly yeshivah after his death, and only Mar Shmuel's intercession on his behalf brought him "inside" the heavenly yeshivah's confines.[128] When Rav Afeiss died, Rav Chanina entered the yeshivah and became its head, as per Rabi's original instructions. Levi, having lost his "outside" learning companion to his new position and not willing to now enter "inside" the yeshivah, left the Land of Israel, and came to Nehardea in Babylonia. He was warmly received.[129] Even in exile, Levi could hear the heavenly spirit moving in his study hall.[130]

This, then, was the Nehardea to which Rav came from the Land of Israel – a city of eminent scholars and of established yeshivos and communal institutions. Though Rav was warmly received by the scholars of Nehardea, he felt uncomfortable, not having any official position. He gave great respect to Mar Shmuel, regretting that he had cursed him when Mar Shmuel attempted to cure his stomach pains.[131] As a temporary means of support for Rav, the *Reish Galusa* (Exilarch, or official head of the Jewish community of Babylonia) appointed him *angramos* – an inspector of weights and measures and of the quality of wine being sold in Nehardea.[132] The Exilarch also wanted Rav to supervise the prices of food as well, to prevent price gouging in times of want. Rav felt that this was not within the purview of his duties – or perhaps even his desires and capabilities – and refused to do so. Stung and angered by this display of independence, the Exilarch had Rav arrested and imprisoned.[133] Karna, the leading judge in Nehardea, attempted to intercede on Rav's behalf. He visited Rav in prison and advised him to fulfill at least the Exilarch's demands on a pro forma basis. Rav remained adamant, and Karna left disappointed and dismayed at the injustice done to Rav.[134] Eventually Rav was released from prison, but he no longer served as an *angramos*. Nehardea was proving to be a difficult place for Rav to function effectively. Things would not immediately improve for him as the following story indicates.

Rav now attended the *sidra* study hall of Rav Sheila in Nehardea. The custom there was that the head of the *sidra* – in this case, Rav Sheila – delivered the Torah lecture and it was then explained to the assembled students by an *amora* or *meturgaman*, literally, a speaker or translator. Rav Sheila's usual *amora* was not present

Be careful in the treatment of the children of the poor, for from them will come forth Torah.

Rav

one day and Rav volunteered to serve in that capacity. However, he interpreted Rav Sheila's words more creatively and differently than was Rav Sheila's intent. Rav was called to task for this and Rav Sheila wished to immediately substitute another *Amora* in his stead.[135] Rav refused to step down as *Amora* until Rav Sheila fully completed his lecture, as he felt that to do so would be degrading.[136]

Because of these unpleasant incidents, Rav soon left Nehardea and moved to the neighboring city of Hutzal.[137] There, a great study hall had been established under the leadership and name of Rav Achi, a member of the last generation of *Tannaim*. Rav Achi was the son and main disciple of Rav Yoshiyah, who himself had been a student of the *Tanna*, Rav Yishmael.[138] Even after Rav Achi died – apparently sometime before Rav arrived in Hutzal[139] – the great study hall nevertheless continued to be called the study hall of Rav Achi. When Rav came to Hutzal, Rav Assi I was active there.[140] In this great study hall, Rav finally found a fitting position for himself and an outlet for his enormous knowledge and talents.

Parthian coins depicting King Mithridates, Parthian ruler, 2nd century CE

Rav was appointed as the advisor and scholarly mentor of the students in Rav Achi's study hall.[141] Rav was very successful in this role and many students flocked to him. Above all else, he preached the necessity for humility as a precondition to Torah greatness.[142] His reputation, not only as a great Torah scholar but also as an outstanding educator, was created and enhanced in the study hall of Hutzal.[143]

When Rav Sheila died, Rav was asked to head the yeshivah in Nehardea. Rav refused to accept the position out of deference to Mar Shmuel, even though Rav was older than Mar Shmuel, was of great renown as a scholar, and was regarded as the chief student of Rabi and Rabi Chiya. Mar Shmuel thus became the head of the study hall in Nehardea, a position that he filled until his death in

254 CE.[144]

After the death of Rabi Yehudah Nesiah, Rabi's grandson, in c. 230 CE, the institution of the *Nasi* in the Land of Israel was greatly weakened and Babylonia took over as the focal point and central location in Jewish life. Rav left Hutzal and moved to Sura,[145] there to establish his own great study hall, which eventually became the center of Torah study for Babylonian Jewry for centuries. He soon became known as the leading head of the *sidra* in Babylonia.[146] With the establishment of his yeshivah in Sura, the mantle of Torah authority also passed from the Land of Israel to the Babylonian yeshivos. Babylonia would continue as the center of Jewish life and Torah study for the next 700 years of Jewish history. Its yeshivos would become the authoritative and decisive voice of Israel in matters of *halachah*, custom and public policy.[147]

Babylonia was part of the Parthian Empire from 129 CE till 226 CE. The Jewish communities fared well under Parthian rule and were almost autonomous in governing themselves. The last of the Parthian rulers, Artban (or Artchan, as he is sometimes known in the Talmud) was particularly friendly to Rav. The Talmud compares their relationship to that of Rabi and Antoninus in the previous generation.[148] We are told that there was an exchange of gifts between this Parthian king and Rabi himself earlier in the generation. The king sent Rabi a diamond and Rabi sent him a *mezuzah* in return.[149] Rabi explained to Artchan that the *mezuzah* was more valuable than the diamond: after all, the diamond requires its owners to guard it, while the *mezuzah* guards its owners![150]

When Rav settled in the area of southwest Babylonia in which Sura is located, the Parthian Empire was already in decline, though still nominally in control of the country. There were Jewish communities in the area of Sura from the time of the destruction of the First Temple. Because of local tribal and dynastic wars, the Jewish community there dwindled in the first century of the Common Era, with most Jews moving to Nehardea and Netzivin. However, by the time of Rav's appearance in Babylonia, almost two centuries later, a large number of Jews once again lived in Sura and its environs.[151] It was not a center of Torah learning, and the Jewish population there

The house of Rav was known as a miniature sanctuary of God.

Talmud

THE FIRST GENERATION OF AMORAIM IN BABYLONIA

was strongly susceptible to assimilation.[152] Rav apparently chose to settle in this location precisely because of its low spiritual state: it afforded greater opportunities for spreading and strengthening Torah amongst its Jewish inhabitants than did older, more established communities already populated with Torah scholars.[153] This pioneering, risk-taking spirit of Rav reflected his own strength of character, self-reliance and deep love of Torah and the Jewish people.[154] His yeshivah in Sura gained great and immediate fame[155] and his two earliest students, Rav Huna[156] and Rav Yehudah bar Yechez-kel[157] helped attract great Jewish minds and hearts to Sura to hear Rav's teachings. Rav and the town of Sura became synonymous. The two great centers of Torah learning and Jewish life were now in Sura, headed by Rav, and in Nehardea, headed by Mar Shmuel.

Within the jurisdiction of Sura a smaller community – almost a suburb – was the town of Masa Machsiya.[158] In addition to heading the yeshivah there, Rav served as the chief judge of the court in Sura, albeit doing so in a reluctant and fearful manner.[159] In a short time, Rav's yeshivah grew to 1200 full-time students.[160] These numbers were swelled by thousands more who came to study in the yeshivah in the months of Elul and Adar – the months of the *kallah*.[161] Apparently, Rav was the founder, or at least the main proponent, of the institution of the *yarchei kallah*.[162] The yeshivah in Sura had a large building, an enclosed colonnade surrounding it,[163] small classrooms adjoining the building[164] and a large vegetable garden nearby.[165] All of this was called "the house of Rav."[166] and was known as a "miniature sanctuary [of God]."[167] For more than twenty years Rav stood at the helm of the great yeshivah in Sura, until his death in c. 246-7 CE. The legacy of Sura was continued by Rav's disciples, especially by his successor as head of the yeshivah, Rav Huna.[168] While Nehardea declined after the death of Mar Shmuel in c. 254 CE, Sura remained as the steadfast fortress of Torah study in Babylonia for centuries.

As mentioned above, the Parthian Empire collapsed in 226 CE and was then replaced by the Persian Empire. This new ruling force at first caused enormous problems for the Jews living in Babylonia. A leading group within the empire was a fanatical Zoroastrian sect called in the Talmud *Amgushei,* or *Chaverim.* Their opposition to Jewish monotheism was fierce and bitter.[169] On the days that they dedicated to the service of their god of darkness they forbade any fire to be lit. Initially, the Jews suffered under their rule so much that they even expressed a preference for Roman rule over that of the *Chaverim.*[170] The Jewish communities in Babylonia were forced to resort to bribing the *Chaverim* in order to allow Jewish religious life to function.[171] Jews no longer held any public office and were not even appointed to the menial tasks of customs collectors or tax agents.[172] However, as we will soon see, Mar Shmuel was able to come to an accommodation with Shevor Malka, the Persian king, and the persecution of the *Chaverim* against the Jews began to abate.

Rav was built of a strong and healthy physical constitution (and lived well into his eighties),[173] but he had a fastidious nature and personality.[174] As mentioned above, he ate meat only at a meal related to a *mitzvah.*[175] With his remarkable insight, Rav saw purpose in every created object that exists in this world.[176] Distinguished and beloved, he traveled throughout the Jewish communities of Babylonia, strengthening and encouraging Torah life amongst them.

However, the infirmities of age did not skip over Rav. His eyesight began to fail,[177] he became stooped over,[178] many of his teeth decayed and fell out[179] and he became subject to forgetfulness.[180] He ruefully stated that "everyone and everything [meaning all afflictions] rules over a person at the end of one's days."[181] Rav accepted the infirmities of advancing age with a tinge of sadness and a great sigh.[182] His students prayed for him regularly[183] and their love and respect for him knew no limits. Rav bade his student, Rav Shmuel bar Sheila[184] (alternatively spelled bar Sheilas) to eulogize him at his funeral, requesting of him to do so emotionally and to touch the hearts of those gathered there. He promised him that "I will be there as well."[185]

Rav was not buried in Sura, but rather in a neighboring town, apparently near where his parents were buried.[186] His grave became a shrine, and the masses of Israel came to take soil from his burial place and use it as a talisman for healing and good fortune.[187] There was some halachic dispute over the propriety of this popular cus-

At my funeral, deliver an emotional eulogy, for I will be there as well.

Rav to Rav Sheila

tom, but Mar Shmuel allowed it.[188] Rav's students grieved bitterly over the death of their teacher and felt his loss keenly and painfully.[189] Mar Shmuel marked the passing of Rav by stating that "the man that I was in awe of has now departed." As customary at the time, he also tore twelve garments in grief.[190] For the duration of the year of mourning over Rav's death, the rabbis decreed that the rejoicing at Jewish weddings should be tempered.[191]

The demise of Rav was seen as a national calamity. Yet Rav lived on in the work of his students and his descendants. His influence and greatness spanned all of the generations of Israel and today he is still what he was in the days of his life – the master of the Talmud and of the Oral Law. As mentioned earlier, Rav Huna and Rav Yehudah bar Yechezkel were his chief disciples.[192] They were primarily responsible for disseminating Rav's statements and opinions to the later generations of *Amoraim*. Rav Yehudah bar Yechezkel quotes his master's teachings no less than 386 times in the Talmud.[193] Rashi is of the opinion that all of the statements of Rav that appear in the Talmud, but were transmitted anonymously, are also the result of Rav Yehudah bar Yechezkel's teachings.[194] Mar Shmuel also transmits Rav's teachings in a reverent and loving fashion.[195] Rav's children and grandchildren also quoted the teachings of Rav extensively and spread those teachings to later generations.[196] Essentially, Rav founded the Talmud – and the Talmud has made Rav forever immortal.

Frieze depicting a captured Parthian, c. 200 CE (detail)

Because of the great magnitude of his role in the formulation of the Talmud, the fact that Rav was also a significant poet and liturgist is sometimes overlooked. The soaring *Musaf* service of Rosh Hashanah called *tekiasa d'bei Rav* – the order of the sounding of the shofar as composed in Rav's yeshivah[197]– remains today as the basis of our Rosh Hashanah liturgy. Rav is also the author, together with Mar Shmuel, of the prayer *Vatodienu* – a prayer that is recited on the night of a holiday when it falls on Saturday night.[198] He is the author of the prayer to God for the provision of all human needs – physical and spiritual – that has become the liturgy of Jews on the Shabbos preceding the beginning of the new month and the "birth" of that new moon.[199] Rav is also the source of the renowned prayer Aleinu[200] that is recited thrice daily in all synagogues and in private prayer. Rav's deeply spiritual prayers, together with the Psalms of David and the compositions of the *Anshei Knesses HaGedolah* (the Men of the Great Assembly) are the backbone of all Jewish liturgy. Rav, therefore, emerges as a multi-faceted and wide-ranging scholar and intellect. Whatever subject or discipline he labored over bears his hallmark of excellence indelibly stamped upon it.

Rav and his school are also known as the editors of many of the major Torah works that complemented and elucidated the Mishnah particularly, and the Oral Law generally. These include:

Are you my beloved Shimi!

Rav to his grandson, Shimi (Talmud)

- *Sifra D'bei Rav, also known as Toras Kohanim, an halachic commentary to Vayikra/Leviticus*
- *Sifrei D'bei Rav, a commentary similar to the Sifra, except it relates to Bamidbar/Numbers and Dvarim/Deuteronomy*
- *Mechilta, again halachic commentary, this time relating to Shemos/Exodus[201]*
- *Aggadata D'bei Rav, a collection of Aggadic interpretations, parables and moral lessons based upon the verses of the Written Torah*
- *Tosefta D'bei Rav, a commentary and restatement of the laws pertaining to certain tractates of the Mishnah – thereby adding to the earlier Tosefta of Rav Oshiya, which was an addition to the Mishnah as edited by Rabi Yehudah HaNasi.*

Rav fathered three sons and three daughters, though his marriage was not an especially happy one.[202] Nevertheless, he treated his wife respectfully and gently and cautioned others against any form of wife abuse.[203] Two of Rav's sons, Chiya and Ayvu, appear on the pages of the Talmud. A third son, whose name is unknown to us, apparently died in Rav's lifetime.[204] Chiya became a much-noted Torah scholar who appears countless times in the Talmud.[205] Ayvu did not find much success in his studies, and Rav therefore counseled him to become a merchant.[206] Rav's wisdom allowed him to see his sons as different individuals with different talents and skills. He taught that one should not differentiate in the treatment of one's children during one's lifetime.[207] Chiya was apparently sickly, and Rav, his devoted father, was greatly concerned about his health and welfare.[208]

Chiya's son, Shimi, studied with his grandfather, Rav.[209] The special relationship between grandfather and grandson is reflected many times in the Talmud when Rav exclaims in happiness: "*Shimi aat!*" "Are you [my beloved] Shimi!"[210] How satisfied Rav must have been to have such a grandson as Shimi – he was taking his place among the first rank of scholars of the *Amoraim* of the next generation. Rav's immortality was guaranteed by his students and his descendants, who preserved his teachings and personality in the pages of the Talmud.

Rav's oldest daughter was married to the son of the *Reish Galusa*, the Exilarch. She bore him two sons, Ukva and Nechemiah. These two of Rav's grandsons are mentioned many times in the Talmud as scholars and aristocrats of note.[211] They were disciples of Rav Chisda,[212] who himself was married to a granddaughter of Rav.[213] A second daughter of Rav was married to one of his outstanding students, Rav Chanan ben Rava.[214] He quotes Rav many times in the Talmud[215] and was a devoted disciple and son-in-law. There are two other grandchildren of Rav, Ayvu and Chezkiyah, who are sons of a daughter, and are mentioned in the Talmud.[216] However, it is not clear to us from the Talmud which daughter of Rav was their mother. Rav Chanan's daughter was married to Rav Chisda, as mentioned above. (Rav Chisda's life and accomplishments will be discussed in detail later in this book.) As can be seen readily from all of the above, the "house of Rav" – his direct descendants and students – became the bulwark of Torah for Babylonian Jewry for centuries to come. The legacy of that great person and of his family continues to light the way of the Jewish people down to our very day.

Mar Shmuel

MAR SHMUEL (SHMUEL BAR ABBA)
c. 230 CE

Teachers
• Rabi Yehudah HaNasi
• Rabi Levi ben Sissas
• Abba bar Abba
• Rabi Chanina bar Chama
• Rabi Elazar ben Shimon
• Rabi Shimon ben Elazar

Colleagues
• Rav
• Rav Sheila
• Karna

Students
• Rav Yehudah bar Yechezkel
• Rav Chiya bar Rav
• Rav Chanan bar Rava
• Rav Huna

Relatives
• Father: Abba bar Abba
• Sons-in-law: Issur Giyora, Rabi Shemen ben Abba
• Grandson: Rav Mari bar Rachel

av's alter ego in the Talmud is Mar Shmuel, the head of the great yeshivah in Nehardea. His father, Abba bar Abba, a noted scholar and resident of Nehardea, sensed that the child born to him was destined to be a brilliant leader of the Jewish nation.[1] As stated earlier, for the rest of his life Abba bar Abba was called *Abuha d'Shmuel* – the father of Shmuel. He was Shmuel's earliest teacher and it is apparent from the Talmud that Abba bar Abba invested extensive time and effort in teaching his prodigal son Torah and educational skills.[2] He then sent Shmuel to Netzivin, the home of the yeshivah of Rabi Yehudah ben Bseira to study Torah.[3] There, the young Shmuel became a member of the *chevra kadisha* – the holy burial society. Upon learning of this, his father reprimanded him, telling him that he sent him to Netzivin to study Torah exclusively: "Are there no graves here in Nehardea that I had to send you to Netzivin?"[4] Shmuel also studied under Levi ben Sissas, the colleague and student of Rabi, and Shmuel quotes him often in the Talmud.[5]

He acquired a good deal of worldly and scientific knowledge as well. He was an astronomer of note who claimed that "the paths of the stars in heaven were as familiar to me as are the streets and pathways of my city of Nehardea."[6] He was also well-versed in mathematics and this skill, when combined with his knowledge of astronomy, allowed him to become the expert in fixing the dates of the Hebrew calendar for decades in advance.[7] Shmuel achieved great fame and notoriety as a gifted physician and healer. He himself stated that he was an expert in diagnosing sicknesses and healing them.[8] I will discuss his skills in worldly matters in greater detail later in this chapter.

When Shmuel traveled to the Land of Israel[9] to study at the yeshivah of Rabi, he found he was one of the younger students there. He studied with some of the *Tannaim* – the illustrious last generation of Mishnah creators.[10] It is probable that this is where he also met Rav, an older student of Rabi, for the first time. Shmuel wanted to receive *semichah* (ordination) from Rabi, who apparently was willing to ordain him. But as in the case of Rav,[11] the attempt never came to fruition. Shmuel was a favorite of Rabi and he helped cure Rabi of an eye ailment, for which Rabi was immensely grateful to him.[12] Yet, "the matter of the *semichah* was unsuccessful."[13] Rashi indicates that the reason was that "the times were dangerous and the scholars could not therefore convene."[14] Rabi evidently desired the assent of the scholars to grant the *semichah,* and outside circumstances prevented it from happening. Other opinions are that Shmuel's expertise in the calendar and astronomy, if coupled with *semichah,* would move the decision-making process regarding the calendar to Babylonia, something which the rabbis of the Land of Israel were then unwilling to do;[15] or that some of the scholars objected to granting him *semichah* because of his worldly knowledge.[16] In any event, Shmuel accepted the matter most graciously, stating that apparently it was not fated that he be called *"Rabi"* and that it was sufficient for him to be called *"Chacham"* – a wise Torah scholar.[17] Because of this incident, he is called throughout the Talmud by the name of *Mar* Shmuel, or more simply, just Shmuel, indicating that he is not *Rabi* Shmuel.[18]

Mar Shmuel returned to Nehardea, at that time the center of Torah activity in Babylonia, and was appointed as a judge on the rabbinical court of the town. Rav Sheila was then the head of the *sidra* (yeshivah) in Nehardea. As mentioned above, Mar Shmuel welcomed Rav to Nehardea, and served as his doctor and patron. In c. 219 CE, Rav Sheila passed away and Mar Shmuel was appointed

The times were dangerous and the scholars could not therefore convene.

Rashi

as the head of the *sidra,* as Rav had deferred to him in this honor and appointment. Shmuel would be the head of the ancient, scholarly, and prestigious Jewish community of Nehardea for the next 35 years, until his death in 254 CE.[19]

Under Mar Shmuel's leadership, Nehardea became the co-equal of Torah learning with Sura, where Rav's prestigious yeshivah was located. In this way, the pattern of Babylonian Jewish life was set for many centuries, with two competing and complementing main yeshivos in operation simultaneously. The yeshivos differed in customs and this was reflected in the life of the two communities: The Talmud points out that the area of Babylonia neighboring Sura followed the opinions and dictates of Rav, while the area of Nehardea followed the opinions and decisions of Mar Shmuel.[20]

Rav and Shmuel established and led the first generation of *Amoraim,* setting the example and standards for all later scholars of the Talmud. Mar Shmuel and Rav were together called "Our rabbis and teachers in Babylonia."[21]

In Nehardea, Mar Shmuel had as his companion and cohort Karna, who served as the chief judge of the rabbinical court of the area.[22] As mentioned earlier, it was he and Mar Shmuel who first welcomed Rav to Nehardea albeit with considerable mutual misunderstanding.[23] The yeshivah in Nehardea that Mar Shmuel headed reached its zenith of authority after the death of Rav. There was an interregnum in Sura when no immediate successor to Rav took control of the yeshivah there. Because of this, many of the students of Sura now came to study under Mar Shmuel in Nehardea. The yeshivah in Sura was held together by Rav's oldest student, Rav Hamnuna,[24] but he did not serve as the official head of the yeshivah, which remained temporarily leaderless. The students who nevertheless remained in Sura after Rav's death now sent their questions to Mar Shmuel in Nehardea for explanation and decision.[25] Rav's own son, Chiya,[26] and Rav's son-in-law, Rav Chanan bar Rava[27] journeyed to Nehardea at this point to study Torah under the direction of Mar Shmuel. Rav Huna, the leading student and eventual heir of Rav as head of the yeshivah in Sura, also studied under Mar Shmuel for a period of time after Rav's death.[28] Rav

> **The ways of the stars in heaven are as familiar to me as the streets of my home city of Nehardea.**
>
> *Mar Shmuel*

Yehudah bar Yechezkel, another of the primary disciples of Rav, also came to study with Mar Shmuel. Rav Yehudah had previously gone to Hutzal to study under Rav Assi I, however Rav Assi I also passed away shortly after Rav's death.[29] Rav Yehudah then made his way to Nehardea to study with Mar Shmuel as well.[30] Rav Yehudah and Rav Huna became the main conduits of their masters' teachings, loyally transmitting the Torah of both Rav and Mar Shmuel, as well as that of Rav Assi I, to the next generation of Babylonian *Amoraim*.[31]

Rav Yehudah was much beloved by Mar Shmuel. Once Mar Shmuel exclaimed: "[Rav Yehudah's greatness is of such a nature] that it is hard to believe that he was born of a woman!"[32] Mar Shmuel many times called Rav Yehudah "*shinanah*" – the sharp, clever one.[33] Rav Yehudah concentrated on explaining, and even correcting, the text of the Mishnah and *breisos,* and was a recognized expert in being able to do so.[34]

Because Mar Shmuel valued the teachings of Rav greatly, he demanded from the former students of Rav in his yeshivah that they faithfully transmit to him all of the teachings that Rav said in Sura. Once, when Mar Shmuel felt that Rav Yehudah neglected to tell him a teaching of Rav, he became cross with him.[35] Even when Mar Shmuel disagreed with the decisions or explanations of Rav, he treasured Rav's opinions and always took them into account when formulating his own decisions, opinions and explanations.[36] Out of deference to the honor of Rav, Mar Shmuel was so respectful of his descendants that he never reprimanded them publicly.[37] Yet he always reserved the right to disagree with Rav, and sometimes expressed himself on a matter quite strongly and vociferously.[38]

As noted previously, Mar Shmuel was the recognized expert in all halachic issues concerning monetary matters, torts, and commercial transactions. The Talmud "compromised" between the two great scholars of Babylonia by stating that in matters of ritual law and prohibitions, the *halachah* would follow the opinion of Rav; whereas in all matters of monetary concern and civil law, the *halachah* would follow the opinion of Mar Shmuel.[39] The views of Mar Shmuel in monetary matters were held to be basic to any understanding of Torah in these matters.[40]

The fact that the Jewish court system operated independently in Babylonia under the tolerance of the Parthian Empire (unlike the Land of Israel, where the Romans did not allow Jewish law and courts to function freely) made Mar Shmuel's opinions especially relevant and necessary in Babylonian Jewish life. Yet, Mar Shmuel recognized the realities of the Jewish people in exile, living as a minority under the rule of non-Jews often inimical to Jewish life: he therefore proclaimed the great Jewish legal principle of *dina d'malchusa dina* – the law of the land is the law for Jews as well.[41] This basic foundation of Jewish law would serve to minimize unnecessary conflicts between the Jewish communities of the Diaspora and the non-Jewish governments that ruled them.

As a corollary of the concept of *dina d'malchusa dina*, Mar Shmuel also upheld the right of government to legally confiscate property from those who had not paid their taxes and to sell that property to others.[42] Mar Shmuel placed great faith in the judgment of the rabbinical court to decide complicated matters when there were no clear proofs present for either party.[43] This concept of *shuda d'dayna*[44] – the best estimation of the judges – became a bulwark for flexibility in order to achieve social justice in monetary matters.

Mar Shmuel upholds the concept that possession is nine-tenths of the law, and that strong proofs are needed to remove property from the possession of the one who is holding it.[45] In monetary matters, Mar Shmuel refuses to follow the principle of *rov* (statistical or psychological probability) [46] when deciding disputed claims.[47] He limits *rov* to matters of ritual law and prohibitions only.[48] In essence, this is a further strengthening of his rule that in monetary matters possession rules, unless clear and convincing proofs against its legality are forthcoming. *Rov* is in itself only a theory, a supposition – circumstantial evidence at best – and is not the clear and convincing proof necessary to override the fact of possession of the property in dispute. However, Mar Shmuel limits the strength of possession alone as a determining factor by stating that if the *safek* – the doubt in question which is the crux of the

The law of the land is the law for Jews as well.

Mar Shmuel

monetary dispute – occurred while the property or animal was in the possession of one of the parties, then that party must assume the burden of proof to prove that he is not liable, or that the property is truly his.[49] All of these judicial principles of law taught by Mar Shmuel were accepted by the Talmud as correct and binding and are the underpinnings of Jewish civil law to this very day.

Safeguarding the rights of women, especially of widows and orphans, was also a major concern of his. In the ancient world (as in our time, perhaps, as well) widows and orphans were often hapless and helpless victims of predators in society who sought to profit from their lack of a defender of their interests. Shmuel allowed an orphaned sister to keep her own earnings, even while she was being supported by her brothers.[50] In a case of a questionable divorce, where the woman was "divorced but not divorced" and in limbo, Mar Shmuel asserted that her husband has to continue to support her until the matter is resolved.[51] He ruled that the clothing and personal effects of a wife are her property, that her husband has no claim to them, and that his heirs may not deduct their value from her share of the estate.[52] The right of support of orphaned daughters was to be extended until they reach their majority.[53] Orphans did not require a *pruzbul* to keep loans owed to them valid and not rendered void by the *shemittah* year.[54] Mar Shmuel also preserved the rights of orphans against the widow herself, stating that the widow could not in effect disinherit the orphans, even when her husband stated that

Frieze depicting a captured Parthian, c. 200 CE

all of his property should go to his wife.[55] Mar Shmuel moreover insisted that the rabbinical court force a husband to support his wife
properly during their marriage.[56] He also originated the statement:
"It is forbidden for a man to be without a wife."[57]

Mar Shmuel was able to craft a relationship with the Persian
ruler Shevor Malka I, the second king of the Persian dynasty who
rose to power in 241 CE. The monarch was a kind and charitable
person,[58] and apparently well-versed in Jewish law and practices.[59]
Mar Shmuel and Shevor Malka I held discussions on many different issues[60] and Mar Shmuel even entertained the king by performing difficult juggling stunts for him![61]

Shevor Malka I embarked on wars of conquest against the Romans, but in the end was forced to retreat before their superior
might. Many thousands of Jews were killed in these wars, though
Shevor Malka I declared that he never willfully persecuted or killed
any Jews.[62] The friendly relationship between Mar Shmuel and
Shevor Malka I led to the rabbis sometimes calling Mar Shmuel
himself Shevor Malka[63] in recognition of his leadership qualities
and legal expertise.[64] During the reign of Shevor Malka I (until
his death in 272 CE), the Jewish community in Babylonia enjoyed
religious autonomy and relative freedom for their communal and
societal organizations. The cultivation of good relations with the
Parthian, and later Persian, rulers by Rav and Mar Shmuel made
a distinct difference for the better in Jewish Babylonia in the third
century CE.

Little is known regarding the wife of Mar Shmuel. However,
Mar Shmuel stated that "the wife of a *chaver* – a Torah scholar
– is to be treated as a *chaver* herself."[65] The father of three daughters, Mar Shmuel had no sons.[66] Great tragedies struck all of them.
His older two daughters were captured by kidnappers, taken to
the Land of Israel, and held there for ransom. Kidnapping Jews
for ransom was common in that era, for the kidnappers knew that
strenuous efforts would be exerted by the Jews to redeem the victims from their kidnappers.[67] When the daughters were redeemed,
the rabbinic court of Rabi Chanina in the Land of Israel questioned
them in order to certify and approve their legitimacy to marry.[68]

The court ruled that they were free to marry even a *kohein*, if they so desired.[69] Rabi Shemen ben Abba, who was a *kohein* and relative of the daughters of Mar Shmuel, married one of them.[70] When she died soon thereafter, Rabi Shemen married the second sister. She, too, died shortly afterward.[71] The rabbis of the Talmud attributed these tragedies to the attempt of the Babylonian rabbis to institute their right to set the Jewish calendar without taking the opinion of the rabbis of the Land of Israel into account.[72] The Land of Israel is zealous of its rights and primary privileges.

Mar Shmuel's third daughter, Rachel, also suffered the same fate as her sisters and was kidnapped. However, her kidnapper, Isur, was intimate with her and later married her. He later converted to Judaism[73] and their son, Rav Mari bar Rachel, became one of the leading scholars of the second generation of *Amoraim*.[74] Both Isur and Rav Mari lived long lives.[75] Rav Mari fathered two sons, Rav Ada Sava and Mar Zutra I, both of whom were great Torah scholars in their own right in the third generation of *Amoraim*.[76] Thus, in spite of all of the turmoil and tragedies of the time that afflicted Mar Shmuel and his family, many generations of Torah scholars emanated from him. God has His ways.

As mentioned earlier, the Talmud also records that Mar Shmuel had a brother, Pinchas.[77] The two brothers married sisters and thus were both brothers and brothers-in-law to each other.[78] Mar Shmuel, as noted above, gained great fame as a physician and his medical and health recommendations are found scattered throughout the pages of the Talmud. His basic medical advice was to encourage hygiene: he advocated cleanliness above all else.[79] He attributed illnesses to "the wind" and the general environment.[80] Though his remedies and potions, especially for eye problems, were in demand,[81] he always cautioned that cleanliness of the body was more effective at preserving health than all of the medicinal potions in the world![82] Moreover, (in the days long before multimillion dollar scientific research bore this out) he deemed washing and wiping one's face carefully as necessary to preserve good skin health.[83] Mar Shmuel's famous dictum was that any sudden change in diet and lifestyle automatically brought upon that person intestinal sickness[84] and he

> **The wife of a chaver – a Torah scholar – is to be treated as a chaver herself.**
>
> *Mar Shmuel*

advocated a moderate lifestyle. It was also his belief that different stages of life required different eating habits.[85] He encouraged good sleeping habits[86] and discouraged fasting.[87] In a world that knew not of x-rays and digital scanning of internal body organs, Mar Shmuel improvised diagnostic tests and methods.[88] The medicine of Mar Shmuel's time, and of many later centuries as well, relied on bloodletting through leeches or other means to cure and even prevent numerous illnesses. Mar Shmuel had many suggestions as to the proper use of this then-accepted medicinal tool.[89] Mar Shmuel's medical knowledge and expertise was well received by the rabbis of the Talmud, even when it concerned matters of *halachah*. Thus, Mar Shmuel's opinion as to what was considered an endangerment of human life, regarding the basic *halachah* allowing the desecration of Shabbos in order to save human life, was accepted.[90] Mar Shmuel prescribed regular exercise for good digestion and good health.[91] He also advanced opinions about animal anatomy, especially as it affected the laws of kashrus,[92] and he sometimes expressed himself bluntly as to his expertise over Rav on this subject.[93] Nevertheless, Mar Shmuel many times bowed to the opinions of Rav in these matters.[94]

Mar Shmuel forbade "stealing another person's mind" [i.e. trust] through false appearances and/or representations, etc., whether the victim is a Jew or a non-Jew.[95] His insights into the psychology of human behavior are also widely quoted in the Talmud:

- *"He who accuses another of a blemish [in family lineage, etc.] is himself probably guilty of that same blemish."*[96]
- *"King Saul's reign was short-lived because he was above reproach and there existed no criticism of his past behavior when he first became king."*[97]
- *"A man should not ask another man regarding the welfare of that man's wife."*[98]

Mar Shmuel envisioned the *yetzer hara* as a stalk of wheat that silently grows next to a person and thus catches him unaware and undefended.[99] In all matters of life and health, both spiritual and physical, he advocated caution and preventive behavior. His medi-

Olive oil press, Beth Guvrin, 4th-6th century CE

cal advice of moderation, cleanliness, and preemptive care applies to the soul just as much as it does to the body.

On the societal level, Mar Shmuel had views on family, government, and history. He cautioned against disinheriting a son that is "bad," for one never knows what the future generations of that son will look like.[100] He observed that once a government decides to undertake a project – even an irrational one, such as leveling a mountain – it will see the project through to its completion, no matter what.[101] Assessing the past, Mar Shmuel saw Rome's eventual triumph over Israel in 70 CE as a result of King Solomon marrying the daughter of the Pharaoh, even though there passed a millennium of time between the two events.[102] Looking toward the future, he envisioned a rather prosaic messianic era when he stated: "There will be no difference between our present world and the world of the messianic era except for the fact that Israel will not be subject to the domination of foreign powers."[103]

Mar Shmuel was especially active in interpreting and clarifying the texts of the Mishnah. We often find in the Talmud the expression *chisurei mechsara* – i.e. "there are words missing in our text of the Mishnah" – attributed to Mar Shmuel.[104]

As noted earlier, Mar Shmuel was a noted astronomer. He therefore stated that he was fully capable of establishing a permanent Jewish calendar for the Jews living in the Diaspora,[105] to the criticism of the scholars in the Land of Israel, as seen in the story above about the unfortunate events that befell his daughters. He felt that the Jewish people is not in any way influenced by the stars, heavenly constellations, or astronomical events.[106] And as a general rule, he did not encourage the study of astrology and astronomy at the expense of devoting time to the study of Torah.[107] His attitude towards dreams was an ambivalent one – a good dream he interpreted literally, and a bad dream was deemed false and unreliable.[108]

Due to Mar Shmuel's wide-ranging expertise and outstanding qualities, different names of affection were bestowed upon him by his colleagues. He was called Shevor Malka,[109] the name of the Persian ruler of Babylonia previously mentioned in this chapter, in recognition of his supreme knowledge and authority in law, torts and commercial matters. He was the "king" in these matters.[110] He was also called by another royal name, *Aryoch*.[111] And we also find him dubbed *"Shakud"* – the diligent one.[112] This name naturally is a reflection of the great diligence and time that Mar Shmuel spent studying and teaching Torah.[113]

When Mar Shmuel died in c. 254 CE,[114] he had outlived Rav by approximately seven years. Unlike Sura – which remained a bastion of Torah scholarship and Jewish life for centuries after the death of Rav – Nehardea declined after the death of Mar Shmuel. In 259 the city was sacked by a Parthian general, Papa bar Netzer (Odenath), the ruler of Palmyra. Many in the Jewish community of Nehardea were put to death, and the survivors fled.[115] Nehardea never recovered its former glory, though its yeshivah did revive in the fourth century, approximately a century after the passing of Mar Shmuel.

The importance of Shevor Malka I in relation to the Jews of

Babylonia cannot be overemphasized. I therefore take the liberty of reviewing some of the facts regarding this ruler. In the year 241 CE Shevor Malka I ascended the throne of the Persian rulers of Babylonia. As noted earlier, he was on friendly and respectful terms with Mar Shmuel[116] as well as Rav.[117] Well-acquainted with Jewish law and customs,[118] he was also an astute observer and saw through the hypocrisy of those who pretended piety while secretly sinning.[119] Mar Shmuel stated that Shevor Malka I deserved merit for his positive attitude towards Jews and testified that the king never willingly killed a Jew.[120] Due to his continuing wars against the Romans, however, thousands of Jews (from outside of the Parthian Empire) who fought on behalf of Rome were killed by his forces. Mar Shmuel felt they had brought tragedy upon themselves by voluntarily fighting for Rome.[121]

Shevor Malka I survived Mar Shmuel by more than twenty years. He was constantly engaged in wars, mainly against the Romans. He succeeded in conquering Syria and much of Asia Minor, but was defeated by the aforementioned Odenath (or Odena).[122] His capital city of Palmyra (known in the Talmud as Tadmor or Tarmod)[123] was a great commercial center in Syria. Odenath was extremely cruel to the Jews: therefore, the Talmud says that the fall of Palmyra will be an occasion of rejoicing for the Jewish people.[124]

Palmyra's rise to power was relatively short-lived, for in 271 CE the Romans sacked the city and carried off Zinovia, the widow of Odenath and regent queen of Palmyra, to Roman captivity. Unlike her husband, she had been especially gracious to the Jews under her rule.[125]

From the history above, it is clear that Rav and Mar Shmuel built their fortresses of Torah and Jewish tradition under the most volatile, and sometimes violent, circumstances. Recognition of the swirling conflicts and changing diplomatic and military circumstances in Babylonia during this century can only increase our respect and awe for the two great men, Rav and Shmuel, the founders of the Babylonian Talmud.

SECTION II

THE FIRST AND SECOND GENERATION OF AMORAIM IN THE LAND OF ISRAEL

250 - 300 CE

The Tabernacle and its Priests. Mural from the synagogue in Dura Europos (eastern Syria), one of the earliest known synagogues, c. 245 CE

Rabi Yochanan

After the death of Rabi, Rav and Mar Shmuel established Babylonia as a renowned Torah center, rivaling those in the Land of Israel. Throughout the third century CE, the Jewish community in the Land of Israel declined in numbers and commercial influence, but not in Torah study. Just as the Babylonian Talmud – *Talmud Bavli* – began to develop as a commentary and elucidation of the Mishnah, so too did the Jerusalem Talmud – *Talmud Yerushalmi*. Both Talmuds were the parallel products of the yeshivos and scholars of those respective locations. The Babylonian Talmud was longer in development – it developed over approximately 300 years – and more extensive and expansive in discussion. Because of its broader development, it became *the* Talmud in later Jewish life and scholarship. Terser in form, language and content than the Babylonian Talmud, the Jerusalem Talmud was compiled over a span of 170 years and is much shorter than its Babylonian brother. The editors and compilers of the Babylonian Talmud were quite aware of the contents and decisions of the Jerusalem Talmud and took its opinions and decisions into account when formulating the *halachah*. Nevertheless, they often chose to rule differently than the Jerusalem Talmud. Since this was the case, the Babylonian Talmud took precedence over the Jerusalem Talmud, and was held to be the authoritative source of *halachah*.[1]

The Jerusalem Talmud was written in the Palestinian dialect

of Aramaic as spoken by the Jews in the Land of Israel in the third and fourth centuries, while the Babylonian Talmud, also written in Aramaic, reflects the slightly different dialect spoken by the Jews living in Babylonia.[2] In the elaborate cross-pollination of the two Talmuds, the opinions of the scholars of the Land of Israel appear in the Babylonian Talmud and the Babylonian scholars are quoted in the Jerusalem Talmud. Interestingly enough, many of those quotations appear exclusively in the "foreign" Talmud and are absent in the Talmud of their home base.[3] In short, even though the two Talmuds disagree with each other on the details of numerous halachic issues, they basically complement each other and can be viewed as being one unified commentary and elucidation of the Mishnah and the Oral Law.

Contemporary with Rav and Mar Shmuel in Babylonia were Rabi Yochanan and Rabi Shimon ben Lakish in the Land of Israel. They were younger than Rav and Mar Shmuel, though both also had studied with Rabi in his yeshivah.[4] In fact, there was a slight overlap, as Rabi Yochanan yet had seen Rav studying with Rabi.[5] The seamless transition of Torah knowledge is demonstrated by the fact that Rav and Mar Shmuel were counted in the first generation of Babylonian *Amoraim*, while Rabi Yochanan and especially Rabi Shimon ben Lakish are counted in the second generation of *Amoraim* of the Land of Israel. Rabi Yochanan had enormous respect for Rav and considered Rav to be greater than him in Torah.[6]

Rabi Yochanan's life was suffused with both tragedy and inspiration. While he was yet in the womb of his mother, Rabi prophesied that the unborn embryo would develop into a great teacher of Torah in Israel.[7] The Talmud tells us that his father

Bronze oil lamp, Beth Shean, 4th century CE (The Israel Museum, Jerusalem)

died before his birth and that his mother died in his childbirth.[8] The tiny orphan was taken to the home of his grandfather and raised there.[9] Born c. 180 CE, Rabi Yochanan lived for more than a century,[10] eventually becoming the leader of the second generation of *Amoraim* in the Land of Israel. Yet his personal sufferings remained unabated: Ten of Rabi Yochanan's sons died during his own lifetime.[11] He carried with him a small piece of bone (or a tooth)[12] of his tenth son who had died, and used it as a means to somehow console other bereaved people.[13]

One of the youngest students at Rabi's yeshivah, Yochanan was only fifteen or sixteen years old at the time of Rabi's passing.[14] Because of his youth, he was not so much a direct student of Rabi as a student of the older disciples of Rabi who were still in attendance at the yeshivah: Rav,[15] Rabi Chiya,[16] Rabi Shimon ben Yehotzadok,[17] and Rabi Banoah.[18] However, his main teachers were Rabi Oshiya,[19] the great master of the *breisos*[20] and expert on the Mishnah;[21] Rabi Yanai,[22] who praised Rabi Yochanan extravagantly;[23] and Rav Chanina bar Chama,[24] who was appointed to serve as the leading scholar in the yeshivah after the death of Rabi, though he originally declined the position in favor of the older Rav Affeis. These teachers of Rabi Yochanan constituted the first generation of *Amoraim* in the Land of Israel. Rabi Yochanan paid great respect to his teachers and bemoaned the fact that his generation of scholars could not be their equals.[25]

His personal qualities are memorable as well. Rabi Yochanan was famous for extending honor and courtesy to every human being, especially to the elderly, whether Jew or non-Jew.[26] He was an extraordinarily handsome person with a shining countenance, though he did not have a bearded face.[27] Women would make it a point to look at him in the belief that, should they conceive, doing so would enhance their child's appearance.[28] While others might flinch at being the object of this practice, Rabi Yochanan claimed immunity from the evil eye – *ayin hara*.[29] He was powerfully built and possessed impressive physical strength. Nevertheless, he took care not to overly exert himself unnecessarily, saying that he must conserve energy for his old age.[30] Apparently, his caution paid off

Even in desperate mortal straits, one should never give up hope.

Rabi Yochanan

as he lived a very long life.

Rabi Yochanan was also the wonder of his generation in piety, scholarship, and longevity. Everyone, even Rabi Yochanan himself, wept at the knowledge that such beauty and greatness was subject to the inexorable law of human mortality and death.[31]

Although he had inherited or otherwise acquired large estates and fields that had previously made him wealthy, he sold off all of his holdings in order to sustain himself in the study of Torah.[32] Rabi Yochanan's love of Torah and enthusiasm for its study knew no bounds.[33] This intense love of Torah even justified in his eyes leaving himself possibly destitute in his old age,[34] against the usual advice of the sages in the Talmud regarding this matter.[35] Eventually, Rabi Yochanan came to a financial crisis that forced him to consider leaving the study hall of Torah and engaging in commerce.[36] In this decision he was joined by his friend and scholarly colleague, Ilfa.[37]

City of Tiberias on the Sea of Galilee, April 22nd 1839, by David Roberts, R.A., England, 1796-1864. A color lithograph published in 1842. (Library of Congress Collection)

While Rabi Yochanan immediately returned to his full-time Torah studies irrespective of his poor financial condition, Ilfa remained in commercial enterprises for a period of time. Ultimately, Rabi Yochanan rose to be the head of the yeshivah in Tiberias while Ilfa did not. Ilfa nevertheless maintained that, in terms of scholarship, he was yet worthy to be appointed as the head.[38] Rabi Yochanan's love and devotion to Torah study was apparent even to the non-Jewish authorities, and they showed him favor because of it.[39]

The great yeshivah in Tiberias was founded c. 235 CE[40] and Rabi Yochanan headed it for more than 50 years.[41] Tiberias was to the study of Torah in the Land of Israel what the yeshivos of Nehardea and Sura were to the study of Torah in Babylonia. It was the bastion of Torah learning and instruction in the Land of Israel for all of the years that Rabi Yochanan lived. It was there that the foundation for the *Talmud Yerushalmi* was laid and most of that Talmud deals with discussions of Torah that took place there during the third century CE.

The sayings and wisdom of Rabi Yochanan are scattered throughout the Talmud. He is quoted many hundreds of times and his opinion in *halachah* is usually considered binding. Rabi Yochanan sought to explain seemingly disparate opinions in the Mishnah in a manner that could reconcile those opinions – so that they really did not disagree![42] A collection of his wise sayings would undoubtedly include the following:

- *Even in desperate mortal straits, one should never give up hope.*[43]

- *The countenance of a person who must rely upon other people for sustenance automatically crusts and darkens.*[44]

- *A clash of cultures and a bad atmosphere of rebellion in one's home is worse than experiencing the great war of Gog and Magog.*[45]

- *Being of service to the scholars of the Torah brings greater merit than even the study of Torah itself.*[46]

- *The reward for those who were righteous their entire lives is greater than that of those who repented of their sins and became righteous.*[47]

Someone who even supplies a patch for the torn pocket of a Torah scholar is entitled to sit in the Heavenly yeshivah.

Rabi Yochanan (Talmud)

- *One should endeavor to see to it that one's daughter should marry a Torah scholar; helping to support a Torah scholar by patronizing his business or profession and by directly helping him monetarily bring great reward. But the reward of the Torah scholar himself for his study of Torah is inestimably greater.[48]*

- *A person should allow himself to be thrown into a fiery furnace rather than be guilty of shaming another person publicly.[49]*

- *Someone who even supplies a patch for the torn pocket of a Torah scholar is entitled to sit in the Heavenly yeshivah.[50]*

- *There are three who merit the World to Come – one who lives in the Land of Israel, one who raises one's children to be Torah scholars and one who makes certain that there is wine for havdalah on Saturday night.[51]*

- *Ruling and lording over others leads to shortening the lives of those rulers.[52]*

- *The "fingernails" of the previous scholars of Torah were greater and larger than the "stomachs" of the later generations of scholars.[53] (His colleague, Rabi Shimon ben Lakish, disagreed with him in this assessment, though Rabi Yochanan summoned history to prove this statement correct.[54])*

- *Repeating words of Torah in the name of a deceased scholar allows that scholar's lips to "move and speak" in the grave.[55]*

- *Better to have a letter in the Torah uprooted, so to speak, than to allow a public desecration of Heaven's Name to take place.[56]*

Rabi Yochanan guaranteed that one who studied Torah in the synagogue, modestly and from the text directly, would not easily forget what he had learned.[57] He is also the author of the famous statement that even if the Torah had not been given to Israel, we would still have been able to learn many positive traits from the animal world around us and thus be held accountable to incorporate those traits in our own lives. [58]

He was also the originator of numerous thoughts and practices that are familiar to the Jewish world today. For example: He declared that one should never enter a home suddenly, without first announcing arrival, even when entering one's own home.[59] Rabi Yochanan also stated that since the destruction of the Temple, the gift of prophecy has been given to the insane and to children.[60] He preached that Torah has to be not only studied and learned, but taught to others as well.[61] Furthermore, if one is fortunate enough to have three consecutive generations of Torah scholars in one's family, then Torah would somehow always find its way to remain within that family.[62] He believed that one's own legs will always deliver that person to the place where God intends that person to come to.[63] He taught that one must be mindful and respectful of the welfare of the woman he divorced, even after their divorce.[64] He allowed the teaching of Greek language to one's daughters, claiming that it was an ornament to them.[65] Perhaps the prediction for which he is best known is that terrible troubles would befall Israel before the coming of the Messiah, and prayed that he be spared having to see them in his lifetime.[66]

His opinions on Torah study and the deportment of Torah scholars were no less exacting. He demanded thorough knowledge of Mishnah as a prerequisite to engaging in Talmudic debate.[67] He set high standards of knowledge and competence for rabbinic scholars who desired public office and/or favorable public treatment,[68] and he felt that rabbinic scholars were the "builders" of society.[69] As such, their clothing should be spotless and they should wear proper shoes; otherwise, people will denigrate them and a desecration of the good name of Torah will occur.[70] Torah was seen by Rabi Yochanan as the means of safeguarding one's soul[71] and humility is the key to retaining one's Torah knowledge and character.[72] Torah is to be studied with joy, melody and enthusiasm,[73] and never be exploited for personal gain or honor.[74] Moreover, the study of Torah purely for its own sake and without any ulterior motive protects all of human society.[75]

Rabi Yochanan also composed prayers, some of which have survived in our present liturgy.[76]

On the subject of personal interaction, Rabi Yochanan was a man of deed as well as word. He stated that the servant of a Torah scholar is to be treated with the same respect as the scholar himself,[77] and he therefore treated his own servants as his equals.[78] His modesty was such that he instructed the burial society that would tend to his body after his death to bury him in colored shrouds – not white nor black – lest he be embarrassed in the World to Come for wearing white among those who were wearing black (a sign of sinners) or for wearing black in the company of those wearing white (a sign of righteousness and purity.)[79] He stressed the importance of dealing with one's fellow human beings in a manner beyond the letter of the law, ascribing the destruction of Jerusalem to the refusal of its population to deal with each other in this manner.[80] He

set a high standard for himself in his own personal behavior as well. He stated that (because of his Torah stature) if he walked publicly a distance of four *amos* (approximately two meters) without Torah study and not wearing *tefillin,* it would be reckoned as a desecration of God's name.[81] In keeping with these high standards, he held that a teacher of Torah must be angelic in

his behavior.[82] He treasured wisdom, accepting knowledge from all sources and readily acknowledged non-Jewish savants as wise men.[83] He was a demanding teacher,[84] yet nevertheless publicly proclaimed that he learned much Torah from his students. Furthermore, he openly asserted that many of his teachings were not original, but rather were derived from the great scholars of Babylonia.[85] Rabi Yochanan revived the life of his dead student, Rabi Kahana, who once fell victim to Rabi Yochanan's stern discipline during his teaching sessions.[86]

Rabi Yochanan is the great decisor of *halachah* in the Talmud,[87] and he laid down the rules as to which opinion of the earlier Torah scholars is to be followed in law and practice.[88] He taught that one should avoid being dependent financially on other human beings, even at the expense of not being able to set a proper table for the Sabbath.[89] In his modesty, he came to recognize that Mar Shmuel was perhaps greater than him in Torah knowledge and he planned to leave the Land of Israel to study with Mar Shmuel in Nehardea,[90] a wish that never was fulfilled. He understood that anti-Semitism was a temporary, but almost certain shortcut taken by those who aspired to rise to power[91] – surely creating a treacherous situation for the Jews – yet, he attempted to interpret the difficult and often pessimistic verses of the prophets in a positive and hopeful fashion.[92] He loved the scholars of Israel and therefore even attempted to mitigate the punishment of the apostate Elisha ben Avuyah (Acher).[93]

Rabi Yochanan was classified as superhuman by his teachers and colleagues,[94] yet when he became profoundly distraught over the death of Rabi Shimon ben Lakish, his colleague and brother-in-law, they thought that he was in danger of losing his mind. They therefore prayed on his behalf, and he soon passed away peacefully.[95] His passing was mourned bitterly by the scholars of his time, and especially by his students and disciples.[96]

It is interesting to note that Rabi Yochanan's physical beauty was described by the rabbis as being one of contrasts – a burnished silver cup and filled with red pomegranate seeds, a red rose adorn-

Rabi Yochanan's beauty was described as "a burnished silver cup and filled with red pomegranate seeds, a red rose adorning it, and it should be placed between sunlight and shade."

Talmud

Relief of a menorah from an Ashkelon synagogue

63

ing it, and it should be placed between sunlight and shade.[97] The Talmud thereby characterized not only his appearance, but his life as well. For Rabi Yochanan's life was one of contrasts, of burnished silver greatness and honor and of blood-red sadness, of great shining light and dark shade. In spite of his personal pain and private anguish, he was *the* teacher of his generation in the Land of Israel and the mentor of generations of scholars thereafter.

When this towering personality died, the rabbis mourned: "All beauty has now been removed from the world,"[98] and "The day of Rabi Yochanan's passing is as difficult for Israel to bear as would be the setting of the sun at midday."[99] Rav Ami, not a blood relative of Rabi Yochanan, nevertheless observed in mourning mode the seven- and 30-day periods of mourning for him.[100] As noted earlier, Rabi Yochanan lived a very long life, passing away in c. 290 CE.[101]

Rabi Yochanan is the founder of the Jerusalem Talmud, though its final editing would not be complete until about a half century after his death. He was one of the most prolific of the teachers of the Talmud; and his imprint and opinions are found throughout this work. As stated earlier, the Jerusalem Talmud is different in kind, degree, and language dialect from the Babylonian Talmud. Therefore, the rabbis cautioned against straying from the study of the Babylonian Talmud to attempt to study the Jerusalem Talmud in the same pedagogic fashion as was employed in the study of the Babylonian Talmud.[102]

Like all of the great men of the Mishnah and the Talmud, Rabi Yochanan carries with himself an aura of mystery and other worldliness. This man of stature and beauty, of long life and many disciples, the creator of the Jerusalem Talmud and the person who brought so much comfort to others is also the person of untold personal tragedy, inner sadness, and great uncompromising moral demands for himself and others. He is witness to the decline of the Jewish community in the Land of Israel and takes great hope and heart in observing the flowering of the great Torah community in Babylonia. His love of Torah, the Land and people of Israel outweighs every other factor in his life's experiences. Rabi Yochanan's

> **Fortunate is the person who was raised in Torah and toiled in Torah study and endeavored to bring satisfaction to one's Creator and departed the world with a good name.**
>
> *Rabi Yochanan (Talmud)*

view of life can be summed up in his own soaring words:

Man's end is always death and the end of the bovine animal is to be slaughtered. Fortunate is the person who was raised in Torah and toiled in Torah study and endeavored to bring satisfaction to one's Creator and departed the world with a good name. It is regarding such a person that Solomon said in Koheles, "A good name is better than the finest of oils, and the day of death is better than the day of birth."[103]

Rabi Yochanan thereby eulogized himself. He remains the symbol of human greatness for all of the later ages of the Jewish people.

Rabi Shimon Ben Lakish

REISH LAKISH
C. 255 CE

Teachers
• Rabi Yochanan
• Rabi Affeis
• Bar Kapara
• Rav Chiya bar Ada
• Rabi Yehudah Nesiah I
• Rabi Yanai
• Rabi Chanina bar Chama

Colleagues
• Rabi Yochanan
• Abba Kohein Bardala
• Rav Ami
• Rav Assi
• Rabi Yehudah Nesiah I

Students
• Rav Chiya bar Ada (He is also
  mentioned as Rabi Shimon
  ben Lakish's teacher)

Relatives
• Brother-in-law: Rabi
  Yochanan

abi Shimon ben Lakish – or as he is commonly called in the Babylonian Talmud, Reish Lakish – was the foremost colleague of Rabi Yochanan in the great yeshivah in Tiberias.[1] Born c. 197 CE, he was younger than Rabi Yochanan, but died before him, either in 277 or 287 CE. Rabi Yochanan sometimes called him "Bar Lakisha,"[2] (possibly a nickname referring to the fact that he became a Torah scholar late in life) a name that Rabi Shimon ben Lakish also used about himself.[3] Lakish is either the name of his father or of his hometown.[4] As a child, he was raised in a house of Torah[5] and even saw the "finger" of the great Rabi Yehudah HaNasi.[6] But unlike his older colleague, Rabi Yochanan, he cannot be counted as a true student of Rabi. Nor was he acquainted with Rav,[7] so he cannot be counted as a bridge figure between the first and second generations of *Amoraim* in the Land of Israel as was Rabi Yochanan. Reish Lakish, then, belongs squarely among the second generation of *Amoraim* in the Land of Israel.[8]

Much of his early life is shrouded in mystery. At one point in his youth, Rabi Shimon ben Lakish left the study halls of Torah[9] and apparently fell into the company of robbers and outlaws. He was physically very strong and powerfully built, and he eventually "sold" himself into joining a group of circus gladiators.[10] All of the gladiators realized that eventually they would be killed, and probably by one another. They agreed among themselves that on the day that a particular one of them would most likely be killed, the doomed man would be granted a final request. When Shimon ben Lakish's day came, he stated his final wish – that he be permitted to tie up the other gladiators and deliver to them each one full blow and one with less force, deemed a "half blow." This ruse allowed him to kill the other gladiators and to escape from the slavery of that circus troupe, gaining his freedom![11] He now stood at a crossroads in his life – whether to continue his life as a criminal/gladiator, or to return to his roots and live a life of Torah.

The Talmud relates[12] that at this juncture of his life, Reish Lakish happened by when Rabi Yochanan – his older friend and mentor from the days of Rabi – was swimming in the Jordan River. Reish Lakish leaped into the water from a high riverbank to swim with Rabi Yochanan, apparently exhibiting impressive physical strength and skill. Rabi Yochanan thereupon challenged him to use his strength for Torah! Reish Lakish answered him mockingly that Rabi Yochanan's physical handsomeness was fitting for women. Rabi Yochanan immediately offered to have his beautiful sister marry him if he would return to the study halls of Torah. In a flash of remorse for his wayward life, Reish Lakish accepted Rabi Yochanan's offer. He then attempted to leap back to the riverbank to fetch his clothes, but now was unable to do so for "[The acceptance of the toil of the study of] Torah saps a person's physical strength."[13] Rabi Yochanan personally taught Torah to Rabi Shimon, and eventually made him into "a great man" in Torah and one of our most fascinating figures in Jewish history.[14]

Even though Rabi Yochanan was considered the primary mentor of Rabi Shimon ben Lakish, Rabi Shimon studied at various stages of his life (both before and after his return to Torah in the waters of the Jordan) with other great Torah scholars. Among his teachers were the "wise men and teachers of the south,"[15] such as Rabi Affeis and his yeshivah. He is quoted in the Talmud relating teachings from his many teachers including no less than Bar Kapara,[16] Bar Kapara's nephew, Rabi Chiya bar Ada,[17] Rabi Affeis,[18] Rabi Yehoshua ben Levi,[19] Chezkiyah,[20] Rabi Yehudah ben Chanina,[21] Abba Kohein Bardala,[22] Rabi Yehudah Nesiah,[23] Rabi Hoshiyahu,[24] Rabi

"Even the evildoers of Israel are as full of good deeds as a pomegranate is full of seeds."
Rabi Yochanan

Chanina bar Chama,[25] and Rabi Yanai.[26] Despite these many influences, Rabi Shimon ben Lakish's fame as a scholar and teacher rests in his connection with Rabi Yochanan and with the great yeshivah located in Tiberias in the third century of the Common Era.

Rabi Shimon ben Lakish is always regarded as Rabi Yochanan's companion and colleague in Torah study,[27] and they appear together throughout the pages of the Talmud, debating and deciding the law. They were known as the "two great men of the world"[28] "great lions of the Torah."[29] While they shared a joint reputation, Rabi Shimon ben Lakish retained his independent identity. He was known as "the strong person in the Land of Israel,"[30] recognition not only of his physical strength, but of his great spiritual stature and enormous Torah knowledge as well.

Rabi Yochanan respected him greatly, and called him "my opposite [equal.]"[31] In fact, Rabi Shimon ben Lakish served as Rabi Yochanan's assistant at the yeshivah in Tiberias and was charged with reviewing and explaining Rabi Yochanan's daily lesson with the students.[32] He also occasionally delivered the main lecture at the yeshivah and had his own *meturgaman* (someone who publicly recited and often simultaneously elucidated the lecture being given by the sage.)[33]

As had been promised to him, Reish Lakish married the sister of Rabi Yochanan. They were parents of a daughter[34] and of a son, the latter born to them when Reish Lakish was already advanced in years.[35] The boy was apparently a very precocious child and his

uncle, Rabi Yochanan, quoted Torah insights that the child told him.[36] Rabi Chiya bar Ada, the beloved student of Reish Lakish,[37] was the chosen teacher of the brilliant young boy.[38]

After years of study and friendship, disaster struck the relationship between Rabi Yochanan and Rabi Shimon ben Lakish! In the midst of a heated halachic discussion between the two, Rabi Yochanan made reference to the past of Reish Lakish as an outlaw and gladiator. Reish Lakish responded by saying, "then I was called 'rabi' – the chief of the outlaws, and now I am also called 'rabi' – the head of the scholars. So, what have I gained by your act [of returning me to the study hall]?" Rabi Yochanan retorted, "I have helped you by bringing you back under the wings of God's presence!" Rabi Yochanan was deeply disappointed and hurt by Reish Lakish's comment; and Reish Lakish was so disturbed by the rupture that he took ill and passed away.

Rabi Yochanan was devastated by the death of his colleague and compatriot. In bitter mourning, he recalled that Reish Lakish used to question him 24 times regarding every halachic statement that he made – and that he was forced to answer him on each of the questions – so the matter then would be truly clarified! But now that Reish Lakish is no longer alive, all he has left are his remaining students, and they only agree with his statements without question or debate! Rabi Yochanan would wander the streets shouting, "Bar Lakish, where are you? Bar Lakish, where are you?" So great was Rabi Yochanan's grief that for three and a half years, he absented himself from the yeshivah and the rabbinic council.[39] Eventu-

"Bar Lakish, where are you? Bar Lakish, where are you?"

Rabi Yochanan (Talmud)

Decorated console from the synagogue in Capernaum (Kfar Nachum), 3rd century CE

69

ally, his mind deteriorated from his anguish. The rabbis prayed for him, so he would soon die as well, and could thus rejoin Rabi Shimon ben Lakish in the yeshivah in heaven.[40]

The Talmud brings us numerous insights into the personality and teachings of Reish Lakish. We know that he spoke directly, and honestly expressed his opinion on all matters.[41] Clearly, he never feared anyone: He criticized the sages of Babylonia in strong words because the Jews of Babylonia did not leave their homes and return to the land of Israel when they had the opportunity to do so at the time of Ezra.[42] When he felt that those who attempted to declare a leap year were not up to the task, he spoke of them in critical terms as well.[43]

The Ark of the Covenant on wheels. Stone carving from the Capernaum (Kfar Nachum) synagogue, 4th-5th century CE

In fact, when he was convinced that a person was not qualified to judge issues regarding the establishment of the calendar, he had that person removed from the court that was then deliberating the matter.[44]

His openness brought him into considerable danger at times. On one famous occasion, he taught that if the *Nasi* sins, he is liable to the punishment of flogging (as was any Jew), even in a court of only three judges. The *Nasi* at the time, Rabi Yehudah Nesiah I, felt that this lesson was somehow meant as a personal insult directed toward him. He sent bailiffs to arrest Reish Lakish, who meanwhile had fled. The absence of Reish Lakish caused considerable hardship to Rabi Yochanan and he told the *Nasi* that he could not function without his "other hand" with him in the study hall. The *Nasi* relented and magnanimously went together with Rabi Yochanan to restore Reish Lakish to favor and return him to the study hall.

Delighted by the personal pardon, Reish Lakish compared Rabi Yehuda Nesia's benevolence towards him to the behavior of God Himself, so to speak, in Egypt when He redeemed Israel Himself and not by agents or messengers. The two were now reconciled, but the *Nasi* asked Reish Lakish why he had publicly taught that particular law regarding the sins and punishment of a *Nasi*. Reish Lakish responded: "Do you think that out of fear of you I would withhold any teaching of God's Torah from my students?"[45]

As mentioned earlier, we find that Reish Lakish quotes halachic statements of this same *Nasi*, Rabi Yehudah Nesiah I, in a number of places in the Talmud,[46] and we find that the *Nasi* asked the advice of Reish Lakish concerning a gift offered to him by a Roman officer. Reish Lakish dissuaded him from accepting, sensing it to be a form of a bribe that would then allow the Romans to increase taxes on the Jews.[47] Reish Lakish and Rabi Yehudah Nesiah I worked together to strengthen Torah education for children in the Land of Israel,[48] stating that even the building of the Temple is secondary to the study of the Torah by Jewish children.[49]

His own life experiences gave Rabi Shimon ben Lakish insight into human nature and potential. He was adamant in defense of the power of human beings to choose and to create either good or evil out of trying situations. What matters greatly is not the circumstances of life as much the attitude and behavior of the people dealing with those circumstances. Even regarding Torah, Rabi Shimon ben Lakish followed the position stated in the Talmud by Rabi Yehoshua ben Levi that Torah could be the elixir of life or a potion of death, depending on one's attitudes and merits.[50] Based on that understanding, he warned that the verses of the Torah should never be viewed in a superficial manner, as though a verse were somehow unnecessary, redundant or uninformative. He taught: "There are many verses in the Torah that people may feel to be worthy of burning [to be removed from the text because of their seeming unimportance], but these very verses are themselves the sources of the structure of the Torah itself."[51] Despite his emphasis on the primacy of Torah in one's life, he also believed that sometimes there are circumstances – such as attending a funeral or a wedding –

when forsaking the study of Torah temporarily is itself the way to preserve Torah.[52]

He endeavored to analyze the causes and nature of sin. He taught that how a person speaks and what he says influences later events; therefore one should never say bad things about himself or others or about events, for Satan will then act upon those statements and cause them to occur.[53] A person's own evil inclinations eventually become the Satan and the Angel of Death, so ultimately everything depends on the person himself.[54] Therefore, it is important to know that a person has the ability to overcome his evil inclination by mobilizing the forces of good within himself.[55] Reish Lakish was of the opinion that even the sinners of Israel would be saved eventually from the fires of Hell and that they were also "full of good deeds as a pomegranate is full of seeds."[56] Rabi Yochanan had stated that the dwelling place of a person finds favor in that person's eyes, even if others may find it repugnant.[57] Reish Lakish agreed with this shrewd and perceptive observation of the inherent differences in human tastes and preferences.[58]

In halachic disputes, Rabi Shimon ben Lakish's opinions were secondary to those of Rabi Yochanan. The decisions of the majority of the scholars of the Talmud favored Rabi Yochanan's opinions in most cases, even when Reish Lakish forcefully and publicly proclaimed the correctness of his own dissenting position. The rabbis generally ignored his contentions and followed Rabi Yochanan's lead.[59]

Yet Rabi Shimon ben Lakish's love for Torah and his enormous concentration and diligence were revered by all. He often literally forgot where he was because of his constant and intense focus on his Torah studies.[60] He would review a Torah matter forty times before entering into a discussion with Rabi Yochanan about it.[61] The Talmud relates that "one who saw Reish Lakish in the study hall when he was studying witnessed a scene [comparable to seeing] Reish Lakish uproot mountains and grind them together into bits."[62] As mentioned earlier, for every opinion advanced by Rabi Yochanan, Reish Lakish would have 24 questions regarding it.[63]

His own industriousness in Torah study is itself the background for some of his most famous statements:

- *"The Torah is preserved only by those who 'die' for it in the study hall."*[64]
- *"The night was only created for the study of Torah..."*[65]
- *"Those that study Torah at night have a special grace from God drawn upon them during the day."*[66]

He was of the opinion that the scholars should not indulge in fasting and physical depriva-tions, for that would weaken their ability to study intently and serve Heaven prop-erly.[67] He taught that everything in the uni-verse was created only for the Torah – espe-cially gold,[68] (which supports Torah study) and even the moon[69] (whose light enables scholars to study even at night.) He was a champi-on of order and diligence in achieving success in studying Torah.[70] Though deeply reverent of earlier scholars, Reish Lakish championed the cause of the "later generations" of Torah scholars over the achieve-ments of earlier generations, for the later generations were bur-dened by foreign rule and persecutions and nevertheless persisted in their studies.[71]

Stone-carved menorah from the Eshtamoa synagogue, 4th-5th century CE

Living entirely in the reality of Torah, the material world mat-tered little to Reish Lakish. He earned a meager livelihood as a watchman of orchards[72] and lived in such poverty, that he slept without even a pillow.[73] At his death, the sole asset comprising his estate was a container of a spice.[74] Even this he regretted, commenting that he thus violated the rueful statement of Psalms (49:11) regarding the folly of leaving over one's wealth to others.[75] Obviously, he never worried about his material needs for the morrow, trusting that his true needs would always be met.[76]

One would expect a person of such physical and intellectual strength to be an overwhelming presence. Yet Rabi Shimon ben Lakish was modest to a fault, and he regretted that he had allowed any scholar or student to serve or help him.[77] In spite of his great prowess in the study hall and his determined halachic opinions, he preached that a scholar of Torah must always remain modest in deportment and in his relationship with others.[78] He taught that when scholars are courteous and sensitive to one another – and are willing to hear and consider another's opinion – they allow God Himself, so to speak, to hear their Torah discussions.[79] Reish Lakish's standing as an upright and honest person of rigorous integrity was such that anyone with whom he would converse with publicly in the marketplace was then in turn seen as a person of honor, trust and integrity.[80] He warned that those who unjustly suspected others of wrongdoing would only bring physical illness and pain on themselves.[81] He stated that anger impairs wisdom,[82] and that the "mere" act of raising one's hand against one's fellow makes one an evil person.[83]

On the nature of sin and repentance, Reish Lakish stated that truly evil people never repent, even when standing at the threshold of Hell.[84] Since that is the case, "first 'decorate' [improve] yourself before attempting to 'decorate' others."[85] A person sins only because a moment of lightheadedness and foolishness overcomes him.[86] If one is tempted to sin, Heaven will neither aid nor stop him, but if he comes to elevate and purify himself, Heaven will assist him in this holy venture.[87] A Torah scholar who has sinned should not be publicly reprimanded, (as it may cause people to lose respect for Torah).[88]

Reish Lakish illuminated the spiritual processes that impact on every Jew, whether or not that process is perceived. He explained that a special "additional" soul enters the body of a Jew with the onset of the Sabbath and departs after the Sabbath ends.[89] Study of Torah is so basic to the Jewish soul that a teacher of Torah to others becomes their spiritual parent.[90] And he described the common phenomenon that if one moves away from the study of Torah, the Torah itself also moves away from him.[91] Yet a Jew may never give up on one's self, for the power of repentance – *teshuvah* – has such strong spiritual strength that it can even convert willful sins into meritorious acts.[92] And, finally, Reish Lakish taught that the entire creation of the universe and its continuance is dependent not upon any physical laws but upon the Jewish people's acceptance of God's Torah.[93]

The Scholars of Caesarea

hough the main center of Torah study and Jewish life in the early third century CE was in Tiberias, under the leadership of Rabi Yochanan, Rabi Shimon ben Lakish, Rabi Elazar ben Pedas and their colleagues and students, another center arose in the Land of Israel. Strangely enough, this center was in the most cosmopolitan, pagan, Roman, and increasingly Christian city in the land – Caesarea. There, many of the students of Rabi Yochanan and Rabi Shimon ben Lakish, as well as students of Rav and Mar Shmuel of Babylonia, settled and lived, establishing a strong Torah community. These scholars were known as *rabanan d'kisri(n)* – the scholars of Caesarea.[1]

A coastal city located between present-day Hadera and Haifa, Caesarea was the busiest port in the Land of Israel, having a breakwater and artificial harbor that had been built by Herod three centuries earlier. It had always been a non-Jewish city, and the Romans used it as a military and governmental headquarters for centuries. It was also a thriving commercial center, and its citizens engaged in trade with all parts of the Mediterranean basin and Asia Minor. Because of its pagan and hedonistic society, Caesarea was considered the antithesis of Jerusalem.[2] Yet it eventually developed a sizable Jewish population of merchants, traders, artisans and shopkeepers. Since the rabbis and scholars of the time all supported themselves by their own labor and ingenuity, a number of the great students of Tiberias and Babylonia settled in Caesarea for economic reasons.

There they became the heads of the Jewish community, contributing with their scholarship to the work of their colleagues in Tiberias in developing the Jerusalem Talmud.

Foremost among these scholars was Rabi Yosi bar Chanina, who was ordained by Rabi Yochanan himself in Tiberias.[3] Rabi Yosi's succinct understatement, "It is difficult to live in a large city,"[4] expresses the problems – both spiritual and physical – of living in the large urban, cosmopolitan, hedonistic environment of third century Caesarea. Indeed, he suffered great tragedies in his lifetime: his children died consecutively over a short period of time.[5] In spite of the difficulties of his life and the circumstances of living in Caesarea, he proclaimed that "the measure of good comes more quickly [from God] than the measure of punishment and tragedy."[6] A keen observer of human nature,[7] he spoke in favor of order and serenity of spirit in prayer and life,[8] and preached the value of studying Torah in a group.[9] Rabi Yosi bar Chanina was such a loyal student of Rabi Yochanan, that even in death he was seated next to Rabi Yochanan in the Heavenly study hall.[10]

Rabi Yosi bar Chanina's chief disciple was Rabi Abahu,[11] who apparently also studied in Tiberias with Rabi Yochanan in his youth.[12] He was noted for his oratorical prowess in *Aggadah* (homiletical interpretations of Torah verses and ideas) and attracted great crowds to listen to his words.[13] A man of great wealth, he was also a person of handsome countenance.[14] Well-respected by the Roman rulers of Caesarea, who dubbed him the spokesman for all Jewish interests in the area,[15] he was equally revered as a leader by the Jewish society of his day.[16] His influence with the authorities regarding Jewish matters became almost legendary,[17] for he stood tall and proud, a prototype for later influential Jews who defended their people in the courts of the mighty with dignity, purpose and success.

Rabi Abahu debated the Christians of Caesarea, flatly denying any of their claims regarding the Bible and challenging their redefinition of pure monotheism to include the concept of a trinity.[18] As he was fluent in Greek,[19] he could deal easily with all elements of society, especially the governing authorities. He made it a point to teach that language to his daughters.[20] We know little else about them.

RABI YOSSI BAR CHANINA

Teachers
Rabi Yochanan

Colleagues
Rav Ami
Rav Assi
Rabi Shimon ben Lakish

Students
Rabi Abahu

RABI ABAHU

Teachers
• Rabi Yosi ben Chanina
• Rabi Tachlifa
• Rabi Yochanan

Colleagues
• Rav Ami
• Rav Assi
• Rabi Chiya bar Abba

Students
• Rabi Zeira II
• Rabi Yirmiyahu
• Rabi Chizkiyah
• Rabi Yonah
• Rabi Pinchas
• Rabi Yosi

Relatives
• Father-in-law: Rabi Tachlifa
• Son: Rav Chanina bar Abahu, of Avimei and of Rabi Zeira (not to be confused with Rav Zeira I and II).

Famed for his sterling character and upright, God-fearing behavior,[21] Rabi Abahu was even guided by Heaven to ask the most unlikely person in Caesarea to pray for rain in a year of drought![22] He was always steadfast in his modesty[23] and in his advice that one should always be one of the oppressed, rather than an oppressor.[24] Pleasant of demeanor to all, he cautioned against being a harsh taskmaster in one's home and family.[25] As a person of influence and public attention, he was known to speak carefully and often somewhat cryptically.[26]

Rabi Abahu married the daughter of one of the leading scholars of Caesarea, Rabi Tachlifa,[27] and three of their sons are known to us in the Talmud. Rabi Chanina ben Abahu studied Torah in Tiberias and was reprimanded by his father for devoting himself to charitable work there instead of concentrating exclusively on his studies.[28] He apparently heeded his father's admonition, for we find halachic statements attributed to him in the Talmud.[29] A second son, Rabi Zeira (not to be confused with Rav Zeira I or II), resided in Caesarea and was a noted scholar and preacher.[30] A third son, Avimei, was a wealthy merchant whose commercial ventures took him to far-flung locations in Asia Minor and the Middle

"It is difficult to live in a large city"
Rabi Yosi bar Chanina

East.[31] He is mentioned numerous times in the Talmud.[32] Avimei in turn, had five sons, all of whom received *semichah* – ordination – in the lifetime of their grandfather, Rabi Abahu,[33] and Avimei himself was famed for the honor and service that he paid to his father.[34]

On his deathbed, Rabi Abahu saw thirteen streams of persimmon balm preceding him to the World to Come. This rare and

> "Those who have repented of their sins are deemed to be higher than those who have never sinned at all."
>
> *Rav Abahu*

Caesarea, Roman theater

expensive perfume signified royalty and wealth, and the sweet fragrance symbolized personal greatness and stature. He asked for whom these streams were intended, and when he was informed that they were for him, in his modesty, he was greatly surprised.[35] Rabi Abahu was so beloved in Caesarea that at his death it was said that even the marble columns of the city wept.[36]

Among the students of Rabi Abahu were Rav Zeira II,[37] Rabi Yirmiyahu,[38] Rabi Chizkiyah,[39] Rabi Yonah,[40] Rabi Pinchas,[41] and Rabi Yosi.[42] Friends and colleagues of Rabi Abahu included Rav Ami, Rav Assi,[43] Rabi Chiya bar Abba[44] and other disciples of Rabi Yochanan. Rabi Abahu was one of the formative figures in the development of the *Talmud Yerushalmi* and he was a rigorous defender of the honor due to the teachers of Torah.[45] In contradistinction to the opinion of Rabi Yochanan quoted earlier, Rabi Abahu held that those who repented from their sins were to be treated with very high esteem – greater even than righteous people who never sinned![46] Deeply aware of spiritual influences, he taught that those who encourage others – whether by example or persuasion – to do good deeds have the reward as though they themselves had done that good deed.[47] And there is no doubt that Rabi Abahu himself was a perfect example

Capital decorated with a menorah from the synagogue in Caesarea, 5th century CE

of this principle and certainly had the reward for countless good deeds. Moreover, he preached that the righteous have special powers, even in countermanding heavenly decrees.[48]

The "Scholars of Caesarea" extended into the third and fourth generations of the *Amoraim* of the Land of Israel. As we will see in a later chapter of this book, the *Talmud Yerushalmi* was mainly a product of the scholars of the two main centers of Jewish life in the Land of Israel – Tiberias and Caesarea. Just as Rabi Yochanan and Rabi Shimon ben Lakish – along with their teachers, colleagues and students – established Tiberias as a center of Torah scholarship, Rabi Yosi bar Chanina and Rabi Abahu established Caesarea as another citadel of Torah study in third century Jewish life. As we have discussed, Caesarea's importance as a trading, commercial center, made its culture very influential throughout Asia Minor. This is equally true regarding the influence of the Torah scholars of Caesarea, whose teachings and ideas reached and influenced the Jewish world far from the perimeters of Caesarea itself.

SECTION III

THE SECOND GENERATION OF AMORAIM IN BABYLONIA

c. 250 - 300 CE

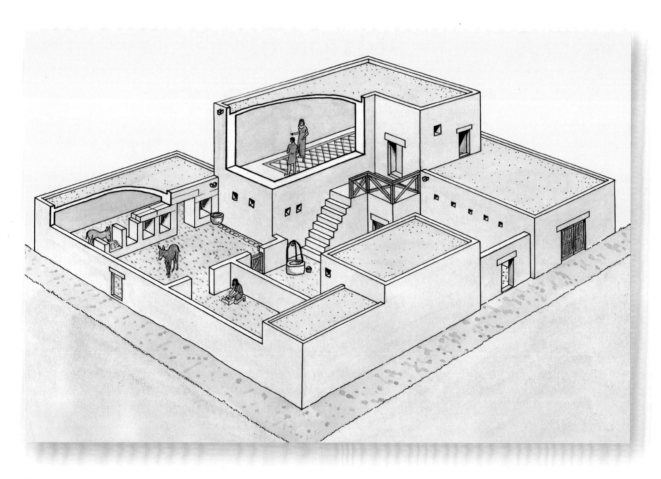

*Reconstruction drawing
of a typical Jewish house
during the Talmudic period,
Capernaum (Kfar Nachum),
3rd-8th centuries CE*

Rav Huna

hen Rav died in c. 246-7 CE, no official *Rosh Yeshivah* was appointed in his place in Sura. Since Mar Shmuel was still alive and his yeshivah in Nehardea was thriving, many of the students of Rav moved to Nehardea to study with the great sage. Sura willingly occupied a secondary position to Nehardea, though the yeshivah in Sura still functioned and housed many students. Rav Hamnuna, one of the elder students of Rav, served as the authority in running the yeshivah, though he never assumed the title of *Rosh Yeshivah*.[1] The remaining students in Sura after the death of Rav were called *chevraya d'bei Rav* – the "collection of students" of the yeshivah of Rav.[2] However, for the next seven years, until the death of Mar Shmuel in c. 254 CE, many of Rav's most devoted students found themselves in Nehardea under the tutelage of Mar Shmuel. These students included Rav's son, Chiya,[3] Rav's son-in-law, Rav Chanan bar Ravah[4] (also named in the Talmud as Chanan bar Rabah), Rav Yehudah bar Yechezkel,[5] Rav Huna[6] and Rav Chiya bar Ashi.[7]

When Mar Shmuel passed away, the students of Rav returned to Sura, to reestablish the supremacy of Rav's yeshivah in Babylonia. The yeshivah at Nehardea never recovered fully from the death of Shmuel, and Sura became the unquestioned center of Torah scholarship in Babylonia. Rav Huna now became the *Rosh Yeshivah* at Sura and the yeshivah flourished under his leadership.[8]

RAV HUNA
c. 280 CE

Teachers
• Rav
• Rav Hamnuna

Colleagues
• Rav Chiya bar Rav
• Rav Yehudah bar Yechezkel
• Rav Chanan bar Rava
• Rav Chiya bar Ashi
• Rav Chisda

Students
• Rav Abba
• Rabah bar Rav Chisda
• Rav Zeira
• Rav Kahana
• Rabah bar Nachmani
• Rav Yosef

Relatives
• Son: Rav Acha bar Rav Huna
• Grandsons: Rabah bar Rav Huna, Rava bar Rav Acha

He became one of the main conduits of the teachings of Rav to all later generations,[9] for wherever we find in the Talmud the phrase *amrei bei Rav* – "thus was said in the yeshivah of Rav" – it is Rav Huna speaking.[10] Rav Huna moved the yeshivah from the city of Sura to the suburb of Masa Machsiya[11] where it eventually had 800 permanent students.[12]

Rav Huna's public lectures were lengthy and well attended.[13] The Talmud states that the *yarchei kallah* months (Adar and Elul) of public Torah study in Rav Huna's yeshivah were so well attended that when the crowd arose after the lecture and shook the dust off of their garments, the dust cloud created could be seen in the Land of Israel![14] Rav Huna had to employ thirteen scholars to transmit his lecture to the assembled masses who came to study Torah during the *yarchei kallah*.[15]

This atmosphere of love of Torah and a thirst for its knowledge, which was so prevalent among the Jews of Babylonia, was the undoubted catalyst and groundwork that facilitated the massive undertaking of compiling the Talmud. It was the work of the great scholars, but they could not have been successful operating in a vacuum. The support and respect for Torah and its scholars exhibited by the Jews of Babylonia created the atmosphere in which the Talmud came into being.

The personal characteristics of Rav Huna have been recorded for us in the Talmud. We know that he was not tall.[16] He was so poor in his early years[17] that his mentor, Rav, blessed him that he someday should be "covered in satin clothing."[18] This blessing came true when, later in life – after his financial situation had improved – Rav Huna was sleeping and his family, who did not notice his small frame lying in the bed, threw their fancy satin wraps on the bed, covering him completely. Upon hearing of the incident, Rav jokingly remarked: "Why did he not return that blessing upon me as well?"[19] Rav Huna earned his living from various kinds of work: shepherding oxen,[20] irrigating fields,[21] and harvesting date palms.[22] When he sat in judgment on a case between litigants, he asked to be paid for the lost wages he might have earned during the time of the trial.[23] This accepted type of payment to some of the judges of

> "A person who has fear of heaven within him will have his opinions heard here on earth."
>
> *Rav Huna*

that time – *schar batala* – (i.e. wages for lost time from work) later became the normal basis in Jewish life for justifying payment to teachers, rabbis, judges and other community officials.[24]

Held in great esteem by his colleagues, Rav Huna was considered the "head" of all of the judges and scholars of his time.[25] He and his companion, Rav Chisda, were considered "the elders of Sura,"[26] and "the pious personages of Babylonia."[27] Rav Huna's reputation for holiness was so remarkable that the Talmud asserts that one who is privileged to see him in a dream is assured of having miracles performed on his behalf.[28] His piety was such that when he discovered that a strap of his *tefillin* had turned inside out while he was wearing them, he fasted for 40 days in repentance![29]

As mentioned above, in later life Rav Huna became a

Wine press, Capernaum (Kfar Nachum), carved from the local black basalt stone

wealthy man, dealing in vineyards and wine.[30] His works of charity[31] and public service were legendary.[32] A *kohein*, he did not take from the priestly tithe for his own use,[33] as he clearly felt responsible for the charity needs and distribution of monies to the poor of his community.[34]

Rav Huna was critical of extravagant living and "holidays" away from the study of Torah.[35] He interpreted the verse in Koheles to "rejoice in one's youth" as being the advice of the *yetzer hara* – the evil inclination within us.[36] He taught that one should study Torah even if motivated by ulterior motives, for the study of Torah itself will eventually lead the student to sincerity and proper dedication.[37] On the subject of the Land of Israel and the Diaspora, he averred that the Jews of Babylonia felt secure and their minds were well settled, while those in other areas of the Diaspora were not so fortunate;[38] and he declared that since the time Rav came to Babylonia, it became equal in halachic authority to the Land of Israel in many instances.[39]

Rav Huna clarified the original authorship of many tractates and opinions in the Mishnah.[40] Many of the most famous statements in the Talmud are attributed to him,[41] among them the advantages of early marriage.[42] He was the supreme advocate and example of holiness of body and spirit.

Although well over 80 years of age, Rav Huna passed away unexpectedly, suddenly and gently.[43] His student, Rav Abba, said of him at his funeral: "Our teacher Rav Huna was worthy that the *Shechinah* should have rested on him, but only because he lived in Babylonia (in exile, outside of the Land of Israel) it did not occur."[44] His body was brought to the Land of Israel where he was buried in the cave where the remains of Rabi Chiya and his sons were interred, "for Rav Huna spread Torah to his generations in the same manner as Rabi Chiya did to his."[45] The rabbis even wished to place a *sefer Torah* on his casket as a sign of his greatness in Torah. However, his colleague and student, Rav Chisda, did not allow this, stating that in his lifetime Rav Huna himself would never have approved of such a ceremony.[46]

Apparently, Rav Huna predeceased his wife, Chova.[47] She was treated with great respect by the rabbis, and it is about her that the Talmud quoted the famous dictum enunciated by Mar Shmuel[48] that "the wife of a Torah scholar is due the same respect as the Torah scholar himself."[49] They had a number of children:[50] Rabah bar Rav Huna, their most noted son, was a great scholar and he appears in many places in the Talmud.[51] Another son, Rav Acha bar Rav Huna, is also quoted numerous times in the Talmud.[52] His grandson, Rava bar Rav Acha, appears in the Talmud many times as well.[53]

Rav Huna served as the *Rosh Yeshivah* of Sura for 40 years, from 258 CE to 298 CE, producing generations of disciples and students. There is no doubt that this extraordinary individual was the leading figure of the second generation of *Amoraim* in Babylonia.

Rav Chisda

A student, and later, the colleague of Rav Huna was Rav Chisda. He was born in 217 CE[1] and lived 92 years,[2] passing away in c. 309 CE. Slightly younger than Rav Huna, Rav Chisda outlived him by twelve years. Like Rav Huna, Rav Chisda was a *kohein*, a member of the priestly clan of Aharon.[3] Even as a child, his genius was noted and a bright future in Torah scholarship was predicted for him by "stargazers."[4] Raised in poverty,[5] he became very wealthy later in life.[6] His experiences as a poor person colored his outlook on life forevermore; though eventually rich, he opposed all types of material extravagance[7] and regarded unnecessary pleasures and luxuries as sinful.[8] His wealth came from the manufacture and sale of date beer,[9] which was the main beverage of the Jews of Babylonia.[10]

Rav Chisda married the granddaughter of Rav, the daughter of Rav Chanan bar Rava. He married at the age of sixteen and regretted not having done so even earlier.[11] While Rav Chisda emphasized the importance of being married,[12] he also bemoaned the lost days of one's youth.[13] In terms of his personal life, we know that miraculous events happened to him because of his great piety.[14] Like the other rabbis of the Talmud, he personally helped prepare food for the honor of the Sabbath meals.[15] Many happy and fortunate things happened to him regularly, and his household was blessed with "60 weddings."[16]

A student in Rav's great yeshivah in Sura,[17] he referred to Rav as

RAV CHISDA
c. 295 CE

Teachers
• Rav
• Rav Yirmiyahu bar Abba
• Avimei
• Zeirei
• Rav Chama bar Gurya
• Rav Chanan bar Rava

Colleagues
• Rav Huna
• Rav Yehudah bar Yechezkel
• Rav Nachman bar Yaakov
• Rav Sheishes
• Rav Hamnuna II

Students
• Rabah bar Nachmani
• Rav Yosef
• Rav Acha bar Yosef
• Raban (Ravna) Ukva
• Raban Nechemiah

Relatives
• Sons: Rav Nachman bar Rav Chisda, Rav Tachlifa, Rav Mari, Rav Pinchas, Mar Yenuka, Mar Kashisha
• Sons-in-law: Rami bar Chama, Mar Ukva bar Cham, Rava
• Father-in-law: Rav Chanan bar Rava, the son-in-law of Rav

Rabeinu HaGadol – Our Great Teacher.[18] He may also have studied in Nehardea under Mar Shmuel.[19] However, since Rav Chisda was still relatively young when he attended the yeshivah of Rav in Sura, most of his teachers there were the older students of Rav. Thus we find that he studied with Rav Yirmiyahu bar Abba,[20] Zeirei,[21] Rav Chama bar Gurya,[22] and Rav Chanan brei d'Rava,[23] all of whom were students of Rav from an earlier generation. Because of his longevity, Rav Chisda saw, studied with and taught during the first, second and third generations of the *Amoraim* of the Babylonia Talmud.

The Head of the Exile (*Reish Galusa*) at the time of Rav Chisda's early years was Mar Ukva, and they both lived in the town of Kafari.[24] Rav Chisda quotes the opinions that he learned from Mar Ukva as well as those of his teachers.[25] In his youth, Rav Chisda also had a teacher, Avimei,[26] who was quite demanding of him.[27] Later in life, in an ironic reversal of roles, Rav Chisda was the teacher of the same Avimei, helping him restore his memory of tractate Menachos.[28]

It is unknown and unlikely that Rav Chisda ever traveled to the Land of Israel to study. He does quote teachings of Rabi Yochanan,[29] but these teachings were most probably transmitted to him by the continual flow of scholars traveling between the yeshivos of Babylonia and the Land of Israel.[30] He remained primarily a devoted student of Sura and later in life he offered to give a double portion of his priestly gifts (as mentioned above, Rav Chisda was a *kohein*) to anyone who would inform him of any of Rav's teachings that was previously unknown to him.[31]

Rav Chisda was approximately thirty years old when Rav passed away. Some years later, Rav Huna assumed the leadership of the yeshivah in Sura and Rav Chisda joined him there. Rav Chisda's renowned devotion to the study of Torah was so great and consistent that even the Angel of Death dared not approach him while he was studying![32]

As noted earlier, Rav Chisda was at first a student of Rav Huna's, but because of his brilliance, he quickly rose to be a colleague. Rav Huna praised him extravagantly, saying: "Your name is Chisda (meaning goodness and generosity) and your words of Torah are also *chasdain* – good, correct and generous."[33] Rav Huna urged his own son, Rabah, to attend the lectures of Rav Chisda, "for his lessons are sharp and clear."[34] At one point, a misunderstanding arose between Rav Huna and Rav Chisda and the two grew distant.[35] However, eventually they reconciled and in regret over the incident and their unnecessary separation, each of them fasted in penance 40 days.[36]

After the death of Rav Huna, the center of Torah learning transferred from Sura to the yeshivah of Rav Yehudah bar Yechezkel,[37] in Pumbedisa.[38] However, Rav Yehudah bar Yechezkel passed away only two years after the death of Rav Huna.[39] After his death, the yeshivah at Sura, now under the leadership of Rav Chisda, regained its preeminence as the Torah center of Babylonia. Rav Chisda would serve as the *Rosh Yeshivah* at Sura for ten years, until his death. Rav Chisda thus preserved the chain of tradition from Rav well into the third generation of *Amoraim:* many, if not most of them, were his direct disciples.

Through this process of direct transmission, the Talmud was composed by great individuals who perpetuated and explained, elucidated and clarified the traditions of Torah received by Moshe at Sinai. Rav Chisda is an important figure in this chain of transmission and tradition. He taught that even the later words of prophets, such as Yechezkel, were based completely upon the traditions transmitted from Sinai.[40] Rav Chisda was 82 years old when he assumed the leadership of Sura, yet even at this advanced age he was vigorous in teaching Torah and helping to create and shape the next generation of Torah scholars.

In regard to Torah study, Rav Chisda was very didactic in his interpretation: Every letter and mark in the Torah represented "piles and piles" of *halachah*.[41] He emphasized the necessity of being stringent regarding one's own doubtful questions in *halachah* as well as to always strive to serve the scholars of Israel in study and deed.[42] He slept little, opting to study far into the night, stating that after this life ends there is much time to sleep, but no ability then to accomplish any more.[43] He advised students to devise "signs"(using

> "One should not destroy an existing synagogue building before the new one is in place"
>
> *Rav Chisda (Talmud)*

mnemonics, abbreviations, and acrostics) to help remember the Torah one studied.[44] Rav Chisda himself signed his name by drawing a *samech* – a circular letter in the Hebrew alphabet.[45] It may have represented the completeness and all-encompassing scope of Torah, or perhaps it simply symbolized his name, since its most prominent letter is a *samech.*

His observations on human behavior are well-known. He warned that a Jew should not walk within four *ells* (an *ell* is 18-24 inches) of places of paganism, immorality and the seats of tyrannical government, lest he be influenced by them.[46] And he warned that people use both wealth and poverty as an excuse for their dissatisfactions.[47] He cautioned against a person in authority exerting power over others unnecessarily and not for the sake of heaven.[48] He also stated that this rule applies as well to the behavior of a husband and a father regarding his relations with his family.[49] He opined that "liars, sycophants, slanderers and cynical mockers will never be privileged to receive the face of Godliness" in their lives,[50] and that one who speaks obscenities only deepens his place in Hell.[51] On the other hand, the prayers of a person who never misleads or insults others with words, are always accepted.[52]

Rav Chisda's wisdom is reflected through many more of his sayings that appear throughout the Talmud and Midrash. Among these: Neither good dreams nor bad dreams are ever fully fulfilled.[53]

Chorazin synagogue, lower Galilee, 4th century CE

One should not destroy an existing synagogue building before the new one is in place.[54] And the nature of women is to attempt to look presentable always, no matter the age of the woman![55]

The father of seven sons and two daughters, Rav Chisda is the author of the famous saying in the Talmud (which has become a Jewish folk expression) that "a first-born daughter is a good sign for later sons."[56] He loved his daughters greatly, stating that he preferred them to sons.[57] His daughters respectively married outstanding Torah scholars, the brothers Rami bar Chama and Mar Ukva bar Chama.[58] After the death of Rami bar Chama, Rav Chisda's daughter married another great scholar, Rava.[59] Rav Chisda is known to have cautioned his daughters on the advantages of modesty in marriage.[60]

Rav Chisda's oldest son was Rav Nachman bar Rav Chisda.[61] His second son was named Rava Chanan[62] bar Rav Chisda, and he learned Torah primarily from his father.[63] Rav Chisda had another son named Tachlifa, also a Torah scholar,[64] about whom little more is known. The Talmud also mentions his other sons: Rav Mari and Rav Pinchas,[65] as well as Mar Yenuka[66] and Mar Kashisha.[67] Rav Chisda's grandson, Rav Mari, the son of Rav Pinchas, is also mentioned in the Talmud.[68] The descendants of Rav Chisda throughout the entire later generations were scholars who contributed actively to the production and editing of the Talmud.[69]

Among some of the well-known statements of Rav Chisda that appear in the Talmud are many that comment on the national travails of the Jewish people. For example: Originally, before the Jewish people sinned, the holy spirit (*Shechinah*) dwelt within each and every Jew. After they sinned, it departed from them.[70] When the Jewish people live in the Land of Israel, the rains that fall there come from God's good treasure house. After the destruction of the Temple and the exiling of the Jews from their land, the rain that falls there is no longer from God's good treasure house.[71] The fact that Nebuchadnezzar exiled the scholars of Jerusalem to Babylonia eleven years before the actual destruction of the First Temple and the great exile of the remaining Jews to Babylonia was in itself a hidden blessing from God – for the earlier exiles created a Torah infrastructure in Babylonia that helped the Jews survive the Babylonian exile.[72] The withholding of giving proper tithes causes droughts to occur.[73]

Hundreds of Rav Chisda's statements, teachings, and opinions are found throughout the pages of the Talmud. Some are meant to guide the individual; others have implications for the entire nation.

A few examples:

- *When one travels, one should always recite the wayfarer's prayer.*[74]

- *Praying in the synagogue on the Sabbath night and reciting the prayer of "Vayechulu" (the prayer that testifies to God's creation of the universe) allows two angels to accompany him home and bless him, removing his sins.*[75]

- *The houses of Torah study that determine halachic practice are even more beloved to God, so to speak, than the houses of prayer or theoretical Torah study.*[76]

- *The soul of a person mourns over its departure from the body at the death of the person for seven days.*[77]

- *Who is a talmid chacham – a wise and knowledgeable student of Torah? One who can decide against his own monetary interest when a question of halachah regarding the kashrus of his own animal arises, even if it is possible to be lenient in the matter.*[78]

With Rav Chisda's death in c. 310 CE,[79] the era of Sura's supremacy as the focal point of Torah study in Babylonia ended. Great was the mourning for Rav Chisda; his students were desolate in their bereavement.[80] Yet the immortality of Torah survives the inevitable passing of all of its scholars and the leaders of any particular generation. The center of Torah in Babylonia would now shift to the great yeshivah located in Pumbedisa.

Rav Yehudah Bar Yechezkel

As noted earlier, Rav Yehudah bar Yechezkel was one of the primary students of both Rav and Mar Shmuel. According to the Talmud, Rabi Yehudah HaNasi predicted the birth of Rav Yehudah[1] and Rav Yehudah was, in fact, born on the day of Rabi's death.[2] His father, Rav Yechezkel was a highly respected scholar and community activist in matters of charity, so much so that even Mar Shmuel stood before him in respect.[3] Though Rav Yehudah obviously began his studies under the tutelage of his father,[4] his main teachers were Rav Assi I, Rav and Mar Shmuel. He first studied in Hutzal in the yeshivah of Rav Assi I, where he became his prime student. Many of the opinions of Rav Assi I that are mentioned in the Talmud are quoted there in the name of Rav Yehudah.[5] After a number of years, Rav Yehudah moved to Sura to study in the great yeshivah of Rav. During the more than twenty years that Rav headed Sura, Rav Yehudah was one of his most distinguished students, accompanying his mentor on his travels[6] and teaching Rav's own son, Chiya.[7]

Rav Yehudah was considered the main conduit of Rav's teachings to such an extent that even when Rav Yehudah's name is not mentioned in the Talmud as the transmitter of Rav's statement, it is nevertheless assumed that the statement came to us through him.[8] More than 300 statements from Rav are related by Rav Yehudah in the Talmud.[9] Rav Yehudah returned to Hutzal to study at the yeshivah of Rav Assi I after the death of Rav, but Rav Assi I also

RAV YEHUDAH BAR YECHEZKEL
c. 285 CE

TEACHERS
- Rav
- Mar Shmuel
- Rav Assi I

Colleagues
- Rav Huna
- Rav Chisda
- Rav Nosson bar Oshiya
- Rav Papa Sava
- Rav Nachman bar Yaakov
- Rav Eyna
- Rav Huna bar Chiya
- Rav Sheishes

Students
- Rabah bar Nachmani
- Rav Yosef
- Rav Zeira I
- Rav Oshiya
- Rav Hamnuna II
- Ravin bar Rav Ada
- Rava bar Rav Ada
- Ravin bar Rav Nachman
- Rava

Relatives
- Brother: Rami bar Yechezkel
- Son: Rav Yitzchak

died shortly after Rav.[10] Rav Yehudah now journeyed to Nehardea to study under Mar Shmuel, where he again became the primary disciple. As mentioned earlier, Mar Shmuel was so impressed with Rav Yehudah's nearly superhuman abilities that he once exclaimed: "Was it possible that this man was born of a woman?"[11] Mar Shmuel dubbed Rav Yehudah "*shinanah*" – the sharp, creative genius.[12] As explained earlier, Mar Shmuel died in 254 CE, seven years after Rav's death. With Mar Shmuel's demise, the yeshivah in Nehardea began a long decline, and Rav Yehudah now left to become the head of the yeshivah in Pumbedisa.

At that time, Pumbedisa was a major trading center in northern Babylonia. Though it possessed a sizable Jewish population, it was not previously known as a center of Torah study and religious piety. After the death of Mar Shmuel and the already noticeable decline of Nehardea – due to internal and external factors discussed previously in this work – many of the students of Nehardea and its yeshivah migrated to Sura and its suburb, Masa Machsiya, to study under Rav Huna and later, Rav Chisda.

Rav Yehudah took the bold step of moving to Pumbedisa and founding a new yeshivah there under seemingly inhospitable circumstances. (As was the custom of all of the scholars of the Talmud, Rav Yehudah took no salary from the yeshivah in Pumbedisa but rather earned his livelihood as a wine merchant.[13]) The yeshivah began with only a few students – colleagues and disciples of Rav Yehudah from his days of learning in Nehardea. Eventually, it grew in numbers and prestige and took the place of Nehardea as the companion and alternative to Rav Huna's yeshivah

Hexagonal glass jar, Palestine, 6th - 7th century CE (The Israel Museum, Jerusalem)

in Sura. Rav Yehudah served as its head for approximately 40 years and his personality, intellect and genius drew hundreds of students. Rav Yehudah outlived Rav Huna by only two years, but even in that short span of time many of Rav Huna's prime disciples came to Pumbedisa to study under him.[14] By then, Rav Yehudah's sight was impaired due to his advanced age,[15] but he nevertheless continued teaching and guiding the yeshivah until his death in c. 300 CE. The great yeshivah of Pumbedisa that he founded was to last as an effective house of Torah study and guidance for almost 800 more years, a testimony to the holiness and genius of its founder, Rav Yehudah bar Yechezkel.

Rav Yehudah was renowned for his sharp mind and genius in explaining and reconciling seemingly contradictory rulings of the different rabbis. He was the *charif* – the sharp genius – par excellence, and he trained his students to follow in his footsteps.[16] The students of Pumbedisa were known as *charifei d'Pumbedisa* – the sharp ones of Pumbedisa who were able to "draw an elephant through the eye of a needle!"[17] Despite his emphasis on excellence in all intellectual matters, Rav Yehudah warned against hubris and arrogance.[18]

As mentioned earlier, Rav Yehudah was one of the significant transmitters of the teachings of both Rav and Mar Shmuel to the next generation of scholars. He quoted many laws and opinions in their names. However, his younger brother, Rami bar Yechezkel, often questioned his brother's transmission of law in the name of Rav and/or Mar Shmuel.[19] Rav Yosef, the disciple of Rav Yehudah, insisted, though that his mentor was careful in transmitting the law in the name of Rav and/or Mar Shmuel; and when sometimes in doubt, Rav Yehudah himself indicated that he was unsure as to the origin of the statement.[20] Rav Yehudah was also the conduit for some of the most famous stories of Rav and Mar Shmuel regarding the events of the Second Temple, its destruction and aftermath.[21]

During the tenure of Rav Yehudah in Pumbedisa, the intense, sharp study of Torah associated with his methodology concentrated on *seder* Nezikin – the laws of torts, damages, commerce, partnerships and the judicial system.[22] Rav Yehudah himself praised the

One should always study Torah, even if at first insincerely, because the study of Torah itself will eventually lead that person to sincerity.
Rav Yehudah Bar Yechezkel

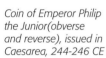

Coin of Emperor Philip the Junior(obverse and reverse), issued in Caesarea, 244-246 CE

study of *nezikin* as being the gateway to becoming a pious person.[23] Like his mentor, Mar Shmuel, Rav Yehudah paid close attention to the correct text and interpretation of the Mishnah,[24] and we find his explanations and insights as to the true meaning of the sometimes cryptic words of the Mishnah throughout the Talmud.[25]

This approach is in line with the general attempt of all of the *Amoraim* of the Talmud to understand the words of the Mishnah, and in the tradition of the Divine Oral Law to transmit those ideas and laws in correct form to the Torah students of later generations.

Several of Rav Yehudah's statements regarding practical personal conduct have come down to us:

- *One should always study Torah, even if at first insincerely, because the study of Torah itself will eventually lead that person to sincerity.*[26]

- *Acts that the rabbis banned to be performed publicly (because they may lead to misinterpretation) are forbidden even if performed in strictest privacy.*[27]

- *A king must always insist on his honor.*[28]

- *Night was created for sleep.*[29]

- *One should not keep incorrect weights or measures in one's home even if they are now used as chamber pots!*[30]

- *[Stated in the name of Rav...] Most people skirt the laws of thievery, a minority of humans are sexually immoral, but all are covered with the dust of slandering others.*[31]

- *Preventing poverty in one's home and thus promoting harmony is of great importance.*[32]

- *One must increase the joy and pleasantness of the celebration and commemoration of the Sabbath.*[33]

Rav Yehudah's personal example during prayer was an inspiration to others. He would carefully prepare and organize his prayers in his mind before actually praying.[34] He would arrange his clothing carefully before praying, as well.[35] He felt that intense concentration while engaged in prayer was essential, and actually "praised" himself as an example to others in this regard.[36]

Rav Yehudah had a son, Rav Yitzchak, who was taught and educated by his father.[37] Rav Yehudah's grandson, Isai – the son of Rav Yitzchak – was also a well-known scholar.[38]

After the death of Rav Yehudah, the center of Torah study gravitated back to Sura, where Rav Chisda was now the head of the yeshivah. After Rav Chisda's death, there was a period of time when neither the yeshivos of Sura nor Pumbedisa were particularly strong and active. Other smaller yeshivos sprung up in different parts of Babylonia.

Among the many other scholars who formed the second generation of *Amoraim* and who were colleagues of Rav Huna, Rav Chisda and Rav Yehudah Bar Yechezkel were:

- Avimei[39]
- Rav Ada[40]
- Rav Ada bar Ahava I[41]
- Rav Ada bar Masna I[42]
- Rav Acha Bardala[43]
- Rav Gidal[44]
- Rav Brona[45]
- Gneiva[46]
- Rav Dimi bar Chinana I[47]
- Rav Dimi bar Yosef[48]
- Rav Hamnuna[49]
- Zeirei II[50]
- Rav Chiya bar Ashi[51]
- Rav Chiya bar Yosef[52]
- Rav Chiya bar Rav[53]
- Rav Chama bar Gurya[54]
- Rav Chana bar Chanilai[55]
- Rav Chanin[56]
- Rav Chanina bar Avdimei[57]
- Rav Chanan bar Ravah[58]
- Rav Chananel[59]
- Rabi Tavla (Tavlai)[60]
- Rav Chanan bar Ami[61]
- Rav Tuvi bar Kisna[62]
- Rav Yeyva Sava[63]
- Rav Yirmiyahu bar Abba I[64]
- Rav Kahana II[65]
- Rav Menashya bar Zvid[66]
- Rav Menashe bar Yirmiyahu[67]
- Mar Ukva[68]
- Rav Nachman bar Yaakov[69]
- Rav Nosson bar Abba[70]
- Rav Nosson bar Oshiya[71]
- Ulla [bar Yishmael][72]
- Rav Eyna[73]
- Rav Amram I[74]
- Rav Anan[75]
- Rav Anan bar Tachlifa[76]
- Rav Papa Sava[77]
- Rabah bar bar Chana[78]
- Rav Katina[79]
- Rabah bar Yirmiyahu[80]
- Rabah bar Rav Huna[81]
- Rami bar Yechezkel[82]
- Rav Sheishes[83]
- Rav Tachlifa bar Avimei (Avdimei)[84]

This list is certainly not complete or exhaustive. Nevertheless, it does highlight for us many of the names of the extraordinary scholars who are the backbone of the Talmud, this famed second generation of *Amoraim*, the worthy successors to their teachers and mentors, Rav, Mar Shmuel and Rabi Yochanan.

The importance of this second generation of *Amoraim* to the formation of the Talmud cannot be overemphasized. Whereas the first generation of *Amoraim* – Rav, Mar Shmuel, Rabi Yochanan and their colleagues – were students of the *Tannaim* who composed and edited the Mishnah and thus had the opportunity to deal with the Mishnah from the direct teachings of its authors and final editors, this second generation of *Amoraim* was removed in time and place from the work and men of the Mishnah. Their work in developing the Talmud was therefore based on the oral traditions received from their teachers, their own holy instinct, their ingenuity in understanding the sometimes cryptic words of the Mishnah, and the give-and-take of the intellectual discussion between scholars from different yeshivos and teachers – all of which led to clarifying and deciding the *halachah*. Thus the Talmud, as we have come to know it, is in a great measure a development of these men of the second generation of *Amoraim*. All later generations of the Talmud followed this pattern of scholarship, debate, question-and-answer format, and analytic learning established by the scholars of the second generation of *Amoraim*.

SECTION IV

THE THIRD GENERATION OF AMORAIM IN BABYLONIA

300 - 330 CE

*Tabarius (Tiberias) from the Walls of Saffet
(Safed) in the distance, April 22nd 1839, by
David Roberts, R.A., England, 1796-1864, a
color lithograph published in 1842.
(Library of Congress Collection)*

Rabah Bar Nachmani

fter the passing of Rav Yehudah bar Yechezkel in c. 300 CE, the position of the head of the yeshivah in Pumbedisa was vacant. The two main students of Pumbedisa were then Rabah bar Nachmani and Rav Yosef. Rabah was famed for his genius, sharpness of mind and intellectual ingenuity. He was *"okeir harim"* – literally, one who is able to uproot mountains and grind them together with his vast talent and intellectual prowess.[1] He was recognized as the greatest expert in matters of complicated rituals of purity, *negaim* and *oholos*.[2] Rav Yosef, on the other hand was famed as *"Sinai"*– one who knew all of the received Torah from Sinai and did not rely on his own creative intellect; rather he determined all questions of *halachah* from previously stated sources and texts.[3] The rabbis of Babylonia debated which of these two great men should be appointed as the successor to Rav Yehudah bar Yechezkel as the leader of the yeshivah in Pumbedisa.

They turned to the rabbis in the Land of Israel for a decision: the ruling was that *Sinai adif* – the one with the wider knowledge of sources and texts is preferable.[4] With intense modesty, Rav Yosef refused to accept the leadership position. In addition, he had been warned by those who foresaw the future that he would serve as head of the yeshivah for only two years, and then he would die. To prolong his life and retain his modesty and privacy, Rav Yosef refused the position and deferred to Rabah bar Nachmani.[5] For the

RABAH BAR NACHMANI
c. 315 CE

Teachers
• Rav Yehudah bar Yechezkel
• Rabi Yochanan
• Rav Huna
• Rav Nachman bar Yaakov
• Rav Sheishes
• Rav Chisda

Colleagues
• Rav Yosef
• Rav Huna bar Chiya
• Rav Ami
• Rav Assi
• Rabi Zeira
• Rav Zeira I

Students
• Abayei
• Rava
• Rav Ada bar Ahava II

Relatives
• Nephew and adopted son: Abayei
• Brother: Rav Oshiya

next 22 years, the yeshivah was headed by Rabah.[6] Upon his death, Rav Yosef became the head of the yeshivah, and true to their prediction, he served in the position for only a little more than two years.[7]

Rabah bar Nachmani was one of the descendants of the house of Eli HaKohein,[8] who were haunted by the Biblical curse[9] that they would not live long lives. Our text of the Talmud states that Rabah lived only until age 40![10] However, Halevi and many others state that Rabah lived 60 years and that our text in the Talmud is a faulty one, corrupted by copyists.[11]

Born in Babylonia, Rabah received his early education there. He had a number of brothers,[12] and they wrote to him that he should forsake Babylonia and come to study Torah with them at the yeshivah of Rabi Yochanan in the Land of Israel.[13] It is apparent that he followed their advice, for Rabah quotes many statements in the name of Rabi Yochanan throughout the Talmud.[14] However, Rabah did not settle permanently in the Land of Israel;[15] he returned to Babylonia to study with Rav Huna in Sura.[16] Already well-known for his genius and innovative prowess, Rabah was treated in a special fashion by Rav Huna, who set high standards for him and his scholastic accomplishments.[17] When Rav Huna passed away, Rabah returned to Pumbedisa, the city of his birth,[18] to study with Rav Yehudah bar Yechezkel.[19] Together with his colleague, Rav Yosef, Rabah also studied with Rav Nachman bar Yaakov.[20] Rav Nachman respected Rabah greatly and called him "*Abba*" – the ruler and great man.[21] We also find Rabah and Rav Yosef studying with Rav Sheishes.[22] Apparently, he also made it a point to occasionally journey to Sura (after the death of Rav Huna) to study with the aged Rav Chisda.[23] Rabah drew inspiration and knowledge from all of these illustrious men of the second generation of *Amoraim*; he was thus poised and primed to become one of the outstanding leaders of the third generation of *Amoraim*.

Little is known about Rabah's personal family life. Abayei, his orphaned nephew was raised in his home, and often quotes the sayings of Rabah's wife, whom he referred to as his mother.[24] Two of Rabah's sons are mentioned in the Talmud as scholars. One son was

"Let the Messiah come, but I do not wish to live at that time of troubles to witness it."
Rabah bar Nachmani

Rabi Chiya bar Rabah bar Nachmani[25] and another was Rava bar Rabah.[26] Rabah slept very little, emulating his mentor of a previous generation, Rav.[27] In fact, in most of his activities and character traits, he followed those of Rav.[28]

Rabah was very strict in his judgments and punishments.[29] Regarding this tendency, he stated that he was born under the influence of the red star (planet Mars), causing him to be strict and demanding with others.[30] It was this nature of Rabah, coupled with the dishonesty and corruption of the townspeople of Pumbedisa, that made for the tension between them, a tension that ultimately resulted in shameful tragedy and Rabah's demise.[31] Yet, despite these difficulties and his austere reputation, Rabah began every Torah lecture to his students with a humorous story! He used this technique to gain their attention and to relax the atmosphere of the lecture hall.[32] Like many others in the Talmud, Rabah foresaw the tragedies that would occur at the time of the Messianic redemption of Israel. It was he who also said this chilling, now well-known, statement: "Let him [the Messiah] come, but I do not wish to be present to witness it!"[33]

While Rabah headed the yeshivah in Pumbedisa for 22 years, Rav Yosef continued to be his colleague and helped Rabah in maintaining the Torah prominence of the institution.[34] With the death of Rav Chisda, the yeshivah in Sura lost its preeminence in the Torah community of Babylonia. The Pumbedisa yeshivah, headed by Rabah, became the central point of Torah study in Babylonia – and even for the Land of Israel as well. While the great Rav Ami[35] and Rav Assi headed the yeshivah in Tiberias after the death of Rabi Yochanan, and were greatly respected and beloved scholars,[36] the economic and social conditions of Jewish life in the Land of Israel were worsening rapidly. This inevitably led to the weakening of Tiberias as a pivotal center of Torah learning and a magnet for students.

Rav Ami and Rav Assi were both of Babylonian origin, but came to the Land of Israel in their early lives. They were both *kohanim*,[37] and became the leading judges and scholars of the Land of Israel.[38] They were students of Rabi Chanina and Rabi Oshiya, as well as of

Rabi Yochanan and Rabi Elazar ben Pedas,[39] all of whom were the founders of the *Talmud Yerushalmi*. They preached acceptance of the personal and national troubles of Jews and remained serenely faithful in the traditions of their predecessors.[40]

But Tiberias was basically now a holding action for the Jews of the Holy Land, while Pumbedisa under Rabah and Rav Yosef blossomed, expanded, and became the standard of excellence in Torah study in the Jewish world. The yeshivah of Pumbedisa had 400 permanent students[41] and in the months of the *kallah* (Adar and Elul) the number of attendees reached 12,000.[42] Ironically, the very success of the *kallah* attendance would be used by Rabah's foes in Pumbedisa to undermine him, eventually causing his death, as we shall soon see.

During the reign of Rabah and Rav Yosef in Pumbedisa, another house of Torah learning also existed in that city. It was headed by Rav Huna bar Chiya.[43] During the early years of Rabah's stewardship of the yeshivah in Pumbedisa, Rav Huna bar Chiya played a prominent role in building the scholarly environment of Pumbedisa, and was considered the leading scholar in that community.[44] However, after a period of time Rav Huna bar Chiya accepted a position with the governmental authorities as a collector of taxes from the Jewish community. Since many tax collectors were considered dishonest, corrupt and even extortionist,[45] Rabah and Rav Yosef felt that Rav Huna bar Chiya erred in accepting such a position; it could bring the Torah and its scholars into public disrepute. They therefore absented themselves from further Torah discussions with him. Seeing their reaction, Rav Huna bar Chiya resigned from the tax collector post. Rabah returned to studying and discussing Torah with Rav Huna bar Chiya, but Rav Yosef did not.[46] After this incident, Rabah became the undisputed leader of the scholars in Pumbedisa.[47]

As mentioned earlier, Rabah was uncompromising in his moral demands on the Jewish community of Pumbedisa. His popularity among the townspeople was so low[48] Abayei warned him that they would not even mourn his passing.[49] The prediction doesn't seem to have fazed him: Rabah was accustomed to difficulties, for he was a victim of ill fortune and tragedies all his life.[50] According to the Talmud, "Sixty tragic deaths were in his house."[51] Rabah was apparently so poor that he did not have sufficient barley bread to feed his family.[52] He could not even participate in joining an *eiruv* community (a legalism that allows many different properties to be considered as one property as far as carrying on the Sabbath is concerned) for he could not contribute towards the necessary purchase of a loaf of bread that is an essential part of creating the *eiruv*.[53]

It is to be remembered that the rabbis of the Talmud never took any public salaries from their communities or yeshivos:[54] Rabah had to eke out his own living and was not very successful at doing so. His uncompromising, critical attitude towards the people of Pumbedisa, who were well-known as dishonest in their dealings with others, earned him their enmity.[55] Eventually, his enemies informed on him to the government with the outrageous claim that because of the great public attendance at his public Torah lectures in the months' of the *yarchei kallah*, the government loses two months worth of tax revenues! Rabah fled to avoid arrest. When he returned to Pumbedisa, he was discovered. He then encountered the Angel of Death, but miraculously escaped from him. He sat near the trunk of a palm tree and studied Torah with such fervor and concentration that the Angel of Death could not take his soul. When a wind rustled through the palm fronds, Rabah mistakenly took it to be the sound of the arresting officers who were pursuing him. He chose rather to fall into the hands of the Angel of Death than be taken prisoner by the government authorities. He died saying the word *tahor* – pure. His body was shaded and protected by the wings of birds until his students, Abayei and Rava, following the sounds of those birds, found his body, and brought it to burial.[56] A great windstorm accompanied his demise, and abated only due to the prayer of a passing Arab – "O Lord, the whole world is Yours and Rabah bar Nachmani is now Yours as well. Why should You destroy Your world?"[57]

In his lifetime, Rabah "uprooted mountains" and thus his death was no different. Though he had a relatively short life span, his personage and influence are felt on almost every page of the Talmud.

"O Lord, the whole world is Yours and Rabah bar Nachmani is now Yours as well. Why should You destroy Your world?"

Talmud, Bava Metzia

Rav Yosef

RAV YOSEF
c. 320 CE

Teachers
• Rav Huna
• Rav Yehudah bar Yechezkel
• Rav Nachman bar Yaakov
• Rav Chisda
• Rav Hamnuna II

Colleagues
• Rabah bar Nachmani
• Rabi Zeira I
• Rav Acha bar Yosef
• Rav Acha bar Ada
• Rava bar Rav Ada
• Rav Yosef bar Chama
• Rav Kahana III
• Rav Dimi I

Students
• Abayei
• Rava
• Rav Bibi

Relatives
• Son: Rav Nechemiah
• Grandson: Rav Dimi bar Nechemiah

av Yosef was the quintessential master of Torah. As mentioned above, he was called *Sinai* – one who knew the entire Torah as given to Moshe on Mount Sinai and based his halachic rulings on his knowledge of the sources, traditions and texts of the Torah. The rabbis of the time decided that *Sinai* – the one with encyclopedic knowledge - is more necessary and preferable to head the yeshivah of Pumbedisa to the *okeir harim* (Rabah), the one who is sharp and brilliant in intellect.[1] Yet, in the halachic discussions between Rabah and Rav Yosef, the law is always as Rabah decides, except for three instances when the law follows the opinion of Rav Yosef.[2] (Why this should be so is a matter of discussion amongst the scholars.[3]) Rav Yosef also taught that in matters that are doubtful, one should see how the people behave and accept that to be the correct law.[4] Rav Yosef's statements appear throughout the Talmud, and in fact, he is quoted more often than Rabah in its pages. As related above, despite the preference of the rabbis, Rav Yosef deferred to Rabah, who served as the head of the yeshivah for 22 years, after which Rav Yosef served in that post, for two years.[5]

Like Rabah, Rav Yosef originally was a student of Rav Huna in Sura.[6] He then studied at the yeshivah of Rav Yehudah bar Yechezkel in Pumbedisa, who was his main mentor.[7] He also studied with Rav Nachman bar Yaakov,[8] Rav Chisda[9] and Rav Hamnuna II.[10]

Aware that Torah knowledge was not a matter of pedigree, he

commented on the fact that the children of great Torah scholars are not always Torah scholars themselves.[11] Due to this conviction, Rav Yosef himself took extraordinary measures – fasting for 40 days at a time – and praying that his descendants would expend the necessary efforts to become Torah scholars.[12] He stated that if there were three consecutive generations of Torah scholars in one's family, the Torah would always find its way back to its "inn" in the descendants of that family.[13]

His reverence for Torah and what it does for a human being was expressed in his statement that if it were not for the Torah that he had studied "there are many Yosefs in the marketplace" and there would be nothing special about him.[14] Rav Yosef had a keen sense of Torah scholarship and was not hesitant to criticize statements and opinions that he felt were incorrect,[15] but he also was willing to admit that his own originally stated opinion was wrong.[16] And he was quick to praise others whose Torah opinions found favor in his eyes.[17]

The study and promulgation of Torah was a supreme value in his life, and he even stated that it supersedes saving human lives.[18] He was full of praise for the scholars of the yeshivos of Babylonia,[19] and very critical of those who did not appreciate the cosmic importance and societal worth of a Torah scholar.[20] As the great *Sinai*, with a commanding encyclopedic knowledge of the entire Torah, he was expert even in counting its letters and discussed with his colleagues which letters were exactly the midpoint of the Torah.[21] He was also famous for his knowledge of *Targum* – Aramaic translations and explanations of the Hebrew Bible.[22]

Ironically, he would be beset by two major physical tragedies in his lifetime that eventually robbed him of his status as a *Sinai*. He was afflicted with blindness,[23] apparently at least partially self-inflicted.[24] Yet despite his blindness, Rav Yosef continued to teach and perform all of the ritual obligations of the Torah.[25] He longed to be informed that even the sightless are obligated in the performance of the commandments of the Torah.[26]

The second ailment was perhaps even more tragic: though he had previously known the entire Torah by heart, he became ill and

"When I hear my mother's footsteps I rise for the Holy Spirit that accompanies her."
Rav Yosef

his memory failed him.[27] His loyal students attempted to regularly remind of him of his previous teachings and halachic opinions.[28] Perhaps in recognition of his own plight, Rav Yosef taught that "the broken pieces of the first tablets of stone that Moses shattered were also preserved in the Holy Ark," i.e., a scholar suffering from dementia and forgetfulness is still worthy of respect.[29]

Rav Yosef credited the act of supporting Torah students as worthy of forgiveness of sin even for such a major sinner as Achav, the king of Israel.[30] He nevertheless taught that Torah scholars should not allow themselves to become poor and if they did need assistance, they should never become beggars.[31] Yet he regarded poverty as a Divine mechanism, a proper goad for the Jewish people to examine their behavior.[32]

Rav Yosef himself had considerable wealth,[33] and he took rigorous measures not to be corrupted by it. He took a public oath to abstain from alcoholic beverages.[34] Like Rabi Akiva generations before him, Rav Yosef was the "hand" of the poor,[35] entrusted to distribute charity to the poor of Pumbedisa.[36] Even the non-Jewish ruler of Pumbedisa sent him money to distribute to the needy.[37]

He described himself as having three major characteristics which made life difficult: being overly merciful; being quick-tempered; and being overly sensitive and of delicate nature.[38] These traits notwithstanding, his hallmark was humility and modesty, characteristics he considered the highest form of *imitatio Dei* – imitating God's ways, so to speak.[39] And true to this conviction, despite his scholarly stature, Rav Yosef was active personally in preparing for the Sabbath in his home, chopping wood to provide the fuel necessary for the holy day of rest.[40] His respect and care for his aged mother was legendary: when she entered the room he stood up, stating that the holy spirit itself – the *Shechinah* – now enters with her.[41]

As a keen observer of human life, Rav Yosef taught that it is not the mouse that is the thief, but rather the hole that allows its entry that is the true cause of the thievery,[42] meaning that creating the opportunity for sin greatly magnifies the likelihood of its occurrence.

"It is not the mouse that is the thief, but rather the hole that allows its entry"

Rav Yosef (Talmud)

Rav Yosef proclaimed that in the future messianic era all of the non-Jewish world will adopt Judaism as converts.[43] Unlike his colleague Rabah bar Nachmani and other scholars, who prayed for the messianic era to arrive but hoped that they did not have to witness its occurrences, Rav Yosef prayed for its arrival and stated that he would feel privileged to sit in the shade of the pile of dung of the Messiah's donkey![44]

Understanding the spiritual ramifications of every activity and event in life, Rav Yosef felt that the reward for visiting the sick was limitless.[45] When his sixtieth birthday arrived, he made a celebration and invited his colleagues and students to participate in rejoicing that he survived past the age of *kareis* – the risk of being "cut off," [a shortened life span], the biblical punishment for certain sins.[46] When he passed away, Rav Yosef was accorded singular and exceptional honors.[47] His son, Rav Nechemiah, is mentioned in the Talmud a number of times as a formidable scholar.[48] His grandson, Rav Dimi bar Nechemiah,[49] is also mentioned a number of times in the Talmud.[50] Thus, Rav Yosef's ardent prayers for three consecutive generations of Torah scholars in his family indeed were fulfilled.

Rav (Rabi) Zeira I

RAV ZEIRA I
c. 280 - 310 CE

Teachers
• Rav Huna
• Rav Yehudah bar Yechezkel
• Ulla bar Yishmael
• Rav Hamnuna
• Rav Masna
• Rabah bar Yirmiyahu

Colleagues
• Rabah bar Nachmani
• Rav Yosef
• Rav Ami
• Rav Assi
• Rabi Elazar ben Pedas

Students
• The scholars of the yeshiva in Tiberias

Family
• Father: Abahu d'Rav Zeira
• Son: Ahava (Achvaah) bar Zeira

An outstanding colleague of Rabah bar Nachmani and Rav Yosef was Rav (Rabi) Zeira I.[51] Like the father of Mar Shmuel, Rav Zeira I's father identified himself not by his given name but rather as "the father of Rav Zeira."[52] He apparently came from a wealthy family:[53] his father was a tax farmer/collector for the Babylonian government.[54] (A tax farmer was one who purchased at a discount from the government the right to collect taxes and then was legally permitted to collect full taxes from the taxpayers.) In this capacity, he went out of his way to try and protect the Torah scholars from the burden of the heavy taxation by the authorities.[55] On his deathbed, he ordered certain monies in his possession, though legally his, to be returned to the taxpayers.[56]

Rabi Zeira I's main teachers were Rav Huna[57] and Rav Yehudah bar Yechezkel,[58] but he also studied with Ulla bar Yishmael,[59] Rav Hamnuna,[60] Rav Masna[61] and Rabah bar Yirmiyahu.[62] Rav Zeira I was in contact with the scholars of the Land of Israel and posed many halachic questions to them.[63] After a period of studying in Babylonia with his companions Rabah bar Nachmani and Rav Yosef, Rav Zeira I decided to leave Babylonia to settle and study in the Land of Israel.[64] He did so, knowing that this was against the wishes of Rav Yehudah bar Yechezkel, who wanted the scholars to remain in Babylonia in order to strengthen the Torah community there, the country of the larger Jewish population of the time.[65] He did not leave for the Land of Israel until he had a favorable dream that showed him that any possible sins of his were already forgiven; therefore he was worthy of living in the Holy Land.[66] His zeal to reach the Land of Israel was so strong that when the ferry to cross the river was unavailable, he refused to wait for the next boat but rather crossed immediately by pulling himself on a rope that was extended between the two banks of the river,[67] notwithstanding the fact that he was garbed in his finest clothing in anticipation of reaching the Land of Israel.[68] He felt that he could not afford to forfeit an opportunity – even for an extra moment – to come to the Land of Israel, an opportunity that was not granted to Moshe and Aharon.[69]

Like many Jews over the centuries, and even in our time, Rav Zeira I did not have an easy "absorption process" initially in the Land of Israel. The Babylonian Jews were not very beloved to the Jews living in the Land of Israel. This attitude stemmed from their initial refusal to emigrate from Babylonia with Ezra at the beginning of Second Temple times.[70] There were Jews there who actually physically abused him,[71] and others who did so verbally.[72]

Nevertheless, Rabi Zeira I found satisfaction in his ability to study in Tiberias and meet the great Torah scholars of the Land of Israel – Rabi Yochanan,[73] Rabi Shimon ben Lakish,[74] Rabi Elazar ben Pedas,[75] Rav Ami[76] and Rav Assi.[77] His love for the Land of Is-

Gold-glass bases, possibly from a Roman catacomb, Rome, Italy, 4th century CE (The Israel Museum, Jerusalem)

115

rael and for its scholars knew no bounds. The Talmud tells us that he fasted 100 times, hoping that God would allow him to forget the methodology of Torah scholarship he had learned in Babylonia so that he would now be able to become expert in the methodology taught in the Land of Israel.[78] The Talmud itself warns that the transition from the style of learning in the Land of Israel – *Talmud Yerushalmi* – to the style of learning in Babylonia – *Talmud Bavli* – and vice versa as well, would be a difficult one.[79]

Yet Rav Zeira I made the transition successfully. His teachers wished to grant him *semichah* – ordination, but Rav Zeira I modestly avoided accepting this honor.[80] However, when he was informed of Rabi Elazar ben Pedas' opinion that accepting a public position is a sign that one's sins are forgiven, he accepted the ordination.[81] A portion of the poem that was recited at the ceremony of Rabi Zeira I's ordination is preserved for us in the Talmud.[82] It reads: "Without any cosmetics or rouge, [meaning without external artifices] still his countenance [meaning his spiritual and intellectual attainments regarding Torah] is most gracious and becoming."[83] From that time onward, he was known as *Rabi* Zeira and no longer *Rav* Zeira.[84]

Physically, Rabi Zeira I was small in stature.[85] There is an opinion[86] that because of his height he was called Zeira – meaning little or short. However, there is another opinion[87] that he was called Zeira from the Hebrew word *zeir* – meaning a golden crown, referred to the "crown of Torah" he had earned. Rabi Zeira I was famed for his piety, reckoned as one of the especially pious Jews of Babylonia.[88] He again fasted 100 times, this time so that the fires of Hell should not have any powers over his body. He tested himself every 30 days in an open oven and was always saved unharmed. Once, however, the rabbis disapproved of such behavior and he was singed on his hips. He thereby earned a nickname "the short one with singed hips" amongst his less than pious neighbors.[89] Rabi Zeira's holiness and sterling character were so overpowering that even these lawless neighbors eventually repented and changed their ways in honor of his memory after he passed away.[90]

His interpersonal relationships were marked by that piety as well. When Rabi Zeira I had a complaint against someone because of that person's words or actions against him, he purposely sought him out so there would be an opportunity for apology and reconciliation.[91] Rabi Zeira I was famed for his trustworthiness in all matters and for his accuracy in transmitting the precise words of Torah and tradition.[92] Because of his constant adherence to truth, he was critical of preachers who, in his opinion, distorted the meaning of biblical verses or sayings of the rabbis for solely homiletical purposes.[93] He called them "purveyors of magic."[94] Rabi Zeira I was a counselor and teacher for the students in the yeshivah in Tiberias.[95] In this, he was a successor to the role of Rabi Shimon ben Lakish there in an earlier time.[96]

Little is known regarding his personal life. He bemoaned the fact that he became an orphan and therefore no longer had the opportunity of honoring his parents in their lifetime.[97] He was descended from a family of *kohanim*.[98] Rabi Zeira I's son Ahava (Achvaah) was a noted scholar and is quoted in the Talmud.[99]

Rabi Zeira I lived a long life,[100] attributing his longevity to various acts of pious behavior and social rectitude.[101] At his passing, he was widely mourned. The moving eulogy of him that is recorded for us in the Talmud is as follows: "The land of Babylonia conceived and gave birth to him. The Land of Israel raised him – our most beloved child – and honored his desirable accomplishments. Woe to us, says the city of Tiberias, for we have lost our most desirable and precious vessel."[102]

Other Amoraim of the Third Generation

**R**av Oshiya [Hoshiyah] was a student of Rav Huna[103] and Rav Yehudah bar Yechezkel.[104] He was a close friend and colleague of Rabah bar Nachmani[105] and often asked him to clarify the law and tradition that he received from Rav Huna and Rav Chisda.[106] Like Rav Zeira I, Rav Oshiya left Babylonia to study and settle in the Land of Israel. He studied in Tiberias and his colleagues there were Rav Ami,[107] Rav Assi[108] and Rav Zeira I.[109] He arrived in Tiberias in time to study under the great Rabi Yochanan. Though Rabi Yochanan wished to ordain him, somehow the ordination never occurred.[110]

Rav Oshiya married the daughter of Rav Shmuel bar Rav Yitzchak, a noted scholar of Tiberias, and through his father-in-law's influence and standing, Rav Oshiya was able to advance opinions regarding the setting of the Jewish calendar – even though he possessed no official ordination – and was allowed to actually vote on the matter.[111] Rav Oshiya was an expert in *breisos* – those teachings that were not included in the Mishnah but were essential for the transmission and explanation of the Oral Law.[112]

He and Rav Chanina were close friends, and their names are mentioned in tandem a number of times in the Talmud.[113] They both earned their livelihoods as shoemakers,[114] and were renowned for their pious behavior, even under the most difficult circumstances.[115] When Rav Oshiya passed away, mourners said, "The great palm tree of Tiberias has fallen!"[116] Even though Rav Oshiya is listed here among the *Amoraim* of Babylonia, his main works and accomplishments were as a member of the *Amoraim* of the Land of Israel in the third century CE.

There are more than 70 other *Amoraim* of this third generation of Babylonian scholars of the Talmud who appear in the Talmud.[117] Among them was Rav Hamnuna II,[118] who was a disciple of Rav Yehudah bar Yechezkel and a colleague of Rav Chisda. Though Rav Chisda told Rav Huna that Rav Hamnuna II was a great man in Torah,[119] Rav Hamnuna II was subject to much controversy, and even insult, in his life.[120] He was also reproved by Rav Huna for not having married by the time he was twenty.[121] He apparently was a frequent visitor at the palace of the *Reish Galusa,* [122] and he was known to speak out strongly against aggressive, brazen people.[123] He preached important lessons regarding the proper methods of prayer.[124] The great confessional prayer that is recited at the conclusion of the *Neilah* Yom Kippur services: "Lord, until I was created I was unworthy and now after I have been created I am still unworthy, I am dust in my life and certainly so after my death… etc." was authored by Rav Hamnuna II.[125]

Rabah bar Huna and Rav Hamnuna II died at the same time. Both of their bodies were placed on camels to be transported to the Land of Israel for burial. Even in death, the scholars honored each other: the camels balked and would not pass each other in crossing a bridge.[126] The one who eulogized Rav Hamnuna II called him and his life "The Book of the Wars of God."[127] This term was a reference to his great knowledge and teachings of Torah, but it may also have been a reference to the turbulent events of his life.

Rav Acha bar Adah was yet a disciple of Rav.[128] He lived a very long life and was still active in the third generation of the *Amoraim* of Babylonia, and even later.[129] He was also a student of Rav Hamnuna I [130] and of Rav Yehudah bar Yechezkel.[131] Well-known for his respect for and love of Torah scholars, he stated that even the ordinary conversation of the scholars is worthy of study and understanding.[132]

Marble pedestal with carving of a menorah, from Ashkelon synagogue

His colleague, Rav Acha bar Yosef, was a student of Rav Huna[133] and Rav Chisda[134] and a close relative and colleague of Rav Nachman bar Yaakov.[135] Rav Acha bar Yosef was of a sickly nature, suffering from a variety of ailments.[136]

A third Rav Acha – Rav Acha bar Yaakov – was also a disciple of Rav Huna.[137] He was a well-known scholar and holy personage and many wondrous events occurred to him.[138] He lived a long life and the Talmud records him still discussing Torah with Abayei and Rava in the fourth generation of the *Amoraim* of Babylonia.[139] He lived in the town of Papunaya, a suburb of Pumbedisa, and is referred to in the Talmud by the name of his town.[140] His son, Rav Yaakov bar Acha, studied Torah with Abayei, but was not successful there in his studies and returned home to his father.[141] Rav

Acha bar Yaakov's grandson, also named Rav Yaakov, was raised by his grandfather.[142] Rav Acha bar Yaakov's main students were Rav Papa[143] and Rav Acha's nephew, Rav Acha breih d'Rav Ika.[144]

Another *Amora* of this third generation was Rav Achdvoi bar Ami. He was mainly a disciple of Rav Sheishes[145] and was famous for his quickness of mind and creativity of intellect. Because of these attributes, he sometimes came into conflict with his teacher, Rav Sheishes, once resulting in his being punished: he became mute and forgot his knowledge.[146] His mother[147] intervened with Rav Sheishes, who forgave him and restored him to normal health.[148]

Some of the other *Amoraim* of Babylonia of that generation are:

- Rav Abba Achva d'Rav Yehudah bar Zavdi[149]
- Rava bar Rav Ada[150]
- Ravin bar Rav Ada[151]
- Ravin bar Rav Nachman[152]
- Rav Idi bar Avin[153]
- Rav Assi [bar Nosson?][154]
- Rav Bibi[155]
- Rav Yosef bar Chama[156]
- Rav Kahana III[157]
- Levi bar Buti[158]
- Rav Malchiya[159]
- Rav Menashe[160]
- Rav Shmuel bar Yehudah[161]
- Rava [Rabah] bar Rav Huna[162]

This list is far from complete, for there were many hundreds of great scholars who were the students of Rav Chisda, Rav Huna and Rav Yehudah bar Yechezkel, and who were the colleagues of Rabah bar Nachmani and Rav Yosef. However, not all of them are mentioned by name in the Talmud and we know almost nothing about their lives and achievements.[163]

SECTION V

THE THIRD GENERATION OF AMORAIM IN THE LAND OF ISRAEL

300 - 330 CE

*Detail of the zodiac mosaic floor from
the synagogue in Hamat Tiberias,
4th–5th century CE*

Rav Ami and Rav Assi

After the passing of Rabi Yochanan and Rabi Shimon ben Lakish, the great yeshivah in Tiberias came under the direction of Rav Ami, a disciple of Rav Yochanan,[1] and Rav Assi. Very little is known about Rav Ami's ancestry, except that his father's name was Nosson[2] and that he was a *kohein*.[3] In his youth, he was yet able to study under Rav in Sura[4] before coming to the Land of Israel. He was ordained and received *semichah*.[5] His main learning experience was in Tiberias under Rabi Yochanan,[6] though he studied there also under Rabi Chanina,[7] Rabi Shimon ben Lakish[8] and Rabi Elazar ben Pedas.[9] He also studied for a time under Rabi Hoshiyahu,[10] probably in Caesarea.

As stated earlier in this work, when Rabi Yochanan died, Rav Ami observed the laws of a mourner as though Rabi Yochanan were a blood relative of his,[11] and later succeeded Rabi Yochanan as the head of the Tiberias yeshivah.[12] During this period, Rav Huna, the head of the Pumbedisa yeshivah in Babylonia was still considered the final authority in halachic matters.[13] With his passing, Rav Ami became the address for halachic decisions.[14]

He became known for certain opinions and practices that were (and still are) held in high regard. For example, Rav Ami gave credit to those who intended to do a good deed, but because of unforeseen circumstances were unable to do so. He felt that they should be considered as though they had actually fulfilled their good intentions.[15] He always prayed in the study hall where he studied To-

RAV AMI AND RAV ASSI
c. 290 CE

Teachers
• Rabi Yochanan
• Rabi Shimon ben Lakish
• Rabi Chanina
• Rabi Elazar ben Pedas
• Rabi Hoshiyahu

Colleagues
• Rabi Yehudah Nesiah I
• Rabi Abba
• Rabi Yitzchak Nafcha
• Rabi Abahu
• Rabi Safra

Students
• Rav Abba bar Zavda
• Rav Avirah
• Rav Shmuel bar Nachmani
• Rachva

rah, even though there were many synagogues and private houses of prayer nearby.[16]

At the end of his life, because of the growing strength of the Christians in Tiberias, Rav Ami was forced to move to Caesarea, where Rav Abahu's influence still protected the scholars from persecution.[17] He lived a very long life[18] and was a beloved figure among both the scholars and the masses of the Jewish people.

Rav Ami's friend, compatriot and colleague in life and throughout the pages of the Talmud was Rav Assi.[19] Like Rav Ami, he was a *kohein*[20] and received *semichah* ordination.[21] Together, he and Rav Ami, were considered the halachic authorities and the judges of the Land of Israel.[22] Along with Rabi Yehudah Nesiah, Rav Ami and Rav Assi worked diligently to improve the Torah education system in the Land of Israel in their time.[23]

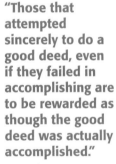

"Those that attempted sincerely to do a good deed, even if they failed in accomplishing are to be rewarded as though the good deed was actually accomplished."

Rav Ami

Rav Assi had deferred to Rav Ami, allowing him to become the sole head of the yeshivah after Rav Yochanan's death, yet on his deathbed Rav Assi wept that perhaps he made the wrong decision in that matter by excusing himself from the yoke and possible merit of public service.[24] Rav Assi was called the "wonder of his generation" by his mentor and colleague, Rabi Elazar ben Pedas,[25] and when he died, the rabbis mourned that "the [great] trees of Tiberias have now been uprooted."[26] They also eulogized him, saying that "the great fortress tower of Tiberias has now collapsed."[27]

Another *Amora* of great prominence at this time in the Land of Israel was Rabi Abba. He was originally of Babylonian origin and had studied under Rav Huna and Rav Yehudah bar Yechezkel.[28] He is

to be counted as one of the scholars of Caesarea, for he settled there permanently after his arrival in the Land of Israel. A wealthy merchant, Rabi Abba dealt in silk and precious stones and traveled often to Babylonia and other places in Asia Minor. He was quite successful in business and had horses and carriages at his disposal.[29] He was involved as a litigant in a number of famous court cases as recorded in the Talmud.[30] Renowned for his charity,[31] his travels also helped spread Torah to the communities he visited. Upon returning from his journeys, his love for the Land of Israel was so great that he kissed the shores of the country when his boat reached the port of Acco (Acre).[32]

Reconstruction drawing of harbor at Capernaum (Kfar Nachum), 1st century CE

Model of Gamla synagogue, 1st century CE

Highly regarded as a Torah scholar, the rabbis attributed many of the Torah statements circulated at that time in the Land of Israel to him.[33] Rabi Abba prayed that his teachings be accepted and honored by the scholars in the Land of Israel.[34] His prayer was accepted and fulfilled. Furthermore, he encouraged the inhabitants of the Land of Israel to be as "strong as iron,"[35] and stated there that the scholars of Israel, wherever they may be, must certainly be as "strong as iron."[36] In many respects, this characteristic of iron will was a personal trait of Rabi Abba himself, in his teachings as well as in his commercial dealings. Little more is known of his personal life, though there is one reference in the Talmud to his family.[37]

Rabi Yitzchak Nafcha was a colleague of Rav Ami and Rav Assi. He may also be classified as a member of the group of the scholars of Caesarea. He was a student of Rabi Yochanan. From Babylonia originally, he was a well-known scholar: his prowess was both in *halachah* – legal and ritual matters – and in *Aggadah* – homiletical interpretations of the Torah and its moral lessons and values. Rav Ami and Rav Assi sat before him to study Torah.[38]

Best known for his statements in *Aggadah*, Rabi Yitzchak Nafcha is the author of the famous Talmudic parable about the man who had two wives, one young and one older. The older one plucked out all of his black hairs, while the younger woman plucked out his gray hairs. The result was that he lost all of his hair and became bald.[39] Rabi Yitzchak Nafcha used that parable to describe his own situation in regard to teaching: he compared himself to that man since Rav Ami and Rav Assi could not agree on whether they wished to hear words of *Aggadah* or *halachah* from him![40]

His profound understanding of *Aggadah* was so impressive that Rabi Shimon ben Lakish told Rabi Yochanan that Rabi Yitzchak Nafcha's interpretations of *Aggadah* were superior even to those of Rabi Yochanan.[41]

Rabi Yitzchak Nafcha traveled throughout the Middle East, and we find him living for a period of time in Antioch.[42] Because of these travels and his advancing age, he sometimes forgot the sources of his aggadic statements.[43] He comforted himself by stating that forgetfulness has a positive side to it: due to forgetfulness a person must constantly study Torah, for if he never forgot what he had learned, he would not consider it necessary to study Torah constantly.[44] The rabbis attested that when the name "Yitzchak" appears in the Talmud – not identified otherwise by any other description – it always refers to Rabi Yitzchak Nafcha.[45] One of the more famous statements in the Talmud regarding the importance of Torah education for Jews is attributed to him: he asserted that by establishing a Torah educational system in Judah during his reign, King Chizkiyah saved Judah from the sword of Sennacherib.[46]

Another *Amora* of the time – also one of the distinguished scholars of Caesarea – was Rav Safra. He, too, was from Babylonia and moved to Caesarea, apparently returning to Babylonia for a time.[47] He studied with Rabi Abahu,[48] Rabi Abba,[49] and the other scholars of Caesarea. He was meticulous in repeating the teachings of his mentors exactly as they had phrased them.[50] He prayed for peace and harmony in the world generally and particularly for peace and harmony amongst the scholars of Israel.[51] And he implored Heaven to allow those who study Torah for lesser motives than purely for the sake of Torah to be allowed to achieve the level of studying Torah in sincerity and for the sake of Torah itself.[52] Rava, the leading *Amora* of fourth-generation Babylonian *Amoraim* said of Rav Safra that he is a "great" man.[53]

In Caesarea, Rabi Abahu attempted to protect Rav Safra from the tax collectors because of his great Torah scholarship,[54] but nevertheless Rav Safra suffered persecution from the Christians there. He is famous in the Talmud for his impeccable honesty, refusing to take more money for an object that he was selling than the amount he had set in his heart originally, even though the non-Jewish buyer now offered him a far greater sum.[55] As such a genuinely pious individual, he was worthy of miraculous events occurring to him.[56] At Rav Safra's passing, Abayei insisted that the rabbis of Babylonia rend their garments as a sign of mourning.[57]

Among the other Amoraim of the period – many who can be counted among the scholars of Caesarea – are:

- Rabi Chanina bar Papa (Papi)[58]
- Rav Acha bar Chanina[59]
- Rav Shimi (Simi)[60]
- Rav Oshiya bar Chama (known as Rav Oshiya Rabah)[61]
- Rabi Yosi d'min Kaeseri (Caesarea)[62]
- Rav Tachlifa m'Kaeseri[63]
- Rabi Zarika(n)[64]
- Rav Abba bar Zavda[65]
- Gidal bar Manyumei[66]
- Rav Avira[67]
- Rabi Yonah[68]
- Rabi Yitzchak ben Elazar (Elaah)[69]
- Rav Shmuel bar Nachman (Nachmani)[70]
- Rachva[71]
- Rav Brechiya[72]

This roll certainly is not meant as a complete listing of the great scholars of the third generation of *Amoraim* in the Land of Israel. However, even in a book such as this, less is sometimes more, and in the people listed and described above, some of the main participants in the final completion of the *Talmud Yerushalmi* are included.

The fourth century CE would not be kind to the Jews living in the Land of Israel. The conversion of the Roman emperor Constantine to Christianity in 312 CE and the subsequent religious and social upheavals in the Roman Empire ushered in a reign of persecution of the Jews in the Holy Land. Unable to convert the Jews to Christianity, the early Church fathers fostered a religious persecution of them that has lasted through the ages.

Because of the heavy hand of the Roman-Byzantine-Christian persecution, the yeshivos in the Land of Israel disbanded, the economic base of the Jews there declined drastically, and many of the Torah scholars who resided in the Land of Israel now fled to Babylonia. The obvious decline of the Jewish community in the Land of Israel forced the Nasi of the time, Hillel II, to create and confirm the permanent Jewish calendar in the year 359 CE. The Sanhedrin could no longer meet in safety and thus was precluded from regularly declaring the new moon's birth and establishing the Jewish calendar on the ancient basis of witnesses appearing before it to testify as to the "birth" of the new moon. The establishment of the permanent calendar, based on astronomically and mathematically produced formulae, proved to be another method of guaranteeing Jewish survival throughout the long exile of Israel.

By the end of the fourth century CE, because of the pressures imposed on the Jews in the Land of Israel at that time, the *Talmud Yerushalmi* was already in its present somewhat abridged and cryptic form. The work on the Babylonian Talmud would continue for almost another two centuries until its final redaction. Thus the remainder of this book, with very few exceptions, will deal with the lives and creativity of the great men of the Babylonian Talmud.

THE FOURTH GENERATION OF AMORAIM IN BABYLONIA

C. 330 - 375 CE

*Detail of mosaic floor
from the synagogue
in Hamat Tiberias,
4th–5th century CE*

Abayei

f there are two names that truly represent the Babylonian Talmud throughout all of the centuries of Jewish life, they are Abayei and Rava. The Talmud styles itself as being the sum of their formulations and discussions.[1] Though Abayei and Rava march in tandem together throughout the pages of the Talmud, I will attempt to deal with their lives separately.

Abayei was born in 279 or 289 CE.[2] He was a *kohein*, descended from the house of Eli, the High Priest, as was his uncle Rabah bar Nachmani.[3] Abayei's father passed away before Abayei was born and his mother died in childbirth with him,[4] so he was raised in the house of his uncle, Rabah bar Nachmani.[5] In the Talmud Abayei is called by the name Nachmani many times, especially by his colleague, Rava.[6] There are numerous interpretations of his name. One opinion is that Nachmani was his given name, and he was named after his grandfather, the father of Rabah.[7] Others say that his real name was Abayei and that he was also called Nachmani due to his being raised in the house of Rabah bar Nachmani.[8] In addition, there is also a possibility that the name "Abayei" was given to children orphaned at their birth for it is an acrostic for the verse in Hosea "*asher becha yerucham yasom* – only in You, God, will the orphan find comfort and mercy."[9] Abayei's father, the brother of Rabah bar Nachmani, was called Baylil (Kaylil), but nothing more is known regarding him.[10] Raised by his foster mother who loved him as he loved her, he called her "mother" and quoted her wisdom and life observations many times in the Talmud.[11]

ABAYEI
c. 330 CE

Teachers
• Rabah bar Nachmani
• Rav Yosef
• Rav Yehudah bar Yechezkel
• Rav Chiya bar Rav
• Rav Kahana III
• Rav Sheishes
• Rav Chisda

Colleagues
• Rava
• Rav Dimi
• Ravin
• Rav Safra
• Rav Zeira II
• Rabah bar Masna
• Rav Abba II

Students
• Rav Zvid
• Rav Papa
• Rav Dimi of Nehardea

Relatives
• Sons: Rav Bibi bar Abayei, Rav Shimi bar Abayei
• Uncle: Rabah bar Nachmani

Living in the house of Rabah bar Nachmani afforded Abayei the opportunity to become a student of that great scholar from his earliest youth – and he was an avid student.[12] He was a precocious child and his cleverness is recorded for us in the Talmud.[13] Apparently, he became well-known as a scholar in his own right while still a very young person: We find him in halachic discussion with Ulla[14] when Abayei was yet only twelve years old.[15] Rabah bar Nachmani shaped Abayei's scholarship and sharpened his abilities to think and analyze Torah,[16] and Abayei considered Rabah his main teacher, referring to him with the respectful title of *Mar* when speaking with or about him.[17] Abayei was also possessed of good humor and a cheerful disposition,[18] regarding which his uncle Rabah somberly cautioned him.[19] Rabah saw the lad's remarkable potential, however; he was convinced that Abayei would be an outstanding Torah scholar and so blessed him in achieving that goal.[20]

The young prodigy also studied with others of the great men of the third and even the second generations of *Amoraim* in Babylonia. We find him with Rav Yehudah bar Yechezkel,[21] Rav Chiya bar Rav,[22] Rav Kahana,[23] Rav Sheishes,[24] Rav Chisda,[25] and Rav Yosef.[26]

In fact, Rav Yosef was considered by Abayei to be a very important teacher of his and accorded him enormous respect.[27] Rav Yosef reciprocated in kind and called Abayei a *gavra rabah* – a great man in Torah scholarship.[28] When the people of Kakonaei asked Rav Yosef to send them an expert in matters of *eiruvin*, Rav Yosef dispatched Abayei to help them.[29] Using his great analytical gifts, Abayei had often disagreed with his uncle and mentor Rabah bar Nachmani, posing difficult questions to him;[30] and we find him having the same type of discussions and halachic arguments with Rav Yosef when the latter assumed the position of the head of the Pumbedisa yeshivah after the passing of Rabah bar Nachmani.[31]

Abayei continually attempted to elicit from Rav Yosef the exact correct text of the Mishnah and *breisos*.[32] When Rav Yosef lost his memory, it was Abayei who refreshed it and reminded him of his previous teachings.[33] Though Abayei slept little during the entire night and day, Rav Yosef remarked to him that King Solomon stated in Proverbs "How long will you, lazy one, continue to sleep? When

"One of them [the scholars of the Land of Israel] is greater than two of us [the scholars of Babylonia.]"

Abayei

will you awake?"[34] In general, we find that Abayei's behavior when learning from Rav Yosef was more reserved than it was when he studied with Rabah bar Nachmani.[35] This may have been because of Rav Yosef's reputation as a strict disciplinarian as compared to Rabah bar Nachmani, who was less stringent with his students.[36] It may also have been a result of Abayei being a relative and an adopted son of Rabah bar Nachmani, while he was understandably more distant from Rav Yosef.

At that time, some of the great scholars of the Land of Israel regularly traveled to Babylonia. These *rabanan nechusei* – scholars who "descended" from the Land of Israel to visit or settle in Babylonia[37]– brought with them the teachings of the great yeshivos of Tiberias and Caesarea. Abayei had contact with two of these legendary scholars, Rav Dimi and Ravin. Rav Dimi was born in Babylonia[38] and spent his youth studying in the Land of Israel. He and Abayei had many discussions that are recorded in the Talmud.[39] Ravin was also a companion of Abayei, and numerous interchanges between them appear in the Talmud.[40] Though Abayei complained to Ravin over the sometimes demeaning attitude of the scholars of the Land of Israel towards their compatriots in Babylonia,[41] he nevertheless stated himself that "one of them [the scholars of the Land of Israel] is greater than two of us [the scholars of Babylonia.]"[42] Abayei relied upon the teachings of Ravin, even granting them greater weight than those of Rav Dimi.[43] Another of the *rabanan nechusei* who was closely associated with Abayei was Rav Safra.[44]

As mentioned above, in the first part of the fourth century

Oil lamp decorated with the motif of a menorah, 4th century CE (The Israel Museum, Jerusalem)

many of the scholars of the Land of Israel immigrated to Babylonia to escape the persecution of the Byzantine Christians. Constantine, the Emperor of Rome, had converted to Christianity and became a zealot in its cause. He repealed all anti-Christian laws and in 325 CE, he convened the Council of Nicea, which formulated Christian doctrine and took a strong stand against Judaism and the Jews. Babylonia was not under his control, but the Land of Israel was, and the persecution of the Jews living there by the newly empowered Christians intensified. These circumstances aborted any further development of *Talmud Yerushalmi* and the Torah scholars living in the Land of Israel fled to Babylonia. Many of them settled in or near Pumbedisa and turned to Abayei in matters of practical life and Torah scholarship.

After the death of Rav Yosef in 326 CE, Abayei was chosen to succeed him as the head of the yeshivah in Pumbedisa.[45] He served in that position for thirteen years until his death.[46] His colleagues, Rav Zeira II, Rabah bar Masna and Rava, all of whom were also considered for this appointment, acknowledged his superiority [47] and saw his selection as being a sign from Heaven.[48] Ironically, despite the fact that Abayei had been appointed the head of the yeshivah over Rava, in halachic discussions between the two, the law always followed the opinion of Rava, except in only six cases, where Abayei's opinion was accepted as binding law.[49] In a moment of honest self-appraisal, Abayei described himself and his knowledge of Torah as comparable to that of Shimon Ben Azai who flourished "in the market places of Tiberias."[50]

Abayei married as a young man, though we have no particular details regarding his wife.[51] They had two sons – Rav Bibi bar Abayei[52] and Rav Shimi bar Abayei[53] – who were scholars in their own right and are mentioned in the Talmud. They apparently also had a daughter.[54] After the death of his wife – and considerably later in his life – Abayei, married a woman named Choma, a great-granddaughter of Rav Yehudah bar Yechezkel[55] and a woman of renowned beauty.[56] She had been already twice widowed when Abayei married her.[57] Abayei too died soon after their marriage[58] and thus she was widowed once more.[59]

Though not wealthy in his early years, Abayei's poverty did not hold him back from striving for excellence in Torah. He was almost unaware of his dire economic situation.[60] During that period of his life, he was a farmer who tended his own fields, and he had no time to take on tutoring others who came to him to study.[61] He also dealt in wine[62] and his financial situation later improved. Eventually he employed many workers for his fields[63] and also leased fields to sharecroppers.[64] Nevertheless, he made it a point to continue to visit his own fields every day in person.[65]

Byzantine coins, Beth Shean

Abayei's love for Torah scholars was legendary and his admiration for them is found in many places in the Talmud.[66] He defended them against their boorish detractors[67] and encouraged their supporters. He is the author of the famous statement that "blessings come immediately to a Torah scholar."[68] He supported 200 Torah scholars in his yeshivah from his own resources.[69]

In addition, Abayei's concern for all others is recorded in many instances in the Talmud. Suffering himself from a sickly disposition, digestive problems[70] and scurvy,[71] one of the things he emphasized was visiting the sick.[72] His deep feeling for others is also reflected in the importance he placed on ransoming captives,[73] never embarrassing anyone publicly,[74] helping the aged,[75] earning one's living (instead of taking from others)[76] and generally dealing peacefully with all human beings.[77] He once stated to his teacher, Rav Yosef, that the entirety of the Torah is based on the principle that all of its paths are ways of pleasantness and its roads are those of peace, and that even the Torah itself was subject to this overriding value of *darkei noam*.[78] He lived his life in accordance with this core belief. His reputation for honesty and goodness endeared him even to non-Jews[79] and he was famous for his kindness and hospitality to all. The Talmud records that this trait lengthened his life,[80] and that Heaven itself greeted this gentle soul every Friday just before Shabbos.[81]

Yet Abayei was far from naïve in his judgment of others and was especially alert to thievery and cheating.[82] Moreover, he never withheld his judgment and guidance of others because his view might be unpopular. On the contrary, an overly popular community rabbi was not doing his job well, according to Abayei.[83] He was especially stringent in matters of *Kiddush Hashem* and *Chilul Hashem* – the enhancement or desecration of the Name of God through human behavior; and he was constantly aware that the behavior and actions of Torah scholars reflect directly in the eyes of the masses on the inherent greatness of Torah and the Creator.[84] Therefore, the scholar must strive for perfection in both his study habits and deportment: he stressed that in order to truly concentrate on Torah, one must do so without any distractions;[85] and that the greater the person, the greater the temptation for evil behavior would be within him.[86]

As stated earlier, Abayei headed the yeshivah in Pumbedisa for thirteen years. He came in contact with almost all of his fellow pillars of the fourth generation of Babylonian *Amoraim*. He was the centerpiece of Torah study in his time. His rare blend of unrivaled scholarship, unlimited compassion, sensitivity to others and wisdom in all aspects of life made him the natural leader of his generation. His presence remains and hovers over all of Jewish life right up to our time. The singsong chant that identifies the study of Talmud throughout the ages is always joined to the words *"Amar Abayei."* *"Amar Abayei"* does not mean only "Abayei said." It means truly that Abayei *still* is saying, in all Jewish study halls and hearts even today.

Rava

RAVA
c. 340 CE

Teachers
• Rav Yosef bar Chama
• Rav Nachman bar Yaakov
• Rav Huna
• Rav Yehudah bar Yechezkel
• Rav Chisda
• Rav Sheishes

Colleagues
• Abayei
• Rabah bar Rav Huna
• Abba bar Manyumi
• Ravin
• Avimei ben Rachva
• Eifah ben Rachva
• Ada Mari
• Rav Nachman bar Yitzchak
• Rav Abba II

Students
• Rav Ada bar Ahava II
• Rav Acha bar Huna
• Rav Huna breih d'Rabi Yehoshua
• Rav Papa
• Rav Kahana IV
• Ravina I
• Avimei of Hagrunya
• Rami bar Chama

Relatives
• Father-in-law: Rav Chisda
• Sons: Rav Yosef ben Rava, Rav Mesharshiya

ava was the son of Rav Yosef bar Chama,[1] one of the leaders of the Jewish community of Mechoza,[2] a trading city on the banks of the Tigris River.[3] It is more than likely that Rava was born there.[4] His main teacher in his youth was Rav Nachman bar Yaakov who was also a resident of Mechoza.[5]

Rava also studied with the aged Rav Huna[6] and was zealous in upholding his opinions in law and practice.[7] After the death of Rav Huna, Rava studied with the revered Rav Yehudah bar Yechezkel.[8] When Rav Yehudah died, Rava then studied under Rav Chisda.[9] Thus he had the benefit of the teachings of the exemplary and influential yeshivos of both Sura and Pumbedisa. Rava also studied under Rav Sheishes[10] and considered him a great man in Torah knowledge.[11]

However, it was finally Rav Yosef who became Rava's chief mentor[12] and Rava's respect for him knew no bounds. Even though Rav Yosef was sightless, Rava always backed out of his presence, not wishing to turn his back on his teacher.[13] In so doing, Rava once injured his foot on the threshold of the room and bled profusely. When Rav Yosef learned of this incident, he thanked Rava for so honoring him and gave him a blessing that he would become a distinguished leader of the Jewish community.[14] Rava was accustomed to serve Rav Yosef food and drink, prepared in a special way.[15] Because of this special relationship, the two reconciled easily when a period of tension arose between them later in life.[16]

It was there, in Pumbedisa under the tutelage of Rav Yosef, that Rava and Abayei first met, studied together, and became lifelong friends and colleagues.

Rava's admiration of Rav Yosef was such that he later sent his own son, also named Yosef, to study under Rav Yosef in Pumbedisa for six years.[17] Rav Yosef's respect for Rava, in turn, is shown in his asking the son what his father's opinion was in certain matters of ritual.[18]

Like Rav Chisda and Rabi (Rabi Yehudah HaNasi, who lived centuries before him), Rava was blessed with Torah greatness and enormous wealth at one and the same time.[19] And like Rabi, Rava used his material, intellectual and spiritual blessings to further the cause of Torah and of the Jewish people.

He inherited wealth from various sources, especially from the family of Mar Shmuel.[20] He also had business dealings with that family and owned and leased fields.[21] Like Abayei, Rava was active in the wine industry,[22] and he also owned ships that plied the Tigris.[23] Because of his wealth and position of honor in the community he was a confidant and friend of the *Reish Galusa* (Exilarch)[24] and received favors and authority from this temporal leader.[25] The son-in law of the *Reish Galusa* was the esteemed scholar, Rav Nachman bar Yaakov[26] and as mentioned here earlier, Rava was a longtime student and colleague of his,[27] zealously according him honor and respect.[28] Undoubtedly, this relationship also contributed to Rava's closeness to the court of the *Reish Galusa*.

He was also a favorite of Queen Ifra Hurmiz of the then-ruling dynasty in Babylonia.[29] Rava performed a miracle at her request, but was reprimanded for it by his father who came to him in a dream and warned him against performing "unnecessary" miracles.[30] Ifra Hurmiz protected Rava from any governmental action against him or the Jewish court that he headed.[31]

Rava cultivated influence in the court of the ruler in order to protect and advance Jewish interests[32] and, in time, the uniqueness and fine qualities of the Jewish community were duly recognized.[33] It was Rava's influence with the ruling authorities – both Jewish[34] and non-Jewish – of the time that helped provide the political and economic stability of the Jewish community in Babylonia, which in turn was necessary for the continuing growth of the yeshivos and the development of the Babylonian Talmud.

Apparently, Rava aspired to the highest standards of personal development, for he bemoaned the fact that he had not achieved the level of humility of Rabah bar Rav Huna.[35] Rava characterized himself generally as being a mere *beinoni* - an average person in behavior, humility and piety.[36] To this, his colleague Abayei retorted: "If that is the case [that you are only average], then you leave no room for ordinary humans to attempt to be considered righteous!" [37] Whenever Rava felt himself threatened by emotions of false pride due to the abundant honors paid to him due to his position of leadership in the Jewish community, he took defensive measures to ward off self-aggrandizement.[38] His famous personal prayer that he recited after his daily prayer service, which illustrates his humility and subservience before his Creator, has become a jewel of Jewish tradition and a part of the Yom Kippur ritual of prayer.[39] Yet despite his extreme sensitivity to this temptation, Rava stated that a Torah scholar must have at least a small amount of obvious self-pride in order to assert himself as a leader in his community.[40]

Rava was lavish in praise of his fellow scholars and held them all in great esteem,[41] rating some of them at times as superior to him in Torah knowledge.[42] He would openly recant opinions or decisions that he had previously maintained as correct, making his change of heart and mind publicly known.[43] He preached the necessity of sincerity and pure altruism in the performance of Torah commandments and study,[44] saying that those who practice hypocrisy or insincerity in their Jewish lives would "have been better off not to have even been born."[45] "God demands our hearts" was his motto.[46] Yet, Rava was tolerant of others, even when they sinned, and looked for exculpatory reasons to mitigate judgment on their behavior.[47]

He searched for people of honesty and integrity, stating that this was a rare commodity in a world that was basically one of falseness and lies.[48] Nevertheless he stressed that the Torah was not given to angels and therefore human conditions and foibles had to be consid-

"God demands our hearts."
Rava (Talmud)

ered, even when making halachic decisions.[49]

Love and respect for Torah scholars was the hallmark of Rava's life and teachings.[50] His power of concentration on the words of the Torah was so great that he actually injured his fingers, crushing them under his leg while seated at his study desk completely engaged in deep analysis of a Torah subject, yet he was unaware of his self-inflicted injury![51] He pointed out that Torah learning creates a protective shield for the student,[52] and is the antidote for the poison of the evil inclination that lies within us all.[53] Moreover, he taught that the study of Torah alone fulfills one's obligation to bring the personal sacrifices that were once brought to the Holy Temple.[54]

We find Rava defending and showing deference to Torah scholars in all matters,[55] even in the court of justice where impartiality is usually manadatory.[56] He felt that even a Torah scholar who became wayward in observance and behavior was yet entitled to respect for his Torah teachings.[57] Rava regarded the time spent in pursuits other than Torah study as wasteful, if not even harmful, and the cause of personal troubles.[58] This even applied to the extra time one spent in prayer![59]

Despite his emphasis on the primacy of Torah study, Rava believed that even if one is well versed in Torah, the important thing is fear of God and dedication to His service.[60] Without it, one would not pass judgment in the World to Come.[61] As mentioned above, Rava himself was the paragon of humility; therefore he was worthy of preaching to others that restraining one's self in response to contentious or insulting situations was a most positive virtue, rewarded by Heaven in the forgiveness of that person's sins.[62]

Incantation bowl with Aramaic inscription, Nippur, Babylonia, 6th century CE.

There are several other abilities (such as the fact that he was an expert in identifying[63] and capturing birds[64]) and words of wisdom attributed to Rava:

- *One should never be quick to judge the words and behavior of another person when that person is in pain or grief.*[65]
- *One needs a cadre of friends and colleagues in life.*[66]
- *The Torah is careful not to abuse or to make unnecessarily high demands on the money of Jews.*[67]
- *Respect and honor for one's wife is a catalyst for worldly success and wealth.*[68]
- *A bad marriage brings harm to a person.*[69]

Rava himself was married twice.[70] His second wife, who was the mother of his sons, was the daughter of Rav Chisda.[71] She was recognized by all as a superlative, intelligent and trustworthy person – so much so, that her opinions affected decisions regarding who could be trusted to take an oath to verify contentions in a court case.[72] Rava had two sons who are mentioned numerous times in the Talmud – Rav Yosef bar Ravah[73] and Rav Mesharshiya.[74] Rava was very proud of their Torah scholarship, and he likened their knowledge of the laws of *treifos* – animals that have diseases or physical infirmities that render their meat ritually unfit to be eaten – to that of the great Rabi Yochanan of Tiberias.[75] Rava's grandsons appear on the pages of the Talmud numerous times as well.[76] His marriage to Rav Chisda's daughter was a happy and loving one and added to his successes as scholar, teacher and community leader, as well as a husband and father.[77]

Rava headed a yeshivah of his own in his hometown of Mechoza,[78] even during the lifetime of his mentor, Rav Yosef and his colleague, Abayei, who were the successive heads of the great yeshivah in Pumbedisa. After the death of Abayei in 339 CE, Rava was named head of the great yeshivah of Pumbedisa, but he moved it to Mechoza,[79] allowing his yeshivah to be absorbed into the larger, greater yeshivah. The commercial lifestyle of Mechoza was not especially suited to allow it to become a center of Torah study.[80]

In addition, there were numerous converts to Judaism in the city, many of whom were not knowledgeable in Torah and ritual.[81] Rava himself realized that, in the main, the people of Mechoza were materialistically oriented and not appreciative of eternal spiritual reward,[82] yet his influence in the city was so great that, in time, it became a more proper host for the yeshivah of Pumbedisa. Highly regarded by the masses of Mechoza, even after he became the leading judge in the city,[83] Rava used his leadership position to bring the yeshivah of Pumbedisa to its zenith in success and influence.[84]

Rava led the yeshivah of Pumbedisa in Mechoza for fourteen years,[85] until he passed away in 353 CE.[86] After his death, he appeared in a dream to his brother and informed him that his moment of death was physically painful to him only as the prick of a bloodletter's needle.[87] The Tigris River was lined with thousands who paid their respects to Rava at his funeral.[88] The great man of that generation had passed from the scene. He now joined his colleague and friend, Abayei, in eternity and in all of the study halls of Israel for all time. There is almost no page in the Talmud upon which his name and teachings do not appear.[89]

It is during his lifetime and reign as head of the yeshivah of Pumbedisa that the Babylonian Talmud began to be edited and take definite form. Though the work would not be completed for approximately another two centuries, Rava is seen as the father of the process of editing and organizing of the Talmud.[90] He had already erased all generational differences in the discussions in the Talmud, making it appear that all of the discussants were actually debating each other face to face – when in reality they all lived at different times and places.[91] This "live" method of discussion and conversation between scholars spanning time and location became the general pattern of recording discussions regarding variant opinions throughout the Talmud.

Other Amoraim of the Fourth Generation

"An overly full stomach leads to many illnesses."

Rav Acha Bar Huna (Talmud)

he fourth generation of *Amoraim* was one of remarkable men and numerous students of Torah – a generation of Torah genius and creativity. It was one of the greatest generations of Torah study and knowledge in the history of the Jewish community in Babylonia. The yeshivah of Pumbedisa reached substantial numbers, and the presence of Abayei and Rava as heads of that institution attracted many to become their colleagues and students. There are over 100 *Amoraim* of that period named in the Talmud itself.[92] Among them were the following great scholars:

- Abba Bar Marta[93] (also known as Abba bar Manyumi[94])
- Abayei bar Avin (Ravin)[95]
- Avimei ben Rachva and his brother Eifah (Cheifah)[96]
- Avimei m'bei Chozai[97]
- Rav Avin (Ravin) bar Sheva[98]
- Rav Ada bar Ahavah (Abba) II[99]
- Rav Ada bar Yitzchak[100]
- Ada Mari[101]
- Rav Avya[102]
- Rav Acha bar Huna[103]
- Rav Dimi of Nehardea[104]
- Rav Hamnuna Zuta (the younger)[105]
- Rav Zvid of Nehardea[106]
- Rav Yehudah Achva D'Rav Sala Chasida[107]

After the death of Rava, there was a period of nineteen years when no main yeshivah held sway in Babylonia. There were then

Wine press, Capernaum, carved from the local black basalt stone

yeshivos in four cities that operated during that period of time – Pumbedisa, Nehardea, Pum Nahara and Narash – but no individual institution was seen as the single main center of Torah scholarship in Babylonia, as was Mechoza during the reign of Rava. It would not be until 372 CE, when Rav Ashi established himself as the head of a reconstituted yeshivah of Sura / Masa Machsiya that a central base of Torah study would arise again in Babylonia.

SECTION VII

THE FIFTH GENERATION OF AMORAIM IN BABYLONIA

C. 360 - 400 CE

Circular gold medallion with Greek inscription, Byzantine Empire, 8th century CE (The Jewish Museum London).

Rav Papa and Rav Huna Breih D'rav Yehoshua

RAV PAPA AND RAV HUNA BREIH D'RAV YEHOSHUA
c. 370 CE

Teachers
• Abayei
• Rava
• Rav Idi bar Avin
• Rav Hamnuna II
• Rav Huna bar Chanina
• Rav Acha bar Yaakov

Colleagues
• Ameimar
• Mar Zutra I
• Rav Kahana IV
• Rav Nachman bar Yitzchak

Students
• Rav Ashi

Relatives
• Son-in-law: Rav Huna bar Rav Nachman
• The ten sons of Rav Papa are immortalized in the service of the siyum (completion) of a tractate of the Talmud.

After the death of Rava, his yeshivah in Mechoza closed. Apparently the fact that it was really the yeshivah of Pumbedisa and had only been transferred to Mechoza as an accommodation to Rava allowed many to still see themselves as bound to Pumbedisa. Another factor in the decline of Mechoza as a Torah center was that, despite Rava's efforts, the inhospitability of the community to the yeshivah in its midst did continue, a fact noted by Rava himself in his lifetime.[1] In any event, after Rava's passing, the yeshivah split into two main groups. One group, led by Rav Papa, one of the premier students of both Abayei[2] and Rava,[3] settled in Narash and created a large yeshivah there. Rav Papa served as the head of the yeshivah in Narash for nineteen years, until his death in 372 CE. The revered and aged Rav Nachman bar Yitzchak, a colleague of Rava, led the second group of Rava's disciples and colleagues back to Pumbedisa, to reestablish its famous yeshivah.[4] Rav Nachman bar Yitzchak died four years later, in 357 CE.[5]

During his lifetime, Rav Nachman bar Yitzchak was famed for his exactitude of behavior and piety,[6] as well as his modesty and humility.[7] He saw the relationship between God, so to speak, and the people of Israel as being one of mutual love, pride and respect.[8] His trait of exactitude carried over into his teachings, as he always

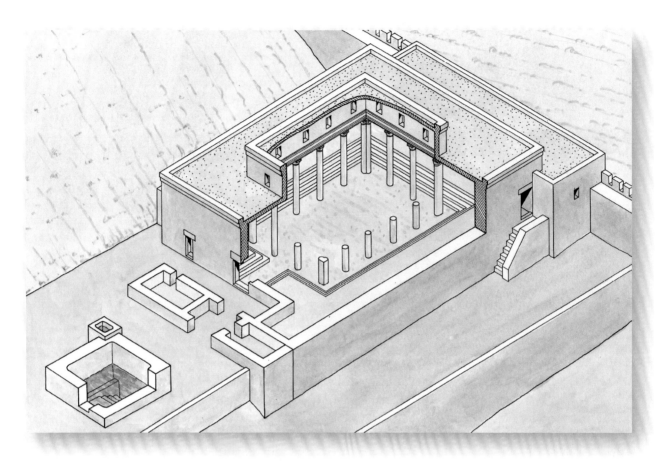

Reconstruction drawing of Gamla synagogue, 1st century CE.

attempted to give his disciples the highest degree of accuracy,[9] seeing himself as an organized teacher and not as a creative genius, seer or abstract thinker.[10] Emphasizing the primacy of Torah study above all, he praised the scholars of Israel for "killing themselves" over the study of Torah.[11] By this, he meant that Torah study requires complete devotion of time and effort, almost to the negation of all else.

After the death of Rav Nachman bar Yitzchak, the yeshivah of Pumbedisa lost its prominence once again, and the yeshivah of Rav Papa in Narash became the leading yeshivah of Babylonia. Yet it never attained the exclusivity and centrality within the Jewish community that Pumbedisa had under Abayei or that Mechoza enjoyed under Rava.

Both Rav Papa and Rav Huna breih d'Rav Yehoshua were child prodigies and while yet youngsters studied with Rav Idi bar Avin in a town called Shachnatzvu.[12] Rav Papa also studied with Rav Hamnuna II,[13] Rav Huna bar Chanina[14] and Rav Acha bar Yaakov.[15]

His main mentors, however, were firstly Abayei[16] and after Abayei's passing, Rava.[17] Rav Papa and Rav Huna breih d'Rav Yehoshua were greatly beloved by Rava who saw them as his spiritual and pedagogical heirs.[18] The Talmud recounts that Rav Papa dreamt that he would become the head of a yeshivah[19] and he realized this dream in his yeshivah in Narash. Rav Huna breih d'Rav Yehoshua dreamt almost the same exact dream. He later became the head of the *yarchei kallah* – the annual months of mass study – in Narash,[20] and, in fact, he became Rav Papa's associate in the administration of the yeshivah. They appear together in the pages of the Talmud, discussing and teaching myriad Torah matters.[21]

Unfortunately, the townspeople of Narash did not enjoy the highest reputation for probity or honesty.[22] They treated Rav Papa and his yeshivah badly and with such disdain that Rav Papa – though known for his piety and mild mannered approach to life – placed a ban upon them and their goods.[23] The yeshivah in Narash numbered 200 permanent students,[24] though during various periods of the year – especially during the months of the *kallah* (Adar and Elul) – there were many hundreds of additional students who came to study under Rav Papa and Rav Huna breih d'Rav Yehoshua.

Both Rav Papa and Rav Huna breih d'Rav Yehoshua were wealthy[25] and they were partners in many successful commercial ventures.[26] Rav Papa however was uniquely famed for his wealth,[27] appetite,[28] girth, and good fortune.[29] His main source of wealth was from the manufacture and sale of *sheichar*[30] – a malt liquor type of beverage made from barley and dates. It was very popular and served as the standard drink of the populace in Babylonia.[31] He also dealt in sesame seeds and sesame oil, and Rav Huna breih d'Rav Yehoshua was his partner in this venture.[32] Active in major financial transactions,[33] Rav Papa was outstanding in his honesty as well as in his compassion toward others. He always dealt in a manner far beyond the minimum that the law required.[34] Of course, despite all of his financial and commercial ventures, the majority of Rav Papa's time and efforts were devoted to his yeshivah in Narash and its students.

Rav Papa's stature was so highly regarded that even Ameimar[35] and Mar Zutra I,[36] the heads of the third yeshivah in Babylonia at that time,[37] located in Nehardea, saw themselves as his disciples and faithfully transmitted his teachings in their yeshivah.[38] Rav Papa, in turn, was very respectful of other Torah scholars, going out of his way to honor them.[39] On one occasion, he fasted as a penance after an incident where he felt he had not been respectful enough to another Torah scholar.[40] He deemed respect for scholars as so fundamental to Judaism that he considered those who disrespect Torah scholars to be *apikorsim* – non-believers.[41]

His sensitivity to human behavior was so strong that he attributed some of the hatred directed at the Jews to the haughtiness and false pride of some of the Jews themselves.[42] His own sensitive nature made him particularly vulnerable to embarrassment;[43] therefore he prayed that he should not be embarrassed by others.[44] Rav Papa was so demanding of himself in self-judgment that when he once slipped on the rung of a ladder and almost fell to the ground: upon righting himself, he stated, "Had I truly fallen to the ground [it would have been an indication that] I am considered [by the Heavenly tribunal] to be one who had committed [a great sin such as] desecrating the Sabbath or worshipping idols!"[45] He also attributed his stumbling on a staircase to his perhaps being lax in giving charity to a poor man.[46] A keen observer of human needs and frailties, he always preached silence as a golden character trait, especially when visiting mourners and those who are grief-stricken.[47] He is also the author of the pithy remark that when foods and goods are being distributed generously, there are many "brothers and loving friends" present; but when there are material and financial losses and poverty, there are no friends and brothers around to share the losses.[48]

The details regarding Rav Papa's personal and family life are sparse. His father is quoted in the Talmud,[49] but not by name. His wife was from a family of *kohanim*[50] and their son, Abba Mar, was known for his honesty and probity.[51] Their daughter was married to Huna bar Rav Nachman (perhaps bar Yitzchak?), a favored student of Rav Papa.[52] After his first wife's death, Rav Papa remarried, this time to the daughter of Abba Suraah,[53] a prominent person

> "The scholars of Israel are to be praised for killing themselves in order to study Torah."
>
> *Rav Nachman bar Yitzchak*

of the time. Eventually, Rav Papa's son, Abba Mar, married another daughter of Abba Suraah.[54] Rav Papa lived for approximately 70 years, passing away in c. 372 CE after heading the yeshivah in Narash for nineteen years.[55]

His beloved comrade, Rav Huna breih d'Rav Yehoshua, was well known as an outstanding scholar and teacher. He was a humble and gentle person who never insisted on honor or position. He attributed his almost miraculous recovery from a serious illness to the efforts he had made to develop the trait of modesty and self-effacement.[56] Very little is known about his personal life, except for his commercial and educational partnership with Rav Papa. He certainly was one of the outstanding individuals who brought the yeshivah of Narash to its exalted position in Babylonian Jewish life in the latter half of the fourth century.

The fourth main yeshivah then existing in Babylonia at this time was in Pum Nahara, headed by Rav Kahana IV.[57] Again, the Talmud is mostly silent about the events of his life and of that yeshivah generally. We do know that Rav Kahana IV stood in prayer in troubled times "as a servant before a master."[58] A student of Rava, he quotes many teachings of his mentor throughout the Talmud,[59] while he was very respectful of the opinions of Rav Huna breih d'Rav Yehoshua and decided halachic matters according to those opinions.[60] Rav Kahana IV also studied under Rav Zvid of Nehardea.[61]

The yeshivah in Pum Nahara attracted many scholars of the time due to Rav Kahana IV's fame as a scholar. But perhaps his highest distinction is that he is recognized as the primary teacher and guide of Rav Ashi, the leading editor of the Talmud. The greatness of teachers is often reflected in the monumental accomplishments of their students. It is through Rav Ashi and his achievements that we are allowed a glimpse of the magnitude of his mentor and teacher, Rav Kahana IV.

SECTION VIII

THE SIXTH GENERATION OF AMORAIM IN BABYLONIA

c. 390 - 430 CE

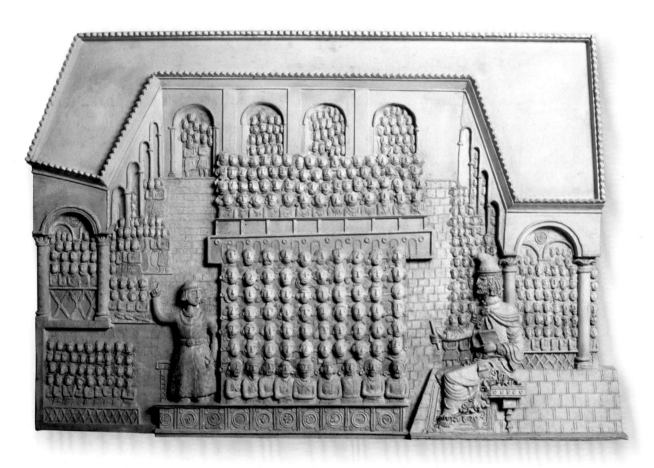

*Relief depicting the
study month at the Sura
Academy in Babylon*

Rav Ashi

f human beings could be "bookends" for great works of scholarship that took centuries to create and edit, the Talmud has at its two ends Rav, the disciple of Rabi, and Rav Ashi. The Talmud characterized their roles as follows: "From the time of Rabi [the editor of the Mishnah] till the time of Rav Ashi [the editor of the Babylonian Talmud] we did not find Torah knowledge, wealth and greatness combined to [such an extent] within one person."[1]

Rav Ashi was born only a few years before the death of Rava in 353 CE,[2] yet, the Talmud attests that as a very young man, he somehow studied under Rava.[3] After Rava's demise, Rav Ashi studied under Rav Nachman bar Yitzchak,[4] who headed the yeshivah in Pumbedisa. Rav Papa and Rav Huna breih d'Rav Yehoshua, the heads of the yeshivah in Narash, also were teachers of Rav Ashi.[5] Rav Ashi also appears in halachic discussions in the yeshivos of Rav Zvid,[6] Ulla II,[7] Rav Papi[8] Rav Masna II[9] and Rabi Chanina of Tzipori.[10] Not surprisingly, Rav Ashi believed that one should study Torah from many masters.[11]

One of his chief mentors was Ameimar, the head of the yeshivah in Nehardea,[12] and Rav Ashi was quite attached to him, following his behavior and actions,[13] and holding his views in great respect.[14] The discussions between Ameimar and Rav Ashi occur throughout the Talmud and in such a vein that it is obvious that the student eventually was considered a colleague.[15]

Even though Rav Ashi was a disciple of so many great schol-

RAV ASHI
c. 410 CE

Teachers
• Rav Papa
• Rav Huna breih d'Rav Yehoshua
• Rav Kahana IV
• Ameimar

Colleagues
• Ravina I
• Rami bar Chama
• Rav Zvid
• Rav Dimi of Nehardea
• Rafram I
• Rav Kahana V
• Rav Acha breih d'Rava
• Rav Huna bar Nosson
• Mar Zutrah II

Students
• Rav Idi bar Avin II
• Mar bar Rav Ashi
• Rav Nachman bar Rav Huna
• Rav Yeymar

Relatives
• Sons: Mar bar Rav Ashi, Rav Sama breih d'Rav Ashi
• Father in law: Rami bar Chama (Abba?)

ars, his main teacher was Rav Kahana IV of Pum Nahara.[16] Rav Ashi shared with Rav Kahana IV many of the teachings that he had learned from other scholars and he received Rav Kahana IV's comments upon these opinions.[17] In the Talmud, Rav Ashi transmits the customs and behavior of his mentor, Rav Kahana IV that he had witnessed.[18] Rav Ashi became part of Rav Kahana IV's rabbinical court[19] and participated jointly with him in rendering halachic decisions.[20] Even after Rav Ashi left the yeshivah of Pum Nahara to reestablish and then head the yeshivah of Sura (by now located in its neighboring suburb of Masa Machsiya[21]) he continued to respectfully visit with Rav Kahana IV.[22] Masa Machsiya was a community of moderate size[23] and by building the yeshivah there to greatness in scholarship and housing it in a magnificently tall and imposing structure,[24] Rav Ashi raised it, physically and spiritually, to fame and eternal Jewish memory.

"One should study Torah from many masters."

Rav Ashi

Because of Rav Ashi's wide acquaintance with all of the illustrious teachers of the previous generation and their students, he became a central figure in the Torah world of Babylonia. He was known personally or by reputation by almost all of the scholars of the time. His great intellect, broad knowledge of Torah received from his many teachers, and wide circle of devoted colleagues allowed him and his colleague, Ravina, to begin the monumental task of editing all of the opinions and discussions of the yeshivos over the past two centuries and placing them into book form. In reestablishing the yeshivah of Sura in Masa Machsiya, Rav Ashi restored this yeshivah to the primacy that it enjoyed in the days of Rav, centuries earlier. Rav Ashi was known as a man of peace[25] and it was his calming and holy influence that brought about the cooperation of the scholars of his generation in this vast undertaking.

But it is Rav Ashi himself who is seen as the final authority on deciding long running disputes and discussions in the Talmud. He, so to speak, sums up the arguments and makes the decision based on logic, knowledge, the majority opinion of the rabbis and certain traditional rules for deciding halachic matters. Rashi explains: "[Rav Ashi and Ravina were at the conclusion of discussion and decision] of the [main] Talmudic period. Until their days, there was no ordered Talmud, but rather whenever a question was raised in the study hall regarding the explanation of a Mishnah or a question regarding the facts and/or decision in a case of money matters, or in matters of the permissible or forbidden ritual law, every scholar advanced his individual opinions and reasonings. Rav Ashi and Ravina edited and ordered the opinions of the *Amoraim* of the generations that preceded them and fixed them according to the tractates involved, each and every one in the proper place following the appropriate Mishnah that related to these discussions. They quoted and discussed all of the questions that were asked regarding the interpretation of the Mishnah as well as all of the answers and solutions to the problems raised by those questions. They, together with their *Amoraim* colleagues, then ordered them in the Talmud, together with proper terminology for the questions and answers discussed."[26]

Rav Ashi, together with Ravina, thus did for the *Amoraim* what Rabi Yehudah HaNasi had done for the *Tannaim* over two centuries earlier when he edited and published the Mishnah. They took centuries of study hall discussions and, following hallowed traditions of learning and halachic decisions, placed them in a generally sequential order and made a written, edited book out of these previously oral debates and explanations. Thus, we can readily understand why Rav Ashi often appears in the Talmud only at the conclusion of a series of discussions and varying opinions on a given subject; he then serves as the final decisor of the matter. Rav Ashi was determined to protect the Torah at all costs and therefore encouraged any strictures that the rabbis would impose in order to safeguard the original halachic decisions.[27]

For more than 55 years (371 CE to 426 CE), Rav Ashi headed the yeshivah in Masa Machsiya.[28] He lived a very long life, well into his nineties,[29] and was quite wealthy.[30] He was married to the daughter of Rami bar Chama[31] and two of their sons, Mar bar Rav Ashi[32] and Rav Sama breih d'Rav Ashi[33] are mentioned numerous times in the Talmud. Sadly, however, Rav Sama died during the Rav Ashi's lifetime.[34]

One of the remarkable qualities of all of the great men of the

Talmud was their ability to deal serenely with their own mortality. The World to Come – the survival of the soul after the body dies – was an actuality to them and not just a matter of faith. Thus, communication between souls that had departed from this world and living beings is an accepted occurrence in the pages of the Talmud; this message of eternity and serenity is part of the mission of the Talmud. It is recorded that Rav Ashi met the Angel of Death and postponed his own demise for 30 days to enable him to review all of his Torah knowledge so that he would come to the Heavenly yeshivah well prepared.[35] Rav Ashi even helped prepare his own eulogy, to be delivered at his funeral.[36]

In his person, Rav Ashi represented the sum total of Talmudic values and knowledge, and he is therefore the fitting role model and paradigm of all of the great sages of the Talmud. Lying in his grave for almost sixteen centuries, Rav Ashi still lives and breathes on every folio of the vast compendium of knowledge that comprises the Babylonian Talmud. He is the guiding spirit that hovers over all of Jewish life since the end of the Talmudic era.

Ravina (The First)

The older of the two, Ravina[37] predeceased Rav Ashi by a number of years. A well-to-do resident of Masa Machsiya[38] he was well-known as the person in charge of collecting monies for the poor and disbursing those funds to them.[39] Ravina was a man of commerce,[40] and also owned real estate.[41] He lived a very long life.[42] His son, Mar bar Ravina, is well-known in the Talmud[43] and he also had a daughter.[44] Apparently, Ravina did not come from a home of great Torah scholarship[45] but his family living after him included numerous Torah scholars.[46]

He was a devoted student and disciple of Rava,[47] and Rava respected him highly and supported him in his judgments and opinions.[48] After the death of Rava, Ravina studied with Rav Nachman bar Yitzchak[49] until the death of the latter four years later. Ravina was recognized as a premier scholar by the great men of his age, even when he was yet quite young.[50] He met Rav Ashi when the latter came to study under Rava.[51] Like Rav Ashi, Ravina also studied under Ameimar.[52] Thus, Rav Ashi and Ravina began a lifelong partnership of Torah study and working on the herculean project of editing the Talmud. Ravina saw himself as a student/colleague of Rav Ashi.[53] While Rav Ashi maintained his residence and yeshivah in Masa Machsiya and traveled little, Ravina is seen in the pages of the Talmud as visiting many Jewish communities in Babylonia on a regular basis.[54]

RAVINA (RAV AVINA) I
c. 420 CE
Teachers
• Rava
• Rav Nachman bar Yitzchak
• Ameimar
Colleagues
• Rav Ashi
• Rav Zvid
• Rav Dimi of Nehardea
• Rafram I
• Rav Kahana V
• Rav Acha breih d'Rava
• Rav Mordechai
• Rav Geviha m'bei Ksil
Students
• Mar breih d'Ravina
• Mreimar
• Rav Idi bar Avin II
• Rav Nachman bar Rav Huna
• Rabah (Rava) Tosefah
• Rav Rechumei II
Relatives
• Son: Mar breih d'Ravina
• Nephew: Ravina II

Seal of Huna bar Nosson (Courtesy of the Hecht Museum, University of Haifa)

"Let us mourn the passing of Ravina night and day in the same manner that he studied Torah night and day."
Moed Katan

The Talmud itself accords Ravina equal status with Rav Ashi in editing the Talmud and determining its laws and instructions.[55] He and Rav Ashi are considered the last of the *Amoraim* in terms of the ability to edit and decide halachic and textual matters in the Talmud.[56]

The final additions and redactions of the Talmud would continue for another two generations, and the Talmud in the exact format that we know it today would not be complete until the seventh century when the input of the *Rabanan Savoraim* – the successors to the *Amoraim* – would be finalized. The eulogy for Ravina at his funeral was, "The dates have lowered their heads in respect to the righteous man who stood tall as the palm tree [in his righteousness.] Let us mourn his passing night and day, in the same manner as he devoted himself in his lifetime night and day to the study of Torah."[57]

Among the colleagues, teachers and scholars of the approximate times of Rav Ashi and Ravina were:

- Rav Zvid[58]
- Rav Dimi of Nehardea[59]
- Rafram I[60]
- Rav Kahana V[61]
- Rav Acha breih d'Ravah[62]

Other scholars of the time who were active in helping Rav Ashi and Ravina in editing the Talmud were:

- Rav Acha Sava[63]
- Rabi Abba III[64]
- Rav Acha breih d'Rav Avya[65]
- Rav Geviha m'bei Ksil[66]
- Rav Acha breih d'Rav Yosef[67]
- Rav Gamda[68]
- Rav Hillel[69]
- Rav Yeymar[70]
- Rav Chanan of Nehardea[71]
- Rav Mordechai[72]

We also find that Rav Ashi was a close colleague of Mar Zutra II, who was also a strong colleague and friend of Ameimar, one of Rav Ashi's mentors, as noted above.[73] The Exilarch of that time was Huna bar Nosson, and both Ameimar and Rav Ashi had excellent relations with him.[74]

This was a special generation of scholars who took upon themselves the monumental task of preserving the Oral Law in all of its details and discussions for the ages. Their work has stood the test of time since the fifth century and has weathered all storms and attacks against it. The Talmud, its thought processes and value system, as fashioned by these intellectual giants, still reigns supreme in the Jewish world.

SECTION IX

THE SEVENTH AND FINAL GENERATION OF AMORAIM IN BABYLONIA

c. 390 - 430 CE

Ruins of the Katzrin synagogue

The Completed Talmud

After the death of Rav Ashi, the rabbis appointed Mreimar, a disciple of Ravina,[1] as the head of the Sura yeshivah located in Masa Machsiya.[2] He returned the yeshivah of Sura from Masa Machsiya to its original home in Sura.[3]

During his lifetime, Mreimar was known as an orator and a public figure,[4] but in the Talmud he is especially noted as the teacher and mentor of Ravina the Latter,[5] the son of the last Rav Huna.[6] There is an opinion that this Rav Huna was, in fact, the brother-in-law of Ravina the First; thus Ravina the Latter was a nephew of Ravina the First.[7] Rav Huna died when Ravina the Latter was yet a young child and so his teachings were transmitted to his son through Mreimar, who was Rav Huna's colleague.[8] Very little more is known about Mreimar personally, except that he died in 432 CE.[9]

After the passing of Mreimar, the rabbis appointed Rav Idi bar Avin II[10] as head of the Sura yeshivah and he served there from 432 to 452 CE.[11] Little is known about his life either, though he also undoubtedly occupied himself with the final redaction of the Talmud. As a colleague of Rav Ashi and Ravina the First, he was part of the group that undertook the massive task of editing the Talmud. It was after his death that the students of Rav Ashi, the true seventh generation of Babylonian *Amoraim*, assumed the leadership of the yeshivah in Sura and of the Jewish community in Babylonia.

As such, following the death of Rav Idi bar Avin II, Rav Nachman bar Rav Huna,[12] was appointed head of the Sura yeshivah. Though his reign was relatively short – only three years until his death in 455 CE – it was during this time[13] that the conditions of Jewish life in Babylonia worsened considerably. Its Persian king promulgated a number of anti-Semitic decrees, including an attempt to forbid the Jews from observing the Sabbath.[14] Fortunately, the decrees were not enforced for long, and Jewish life returned to its accustomed pace shortly before or directly after the death of Rav Nachman bar Rav Huna.

Mar bar Rav Ashi, a son of Rav Ashi, was one of the leading scholars of the generation, yet he was not immediately appointed to succeed his father as the head of the Sura yeshivah upon Rav Ashi's passing. As outlined above, three other scholars filled that role in succession for a period of 28 years. After the death of Rav Nachman bar Rav Huna, the rabbis deliberated over who should succeed him. A deranged person had predicted to Mar bar Rav Ashi that he would be appointed to head the yeshivah, and true to the opinion of the rabbis that the gift of forecasting events is sometimes given to the mentally disturbed, Mar bar Rav Ashi came to his colleagues to claim the position. In the interim, the rabbis had tentatively decided to nominate Rav Acha M'difti.[15] However, upon the arrival of Mar bar Rav Ashi to the rabbinic meeting, the rabbis chose Mar bar Rav Ashi to head the Sura yeshivah after all.[16] Though the rabbis stated that greatness in Torah has to be earned and is not a matter of pure inheritance,[17] it was clear that Mar bar Rav Ashi indeed deserved the position.

Following the lead of his father, Mar bar Rav Ashi moved the Sura yeshivah back to the town of Masa Machsiya.[18] He was a devoted student of his great father, and many statements of Rav Ashi were transmitted and clarified by Mar bar Rav Ashi.[19] He was enormously respectful of his father, calling him "My master, my father" and did not refer to him by name when quoting his opinions.[20] He became beloved and revered throughout Babylonia and in all later years, the Jewish people in its masses, when wishing to determine if a certain person was a Torah scholar would ask "Is he Mar bar Rav Ashi?"

Despite his 28-year wait to be installed as the head of the Sura yeshivah, Mar bar Rav Ashi became the symbol of Torah greatness and sterling character traits for all time amongst the Jewish people. Contributing to this aura was the love that Mar bar Rav Ashi himself displayed towards all Torah scholars, to the extent that he disqualified himself from sitting on a court that had to judge a case where a Torah scholar was one of the litigants.[21]

Very little is known about his personal or family life, though apparently his given name was Tavyumei as he signed himself so.[22] The Talmud also informs us that he had a daughter for whom he created a crown on her wedding day.[23] He served as the head of the Sura yeshivah for thirteen years, until his death in 468 CE.[24] He passed away immediately after Yom Kippur of that year.[25] Mar bar Rav Ashi is truly a legendary figure, surrounded by awe and mystery. Such figures are usually only glimpsed and are not subject to minute and detailed examination.

Ravina the First also had a son called Mar (breih d'Ravina). Raised in luxury, great care was taken to afford him the optimum opportunity to excel in his Torah studies.[26] He studied as a youth

A lintel of a tomb from the ancient cemetery of Tzipori, with inscription "This is the tomb of Rabi Tan[huma] and Rabi Shimon the priest, Huna, Sh[alom]," 3rd-4th century CE.

with Rav Sheishes and Rav Nachman bar Yitzchak. The latter called him "a person who has truly attained fear of heaven."[27] He was so well-known and respected for his integrity and honesty that if a document or other type of written issue were suspect, it would not be approved by the court of his time unless his signature appeared on it.[28] Though little is known of him, there are two wedding-related stories concerning him in the Talmud. The first is a discussion between the rabbis as to the proper song to sing to him at his wedding.[29] The second is that at the wedding of his own son, Mar breih d'Ravina intentionally shattered a precious glass in order to dampen any unwanted levity at the affair.[30]

Byzantine menorah from the synagogue in Hamat Tiberias, 5th century CE (The Israel Museum, Jerusalem)

Like Mar bar Rav Ashi, the life of Mar breih d'Ravina is shrouded in mystery and holiness. He fasted most days of the year,[31] mainly because of his tendency to have nightmares.[32] He is the author of the famous prayer *Elokai netzor* – God, guard my tongue from speaking evil…" that is recited thrice daily at the conclusion of the *Amidah* (eighteen blessings) series of prayer.[33] He is one of the human beings who rose to become almost supernatural in his behavior, demeanor and accomplishments. Miraculous escapes from dangerous situations were common to him.[34]

After the death of Mar bar Rav Ashi, Rabah (Rava) Tosefah was appointed as the head of the Sura yeshivah located in Masa Machsiya.[35] He served in that position for six years from 468 to 474.[36] A disciple of Ravina the First, he appears in discussions with him in a number of places in the Talmud.[37] His companion was Ravina the Latter, who succeeded him after his death as the head of the Sura yeshivah.[38]

Ravina the Latter headed the yeshivah for only one year, passing away in 475 CE.[39] As mentioned earlier, Ravina the Latter was a nephew of Ravina the First and he was the son of the last Rav Huna. His father died while Ravina the Latter was a young child and it was his mother who transmitted to him some of Rav Huna's teachings.[40] He was a student of Mreimar,[41] who also conveyed to him the teachings of his father.[42]

Rav Sherira Gaon, in his *Iggeres* ("letter" of history of the Jewish people), writes, "With the death of Ravina the Latter, the son of Rav Huna, the period of [talmudic] teachings and decisions ended."[43] The period of the *Amoraim* ended, and the students of this seventh generation of *Amoraim* would now be called *Rabanan Savoraim*, the rabbis who commented upon, explained and elucidated the Talmud.[44] Some of them still appear in the Talmud in discussions with their *Amoraim* teachers, and they also put the final touches on the editing of the Talmud.

But with the death of Ravina the Latter, the Talmud in the form that we have it today was finally and substantially completed.[45]

The last heads of the yeshivah in Pumbedisa during this generation were Rav Geviha m'bei Ksil who succeeded Rav Acha breih d'Rava when the latter died in 419 CE. Rav Geviha m'bei Ksil is mentioned many times in the Talmud,[46] and he headed the yeshivah for fourteen years until his passing in 433 CE.[47]

His successor was Rafram II, and he served in that post for ten years until his death in 443 CE.[48] He, in turn, was succeeded by Rav Rechumei II,[49] a student of Ravina the First,[50] who headed the Pumbedisa yeshivah until his passing in 455 CE.[51] After the passing of Rav Rechumei II, Rav Sama breih d'Rava became the head of the yeshivah. As noted earlier, he was the son of the great Rava and is also mentioned a number of times in the Talmud.[52] He passed away in 476 CE.[53]

Rav Yosef (Yossi), served as a bridge figure between the last generation of the *Amoraim* and the first generation of *Savoraim* in the yeshivah of Pumbedisa. The Talmud was completed in his time.[54] He lived a long life and passed away in 514 CE.[55]

It is most understandable that no specific line of cutoff dates can be drawn between the last of the *Amoraim* and their students, the first generation of *Savoraim*. However, a bridge group of scholars of the late fifth century is generally regarded as already being *Rabanan Savoraim*.[56] In addition to Rav Yosef, mentioned above, the leading members of the first and transitional generation include Rav Rechumei III, Rabah (Tosefah), Rav Achaei m'bei Chatim and Rav Ravai m'Rov.[57] As mentioned above and in the footnotes, many of their statements are found in our text of the Talmud itself.

The situation of the Jewish community in Babylonia deteriorated sharply in the fifth century. The Persian rulers attempted to crush Jewish practice under their extreme Zoroastrian pagan beliefs. The Jewish world was under siege from the Byzantine Christians on one hand, and the Zoroastrian Persians on the other. It would only be with the coming of Islam in the seventh century that both of these foes of Judaism would themselves be defeated in the Middle East. The Jewish world would enter into the period of

"With the death of Ravina the Latter, the son of Rav Huna, the period of [talmudic] teachings and decisions ended."

Rav Sherira Gaon (Iggeres)

Moslem rule, a future no less daunting than the situation in fifth century Babylonia.

The Byzantine rulers and the Persian Zoroastrian tyrants are long since gone from the world scene, and from most human memory – and today there are hundreds of thousands of Jews who devote themselves daily to the study of the immortal and holy words of the Talmud. Yes, there is certainly a God in the world!

APPENDICES

Epilogue

fter the completion of the Babylonian Talmud, the continuing development, transmission, and explanation of the Oral Law continued to be the focus of Jewish scholarship. The *Rabanan Savoraim* gave way to the era of the *Geonim* who were active from the seventh to the eleventh centuries, mainly in Babylonia. With the decline of Babylonia as the center of Jewish life, the era of the *Rishonim* began. It extended roughly from the eleventh to the beginning of the sixteenth centuries.

The giants of this era devoted their unbelievable talents and immense energies to cleansing the text of the Talmud from the copyists' errors that had crept in over the centuries, and in explaining and elucidating the words, ideas and patterns of logic of the Talmud itself. In Spain, Morocco, France and the Rhineland, the work of the great *Rishonim* went on unabated by the stormy times and persecutions that marked Jewish life in the Early Middle Ages. In the eleventh century, Rabbi Shlomo Yitzchaki (Rashi) composed his unmatched commentary to the Talmud, opening it for study by all Jews. His descendants, the Tosafists of France and Germany spent the next two centuries establishing and explaining the intricacies of the Talmud, revealing the skeleton, so to speak, that lies beneath the flesh of the written words.

The early *Achronim* continued to comment upon the Talmud while devoting themselves to codifying its halachic decisions, following the lead of the great codifiers of Jewish law in the Middle Ages, Rabbis Yitzchak Alfasi, Moshe ben Maimon, Asher ben Yechiel and his son Yaakov ben Asher (*Tur*). The middle era of *Achronim* culminated with the glosses of the Gaon of Vilna, Rabbi Eliyahu Kramer, and Rabbi Akiva Eiger to the text of the Talmud and the comments and explanations of other great geniuses and scholars to the text of the Talmud and the words of its earlier commentators.

The rise of the modern yeshivah movement in the nineteenth century provided the milieu for intense study of the Talmud in increasing depth and creativity by elite scholars. In Lithuania, Poland, Hungary, Slovakia, Germany, and later in England, the United States, South Africa and South America, Australia and the Land of Israel, the yeshivah movement flourished. With it, a whole new era of authors, scholars and commentators – the latter *Achronim* – took its place in the unending chain of tradition of Torah study that emanates from Moshe and Sinai. Wherever there are Jews in the world, the Talmud has accompanied them there.

Today's yeshivah world, which has a much wider student base than ever before in recent centuries, numbers tens of thousands of students – perhaps the largest number in millennia – devoted to the full-time study of the Talmud and its commentators. There are hundreds of books published every year on the Talmud and its related subjects, and its presence is felt even in secular and non-Jewish universities and schools. Except for the Bible itself, no other book of knowledge, so all-encompassing in its sweep of human life and complex legal subject matter, has survived so long and so well and remained truly beloved and relevant.

The Talmud is constructed as a palace with many rooms, and each room is slightly different from the other. There are rooms that are more frequently used and visited, others less visited, and there are open spaces in the palace as well. Naturally, to appreciate truly the grandeur of the palace, one has to see it all and visit all of its rooms. Yet, just as tourists to grand palaces throughout the world sometimes are only able to visit a small portion of the palace – and nevertheless they are able to absorb the magnificence of the place – so too does even a glimpse of the Talmud reveal its richness.

A great Chasidic master once spent some weeks studying the same page of the Talmud. When asked why he did not move on to other pages, he responded: "What is wrong with staying with this page? My pleasure in studying it is still not satiated!" In the holy palace of Talmud, constructed painstakingly by superior minds over hundreds of years, both the occasional visitor and the full-time resident will find satisfaction, knowledge, and inspiration forever.

Amoraim Timeline

Eretz Yisrael

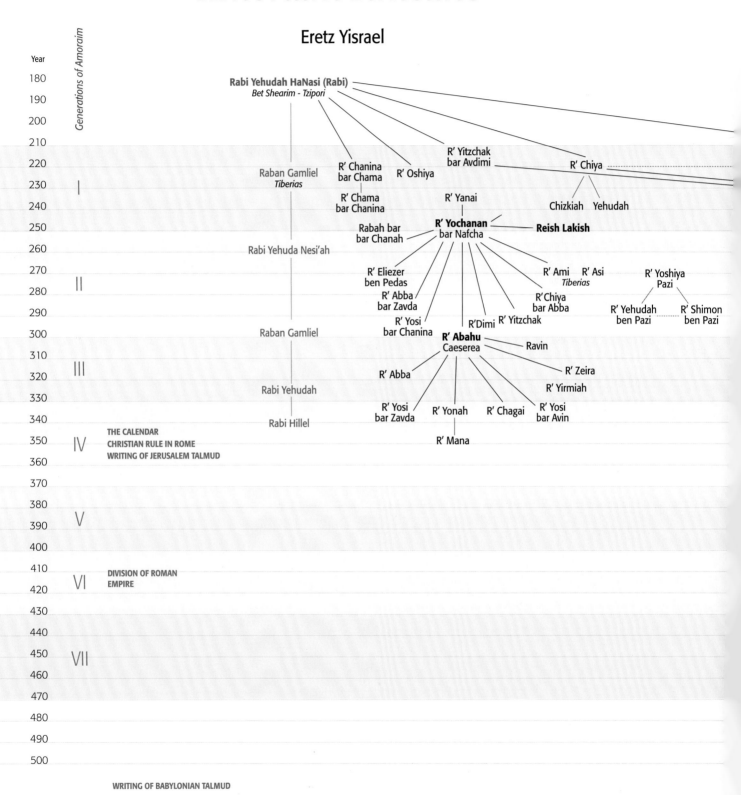

Year	Generations of Amoraim		
180		**Rabi Yehudah HaNasi (Rabi)**	
190		*Bet Shearim - Tzipori*	
200			
210			
220	I	R' Chanina bar Chama / R' Oshiya / R' Yitzchak bar Avdimi / R' Chiya	
230		Raban Gamliel *Tiberias*	
240		R' Chama bar Chanina / R' Yanai	Chizkiah Yehudah
250		Rabah bar bar Chanah / **R' Yochanan bar Nafcha** / **Reish Lakish**	
260	II	Rabi Yehuda Nesi'ah	
270		R' Eliezer ben Pedas / R' Ami R' Asi *Tiberias* / R' Yoshiya Pazi	
280		R' Abba bar Zavda / R'Chiya bar Abba	R' Yehudah ben Pazi R' Shimon ben Pazi
290		R' Yosi bar Chanina / R'Dimi R' Yitzchak	
300		Raban Gamliel / **R' Abahu** Caeserea / Ravin	
310	III		
320		R' Abba / R' Zeira	
330		Rabi Yehudah / R' Yirmiah	
340		Rabi Hillel / R' Yosi bar Zavda R' Yonah R' Chagai R' Yosi bar Avin	
350	IV	THE CALENDAR / R' Mana	
360		CHRISTIAN RULE IN ROME / WRITING OF JERUSALEM TALMUD	
370			
380			
390	V		
400			
410			
420	VI	DIVISION OF ROMAN EMPIRE	
430			
440			
450			
460	VII		
470			
480			
490			
500			
		WRITING OF BABYLONIAN TALMUD	

184

Babylonia

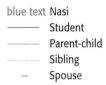

blue text Nasi
——— Student
——— Parent-child
·········· Sibling
-- Spouse

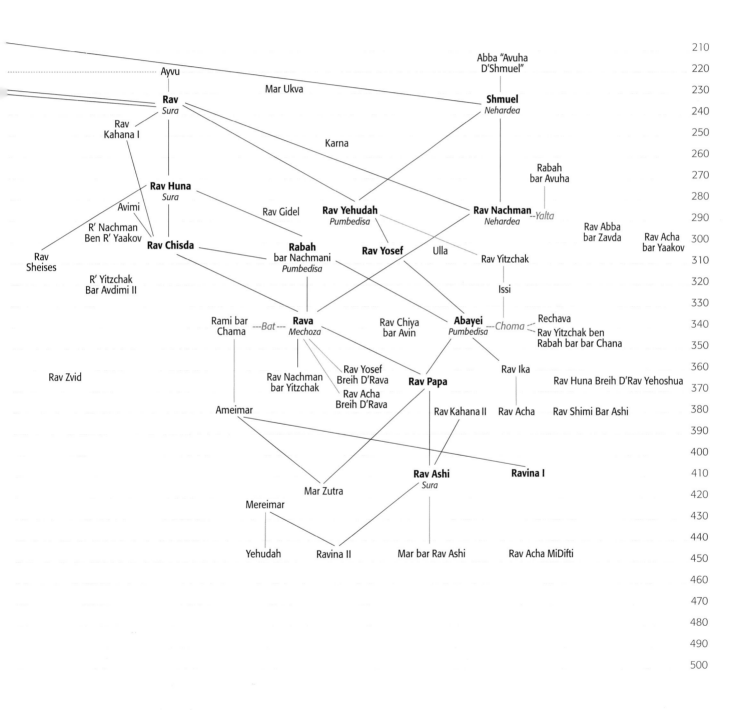

	210
Abba "Avuha D'Shmuel"	220
Ayvu Mar Ukva	230
Rav **Shmuel**	240
Sura *Nehardea*	
Rav Kahana I	250
Karna	260
Rabah bar Avuha	270
Rav Huna **Rav Nachman** --*Yalta*	280
Sura Rav Gidel **Rav Yehudah** *Nehardea*	290
Avimi *Pumbedisa* Rav Abba bar Zavda Rav Acha bar Yaakov	300
R' Nachman Ben R' Yaakov **Rav Chisda** **Rabah** **Rav Yosef** Ulla Rav Yitzchak	310
Rav Sheises bar Nachmani *Pumbedisa*	
R' Yitzchak Bar Avdimi II	320
Issi	330
Rami bar Chama ---*Bat*--- **Rava** Rav Chiya bar Avin **Abayei** ---*Choma* --- Rechava	340
Mechoza *Pumbedisa* Rav Yitzchak ben Rabah bar bar Chana	350
Rav Nachman bar Yitzchak Rav Yosef Breih D'Rava Rav Ika	360
Rav Zvid Rav Acha Breih D'Rava **Rav Papa** Rav Huna Breih D'Rav Yehoshua	370
Ameimar Rav Kahana II Rav Acha Rav Shimi Bar Ashi	380
	390
	400
Rav Ashi **Ravina I**	410
Mar Zutra *Sura*	420
Mereimar	430
	440
Yehudah Ravina II Mar bar Rav Ashi Rav Acha MiDifti	450
	460
	470
	480
	490
	500

185

NOTES

SECTION I

Talmud Introduction

1. Sanhedrin 24a. See also Midrash Tanchuma, Noach, section 3.
2. Moshe ibn Ezra lived in the twelfth century and included this thought in a poem. Though this popular and often-used expression sounds Talmudic, it is not found anywhere in the Talmud.
3. In the late nineteenth century there was a bitter contest over the introduction of *mussar* – studies of works of ethics and personal spiritual development - into the yeshivos of the time. The opponents of *mussar* stated pithily that the Talmud was by itself the premier work of mussar. Even though they lost the *mussar* battle, they certainly had a point.
4. Midrash Rabah, Shmos, chapter 47, section 1.
5. Eiruvin 54a.
6. Shabbos 30a.
7. Chagigah 3a.
8. Berachos 8a.
9. Ibid.
10. See, for instance, Peah, chapter 2, mishnah 6 or Yadayim, chapter 4, mishnah 3.
11. Chagigah, chapter 1, mishnah 8.
12. Ibid.
13. Shabbos 28b, and many other places in the Talmud.
14. Midrash Rabah, Vayikra, chapter 22, section 1.
15. Avos, chapter 5, mishnah 19.
16. See Yevamos 76b. The exact and popularly known phrase *im kabala hee n'kabel* regarding a tradition is not found in those words in the Talmud. The phrase in Yevamos speaks about accepting a *halachah* derived by Moshe at Sinai.
17. See, Naftal, *HaTalmud V'yotzrav*, Doros Amoraim, volume 1, page 233.
18. Midrash Rabah, Bamidbar, chapter 21, section 2; also see Berachos 58a.
19. Taanis 7a – the words of Rabi Meir.
20. Psalms, the concluding verse of chapter 90.

Rav and His Colleagues

1. As a rule of thumb – though there are some exceptions – the *Tannaim* who are the authors of the Mishnah are called Rabi, while the *Amoraim* of the Talmud are called Rav.
2. Kesubos 62b.
3. Sanhedrin 5a.
4. See Bava Metzia 6b, that in later times Rav Chisda was the head of the court and yeshivah located there. See also Eiruvin 62a.

5. Avraham Moshe Naftal, *HaTalmud V'yotzrav, Doros HaAmoraim,* volume 2 (Tel Aviv: Yavneh Publishing House,1972), p. 21.

6. Sanhedrin 5a.

7. Ibid.

8. Nazir 59a; Berachos 13b and 43a; Shabbos 3b and other places in the Talmud as well.

9. Naftal, volume2, chapter 1.

10. Yevamos 102a; Chulin 32a; Bava Basra 41b; Makkos 11a; Pesachim 117a, and many other places in the Talmud.

11. Naftal, p. 23. See also *Doros HaRishonim* by Yitzchak Isaac Halevi, volume 2, p. 403, for an estimate of the time of Rabi Chiya's first arrival in the Land of Israel.

12. Yoma 87a.

13. Chulin 110a. There is a later Rav Yitzchak bar Avdimi who lived and flourished two generations after Rav. See Sanhedrin 56b and 100a, among other places in the Talmud, where this latter Rav Yitzchak is quoted. The former Rabi Yitzchak ben Avdimi, the teacher of Rav, was highly regarded by Rabi Yehudah HaNasi for his erudition and wide knowledge. See Yerushalmi, Maaser Sheni, chapter 5, at the beginning of section 1.

14. Succah 20a.

15. Yerushalmi Maaser Sheni, chapter 5, section 5.

16. Bereshis Rabah, chapter 77, section 2.

17. Beitzah 9b, see Rashi's commentary there. The major crop of Rabi Chiya and his sons was flax, used for the manufacture (and later export) of linen. See Yerushalmi Bava Metzia, chapter 5, section 6, and chapter 6, section 1.

18. Midrash Rabah, Rus, chapter 5, section 12.

19. Yerushalmi Bava Metzia, chapter 6, section 1; Beitzah, chapter 3, section 2.

20. Taanis 29b.

21. Yoma 87a; Berachos 43a.

22. Menachos, 88b; Eiruvin 73a; Nedarim 41a; Avodah Zarah 36b; Bava Metzia 85b; Yerushalmi, Kesubos, chapter 12, section 3.

23. Sanhedrin 98b.

24. Chulin 137b, and many other places in the Talmud. See also Niddah 24b that Rav was the tallest scholar of his generation. There in Chulin 137b, it is related that Rabi Yochanan criticized a colleague who called Rav by this nickname of *Abba Aricha.*

25. Yerushalmi Gittin, chapter 4, section 3, where he describes himself as *vatran*– someone who is free, forgiving, and unconcerned about monetary matters. See also Yerushalmi Bava Metzia, chapter 4, section 2 where he commands his aide to be a check over him when Rav granted gifts or charity to others.

26. Sanhedrin 7b.

27. Yevamos 63a. Rav's wife was of an independent and contrarian personality who often did the opposite of her husband's will and requests. Rav tolerated this behavior without visible complaint or animosity. See also Yoma 87a that Rav went to ask forgiveness before Yom Kippur from a butcher who had in reality harmed him! When the butcher did not come to Rav to reconcile the matter, Rav went to the butcher.

28. Ibid.

29. Chulin 107b.

30. Chulin 95b.

31. Gittin 59a.

32. Sanhedrin 5a.

33. Ibid.
34. Yerushalmi Chagigah, chapter 1, section 8.
35. He is not to be confused with a later *Amora*, Rabah bar Chana, who lived 50 years after this Rabah bar Chana.
36. Sanhedrin 5b.
37. This is somewhat analogous to what the Talmud Eiruvin 13b states regarding Rabi Meir: "It is clear to the Creator of the world that Rabi Meir is the greatest scholar of the generation. Yet, we cannot establish that the *halachah* follows his opinions, for his knowledge and opinions are too erudite and deep for the others scholars to truly follow and understand [and therefore they would be subject to misinterpretation]."
38. Sanhedrin 5a.
39. Naftal, volume 2, p. 40, surmises that it might have been to find a wife. Rav always preached the advantages of marriage and never wanted to be alone without a wife. See Yoma 18b.
40. Yerushalmi Sotah, chapter 9, section 2. See Sotah 45a, where Abaye also boasts about his erudition in similar words, and see Eiruvin 29a, where Rava makes the same statement about his own great knowledge of Torah. Rashi explains there in Sotah that this statement was made when the scholar's mind was absolutely clear in resolving scholarly problems and his mood was therefore exultant. He then declared that he was prepared to answer any question in Torah just as Ben Azai was able to do in a previous generation.
41. Yerushalmi Sotah, chapter 9, section 2.
42. Ibid.
43. Pesachim 4a. See also the opening paragraph here in the text regarding the complicated family relationship of Rav's father, mother and Rabi Chiya.
44. Chulin 137b. See there that "sparks" of holiness flashed between Rav and Rabi when they discussed Torah.
45. Chulin 54a.
46. See Naftal, volume 2, p. 46 in the footnotes, for other opinions of various scholars as to the date of the death of Rabi. They range from 190 CE to 220 CE.
47. Kesubos 103a-b.
48. Yevamos 32b. However, see Kesubos 103b, where there are different opinions as to whether Rabi Chiya survived Rabi or predeceased him.
49. Halevi in *Doros Rishonim*, volume 2, p. 258, states that Rabi Yehudah Nesiah I died before the year 230 CE, probably in 228 CE. See Bava Basra 139b. See also the commentary of Ritva (Rabbi Yom Tov ibn Asbili of fourteenth-century Spain) that the Raban Gamliel mentioned there in the mishnah is the son of Rabi.
    Therefore, the inference may be drawn from this that Rav heard the *halachah* under discussion there from Raban Gamliel III himself.
50. Yerushalmi Shabbos, chapter 3, section 1.
51. Kesubos 103a.
52. See Niddah 45b; Sanhedrin 99b; and other places in the Talmud.
53. Yoma 87a.
54. Yoma 87b.
55. Ibid.
56. Iggeres Rav Sherira Gaon, Levin edition, p. 78.
57. Ibid.
58. Bava Basra 91a.
59. Eiruvin 50b and many other places in the Talmud.

60. Taanis 26b.
61. There are three people, each named Rav Assi, mentioned in the Talmud. Rav Assi I is a contemporary of Rav and Shmuel; Rav Assi II is a disciple of Rav Yochanan of Tiberias and is buried in that city next to his comrade, Rav Ami; and Rav Assi III, who lived at the time of the sixth generation of *Amoraim* and was a colleague of Rav Ashi at the time of the editing of the Talmud. Rav Assi I was also known as Eesai ben Yehudah. See Niddah 36b.
62. Eiruvin 6a. See Rashi there that previously in Babylonia the unlearned Jews treated the Torah commandments lightly and with disdain. Rav's "fence" was to correct that situation.
63. Sanhedrin 17b.
64. Bava Kama 47b; Sanhedrin 30b. His rulings are called in the Talmud *nezikin dbei Karna* – the laws of torts emanating from the school of Karna.
65. Sanhedrin 17b.
66. Ibid. Iggeres Rav Sherira Gaon.
67. Shabbos 108a.
68. Yerushalmi Bava Basra, chapter 5, section 5. Karna there intercedes on behalf of Rav with the Exilarch/*Reish Galusa*.
69. Bava Kama 80b.
70. Megillah 5b. See also Chulin 26b and 107a regarding his association with Hutzal.
71. Yerushalmi Succah, chapter 4, section 2 and other places in Yerushalmi.
72. Megillah 5a; Sanhedrin 29b.
73. See for example, Megillah 5a, Kiddushin 45b, Gittin 25a, Sanhedrin 29b.
74. Kiddushin 46a.
75. Bava Kama 80a-b.
76. For example, see Bava Basra 126a and Chulin 19a regarding Rav Huna; and Shabbos 22a, Yevamos 16b, and Kesubos 77a as to Rav Yehudah bar Yechezkel.
77. Naftal p. 73.
78. Niddah 36b - 37a.
79. There are fives scholars noted in the Talmud with the name Rav Kahana. This one, Rav Kahana I, was a colleague of Rav, Mar Shmuel, and Rav Assi I. Thus he was of the first generation of the Babylonian *Amoraim*. Rav Kahana II was a student of Rav and a member of the second generation of Babylonian *Amoraim*. Rav Kahana III was the student of Rabah bar Nachmani and a member of the fourth generation of Babylonian *Amoraim*. Rav Kahana IV was the main disciple of Rava, and he lived in the fifth generation of the Babylonian *Amoraim*. And finally, Rav Kahana V was a colleague of Rav Ashi, one of the editors of the Talmud and a member of the sixth generation of Babylonian *Amoraim*. The name itself was often used to indicate that the person was a *kohein*, a direct paternal descendant of the priestly family of Aharon. See Pesachim113a, where Rav indicates that Rav Kahana I was a *kohein*. In Talmud Yerushalmi, he is mainly referred to as "Kahana" without any titles placed before his name.
80. Succah 6b; Beitzah 6a, and many other places in the Talmud.
81. Menachos 23b; Zevachim 59a.
82. Yerushalmi Rosh Hashanah, chapter 4, section 1.
83. Menachos 23b; Yerushalmi Orlah, chapter 1, section 5.
84. Zevachim 59a.
85. Sanhedrin 36b.
86. Succah, 6b-7a.
87. Sanhedrin 36b.

88. There are two scholars mentioned in the Talmud by this name. This one was a colleague of Rav who lived in Babylonia and was a member of the first generation of *Amoraim*. The second one was a member of the second generation of *Amoraim* and lived in the Land of Israel. It is often difficult to determine in the Talmud which Zeirei is being quoted. The name Zeirei literally means "little" or "small." Perhaps it was a reflection of his physical size or his great spiritual modesty. There are those who think that the name reflects his position in the family, namely that he was the "baby," the youngest child born to his family.

89. Shabbos 156a.

90. See, for example, Yevamos 21a.

91. See, for example, Bava Kama 30b; Kesubos 13a; Gittin 24b-25a.

92. Zevachim 43b.

93. Menachos 21a, and other places in the Talmud.

94. Yoma 77b, and other places in the Talmud.

95. Menachos 21a.

96. Berachos 43a, and many other places in the Talmud.

97. Yerushalmi Kilayim, chapter 9, section 1.

98. Berachos 18b.

99. Sanhedrin 67b. Naftal, p. 82, in the footnotes on that page, questions whether these stories refer to Zeirei I or to Zeirei II.

100. See *Halachos Gedolos*, Hilchos Gittin, at the end (in the Berlin edition, it is on pp. 337-8.) See also Rosh, Kiddushin, chapter 4, section 7, and Tosfos, Kiddushin 73a. In these latter sources the story is quoted from Yerushalmi. For another version, see Midrash Shmuel, chapter 10, section 3.

101. Chulin 105a.

102. Pesachim 103a; Yerushalmi Rosh Hashanah, chapter 3, section 6.

103. Yerushalmi Bava Metzia, chapter 4, section 1.

104. Berachos 18b.

105. Ibid.

106. Kesubos 51b.

107. Bava Basra 42b; Yerushalmi Yevamos, chapter 4, section 11.

108. Bava Metzia 24b.

109. Moed Katan 18a.

110. Moed Katan 26b; Shabbos 108b.

111. Yerushalmi Berachos, chapter 2, section 8.

112. Berachos 18b.

113. Ibid.

114. However, see Iggeres Rav Sherira Gaon, Levin edition, p. 82, where the date of Shmuel's death is given as 254 CE. See Naftal on this in volume 2, p. 205.

115. Shabbos 59b.

116. Yerushalmi Yevamos, chapter 12, section 6. The Yerushalmi there records Levi's unsuccessful and short tenure as rabbi of the community of Simoniya, a town in the Lower Galilee. Levi's great modesty and honesty shine through that story. See also Kesubos 8a, where Levi is honored to recite the wedding blessings at the wedding ceremony of Rabi Shimon, the son of Rabi.

117. Sanhedrin 17b.

118. For example, Yoma 24a; Kesubos 53b and other places in the Talmud. See Rashi there in Kesubos 53b that Levi authored and organized *breisos* on all six orders of the Mishnah.

119. See Shabbos 108b; Eiruvin 10a; Succah 7a and other places in the Talmud.

120. A festive gathering held on the nights of the intermediate days of *Succos* to commemorate the great joy and spectacle of the drawing of the water and its procession from the Shiloach spring, outside of Jerusalem, to be brought as a libation on the altar of the Temple. The custom of holding this festive gathering is still practiced today throughout the Jewish world.
121. Succah 53a.
122. Ibid.
123. Taanis 25a.
124. Ibid.
125. Shabbos 59b.
126. See Rashi there at Shabbos 59b.
127. Shabbos 59b and there again in Rashi. See Kesubos 103b.
128. See Berachos 18b.
129. Shabbos 59b.
130. Megillah 29a.
131. Bava Kama 80b, and see Rashi there.
132. Yerushalmi Bava Basra, chapter 5, section 5. Rav was known to be very strict in matters of weights and measures, even not allowing one to keep a faulty measure in one's home, even for use as a chamber pot! See Bava Basra 89b.
133. Ibid.
134. Ibid.
135. There is opinion that he wanted to do so in order to honor Rav, having discovered who this *Amora* was and feeling that it was beneath Rav's dignity to serve as an *Amora* for him.
136. Yoma 20b.
137. Rav Sherira Gaon cites Hutzal as being the place of the study hall of the great Ezra the Scribe. See Iggeres Rav Sherira Gaon, Levin edition, p. 73. See also Megillah 29a, where Hutzal is mentioned as one of the two places in Babylonia where the holy spirit of God, so to speak, can be found. Nehardea, with its ancient synagogue dating back to the time of the prophet Yechezkel, is the other place mentioned there in the Talmud.
138. Menachos 57b.
139. See Naftal, volume 2, p. 108.
140. Yerushalmi Beitzah, chapter 1, section 7.
141. In today's yeshivah world, it would be equivalent to a type of *mashgiach/nosei v'nosen/chazara* of the *shiur* position. He was responsible for the spiritual and physical welfare of the students and helped them in grasping the fundamentals of Talmudic study and in reviewing the lecture that was delivered daily in the study hall. See Yerushalmi Succah, chapter 4, section 2.
142. Succah 29b; Pesachim 66b.
143. Rav's advice on educational matters may be found scattered throughout the pages of the Talmud. See, for example, Eiruvin 100b and 53a; Nedarim 32a; Sanhedrin 44b; Avodah Zarah 19a; Pesachim 3b; Chulin 133a and many other places in the Talmud.
144. There are varying opinions given as to the date of the death of Shmuel. They range from 249 CE to 254 CE. Naftal and Halevi adopt this last date. I used 249 CE as his date of death earlier in this chapter based upon the opinion that Mar Shmuel passed away shortly after his father's death in 248 CE. However, all matters of dating regarding the people of the Talmud are somewhat approximate and a spread of five years in estimating the correct date of an event in the third century CE is not uncommon.

145. Halevi, section 2, chapter 17, p. 222, gives the date of Rav's arrival in Sura as 225 CE.

146. Chulin 137b.

147. The differences between *sidra, mesivta* and *yeshivah* are dealt with in detail in Naftal's book However, this rather technical subject is beyond the purview of this book and I have let these technical differences rest. Suffice it to say that the institution of the *mesivta/yeshivah* as the central place of halachic authority did not take official form until after the death of Rabi Yehudah Nesiah I and the decline of the Jewish community in the Land of Israel.

148. Avodah Zarah 10b-11a.

149. Yerushalmi Peah, chapter 1, section 1.

150. Ibid.

151. Iggeres Rav Sherira Gaon, Levin edition, p. 79. He states there, however, that the inhabitants of Sura were ignorant of Jewish law, not knowing what was permissible or forbidden according to Torah law.

152. See Rav's comment in Makkos 24a on the situation, couched as a homiletical interpretation of a verse in the Torah.

153. Ibid. Iggeres Rav Sherira Gaon.

154. Rav was known for his hospitality to strangers. See Shabbos 127a. He also greatly encouraged visiting of the sick and indisposed. See Nedarim 40a. He also was very tolerant and forthcoming to converts to Judaism, even if their original motives for converting were somewhat questionable. See Yerushalmi Kiddushin, chapter 4, section 1. Rav was a staunch defender of the rights of workers, and that they should be accorded just treatment. See Succah 29b. Rav cautioned against discriminating against the children of the poor, for "from them will Torah go forth." See Nedarim 81a. It is no wonder that Rav became the central figure for all of Babylonian Jewry, and not only of his scholarly colleagues alone.

155. Chulin 137b.

156. Eventually Rav's successor as the head of the yeshivah in Sura.

157. One of the great teachers of the second generation of *Amoraim.* After Rav's death, he traveled to Nehardea to study under Mar Shmuel.

158. See Kesubos 4a. Masa Machsiya became famous as a central locality of Torah learning, and the yeshivah of Sura often met there as well. See Krisus 6a.

159. Sanhedrin 7b.

160. Kesubos 106a.

161. The institution of *yarchei kallah* (the months of the *kallah* – the gathering) operated for centuries. Thousands of Jews visited the main yeshivos of Babylonia and spent a month in Torah study in *Adar* and *Elul.* There are many references to the *yarchei kallah* throughout the Talmud. The months of Elul and Adar were chosen for the time of the *kallah,* so as not to interfere with the agricultural seasons of plowing, sowing, harvesting, threshing, and pressing. See Berachos 35b. Large crowds gathered for the months of the *kallah* and all of the facilities of Sura and Masa Machsiya were crowded and cramped. See Berachos 6a-b. As many as 12,000 students came to study in the month of the *kallah.* See Bava Metzia 86a. Such was the greatness of the sight of the Jewish scholars of Babylonia gathering for the *kallah* that the Talmud wondered why the non-Jewish population of Masa Machsiya did not convert to Judaism! See Berachos 17b. When the students of the *kallah* arose from hearing the lecture and shook off the dust that had gathered on their garments, the dust cloud was felt even in the Land of Israel, many kilometers distant. See Kesubos 106a. The Talmud there also points out that many lecturers were required to meet the demands of

the large numbers of attendees. In the months of the *kallah*, those who attended
were immune from any legal procedures against them. See Bava Kama 113a.
There was a specific tractate of the Oral Law that was covered during every
kallah meeting. See Taanis 10b, Kiddushin 49b and Shabbos 114a and in Tosfos
there in Shabbos. The institution of the *kallah* lasted for centuries in Babylonia.
It was revived in our times by Rabbi Yosef Kahaneman, the "Ponovezher Rav"
and is now held annually at the great yeshivah of Ponovezh in Bnei Brak, Israel.

162. See Naftal, volume 2, p. 348.
163. Bava Basra 135b.
164. Shabbos 66a; Nedarim 77a-b.
165. Kiddushin 39a; Bava Basra 54a. Apparently, the garden's produce was used to
help feed the students of the yeshivah.
166. See above notes 162,163, and 164.
167. Megillah 29a and there in Rashi.
168. See more about him in a later chapter of this book.
169. Shabbos 75a.
170. Gittin 16b-17a.
171. Yevamos 63b.
172. Taanis 20a.
173. Chulin 84a.
174. Chulin 107b.
175. Chulin 95b.
176. Shabbos 77b.
177. Chulin 111b.
178. Shabbos 152a.
179. Niddah 65a.
180. Sanhedrin 82a.
181. Nedarim 41a.
182. Shabbos 152a.
183. Their prayer for Rav's health was illustrated and manifested in the fact that now
whenever mentioning the name of their master, Rav, they would add, "May God
be of help to him." Succah 33a and 35b, and other places in the Talmud.
184. One of the primary disciples of Rav. Rav praised him highly for his skill and
devotion as a teacher of young children. See Bava Basra 8b.
185. Shabbos 153a.
186. See Rashi, Berachos 52b.
187. Sanhedrin 47b.
188. Ibid.
189. Berachos 42b.
190. Moed Katan 24a.
191. Shabbos 109b and 110a. See Rashi there.
192. Eliezer Shteinman, *Be'er HaTalmud* (Tel Aviv: Masada Press, 1967), volume 3,
p. 236, lists 34 main students of Rav whose opinions are quoted throughout the
Talmud.
193. Naftal, volume 2, p. 148.
194. Rashi, Chulin 44a.
195. Chagigah 14a; Avodah Zarah 31b; Yerushalmi Berachos, chapter 1, section 5.
196. Chief among them is Rav Chisda, who was married to Rav's granddaughter. He
offered a reward to anyone who would inform him of a teaching of Rav that he
had not heard before. See Shabbos 10b.
197. Yerushalmi Rosh Hashanah, chapter 1, section 3.

198. Berachos 33b.
199. Berachos 16b.
200. This prayer is taken from the *tekiasa d'bei Rav* in the *Musaf* service of Rosh Hashanah. By tradition, the authorship of this prayer is ascribed to Yehoshua bin Nun at the time of the fall of the city of Jericho to the Israelites. However, it apparently was forgotten over the ages – or at least not used in prayer – and it was Rav who restored it to its primacy in Jewish liturgy.
201. See Rashbam, Bava Basra 124b.
202. Yevamos 63a.
203. Bava Metzia 59a.
204. Shteinman, volume 3, p. 235.
205. See, for example, Bava Metzia 16a; Shabbos 69b; and Arachin 20b and numerous other places in the Talmud.
206. Pesachim 113a. As stated above, Rav was wise enough to recognize the differences in talent and intellect of his sons and attempted to make each of them productive and holy people, each according to the abilities, interests, and talents.
207. Shabbos 10b.
208. Avodah Zarah 31b; Pesachim 113a.
209. Kiddushin 12a; Yoma 28b; Niddah 14a and other places in the Talmud.
210. Menachos 29a and 110a; Bechoros 43b; Niddah 24a. Rashi is of the opinion that this was a statement of affection and recognition of Shimi's scholarship by Rav. In Niddah 24b, Rashi treats the phrase as a pure declarative statement rather than as an expression of wonderment.
211. Chulin 92a.
212. Pesachim 115b; Beitzah 29a; Bava Basra 51b.
213. Kiddushin 81b.
214. Chulin 95b.
215. For example, see Eiruvin 5b; Yevamos 63b; Rosh Hashanah 31a and numerous other places in the Talmud.
216. Succah 44b.

Mar Shmuel

1. See the differing legends about the birth of Mar Shmuel in Midrash Shmuel, chapter 10, section 3 and in *Halachos Gedolos*, Berlin edition, pp. 337-8.
2. Chulin 107b; Zevachim 26a; Yerushalmi Shabbos, chapter 6, section 6.
3. See Mordechai, Moed Katan, section 889. The Rosh in Moed Katan, chapter 3, section 61 also quotes this story. However, it is based on a story in Yerushalmi Pesachim, chapter 3, section 7. In our editions of Yerushalmi, the father and son in the story are Rabi Abahu and his son Chanina. See the attempted emendation to Rosh in order to conform his words to our Yerushalmi. Mordechai has Abba bar Abba sending Shmuel to Netzivin from their home in Tiberias. But Abba bar Abba and Shmuel lived then in Nehardea, and not in Tiberias. See the emendation made in Yerushalmi itself to substitute Caesarea for Tiberias. The matter is clouded by different texts and traditions.
4. Ibid.
5. Menachos 39b; Gittin 13b; Shabbos 108b; Eiruvin 10a, and other places in the Talmud.

6. Berachos 58b.
7. See Chulin 95b where it is related that Mar Shmuel established a calendar for the forthcoming 60 years. He was severely criticized for so doing, since the Sanhedrin in the Land of Israel still existed, and the right to determine the calendar was deemed to be exclusively in its powers. See Yerushalmi Kesubos, chapter 2, section 6, that this was perhaps the cause of Mar Shmuel's personal family tragedy: his daughters were taken captive by non-Jews, one of whom then married her. None of the above diminishes his mathematical/astronomical achievement at being able to produce such a complicated calendar.
8. Bava Metzia 113b.
9. Bava Metzia 85b.
10. See, for example, Avodah Zarah 22b (Rabi Chanina bar Chama); Shabbos 138a (Rabi Chiya); Kesubos 44a (Rabi Elazar ben Shimon); Kesubos 10a (Rabi Shimon ben Elazar) and other places in the Talmud.
11. Rav did, however, receive the two lower forms of *semichah*, while Mar Shmuel apparently received no form of *semichah* whatsoever.
12. Bava Metzia 85b – 86a.
13. Ibid.
14. Rashi, Bava Metzia 65b.
15. An inference to this may be derived from Mar Shmuel calling himself "*yarchinai*" – astronomer – in his conversation with Rabi there in Bava Metzia 85b.
16. Naftal, *HaTalmud V'yotzrav, Doros HaAmoraim*, volume 2 (Tel Aviv: Yavneh Publishing House,1972), p. 161.
17. Bava Metzia 86b.
18. However, see Naftal, volume 2, p. 171, where he attempts to cite two places in Yerushalmi where he was called *Rabi* Shmuel. However, Naftal himself admits that the texts for this are in question. Seventeen hundred years later, one of the great pioneers of Torah in American Jewish life, Shraga Feivel Mendlowitz, would emulate Mar Shmuel's action and only allow himself to be called "*Mister*" Mendlowitz.
19. See footnote 142 in the chapter on Rav for conflicting dates as to Mar Shmuel's date of death.
20. Kesubos 54a.
21. Sanhedrin 17b.
22. Ibid. However, see Rashbam, Bava Basra 70b and other places in his commentary to that tractate where he is of the opinion that Mar Shmuel served as a co-equal with Karna in the role as chief judge.
23. Shabbos 108a.
24. Yerushalmi Succah, chapter 4, section 2, and other places in Yerushalmi.
25. Gittin 66b and other places in the Talmud.
26. Berachos 12a; Chagigah 14a.
27. Yerushalmi Berachos, chapter 1, section 5.
28. Arachin 16b. See also Rosh Hashanah 32a, Succah 32b, Kiddushin 6a and many other places in the Talmud where Rav Huna quotes the teachings of Mar Shmuel.
29. Niddah 36b.
30. Yevamos 16b-17a, there in Rashi.
31. Rashi, Succah 9a.
32. Niddah 13a.
33. Berachos 36a; Chagigah 15b and many other places in the Talmud. There is an

alternative explanation to the word *shinanah*, attributed to Rav Hai Gaon, that the word means "the toothy one." Rav Yehudah apparently had large protruding front teeth. See *Aruch HaShalem* under the title *shen* and Iggeres Rav Sherira Gaon, Levin Edition, p. 78, note 1.

34. See, for example, Shabbos 134b. See also Beitzah 31b and other places in the Talmud where he expands on cryptic texts in the Mishnah.
35. Niddah 26b.
36. Berachos 53b; Kesubos 22a; Bava Metzia 15b and many other places in the Talmud where Mar Shmuel himself submits a question to Rav for explanation. Mar Shmuel held Rav in awe and respect .
37. Arachin 16b.
38. For example, see Shabbos 53a, Chulin 45b.
39. Bechoros 49b.
40. Yerushalmi Kiddushin, chapter 1, section 6: "One who does not understand and agree with his [Mar Shmuel's] opinions in matters of tort law does not understand tort law at all."
41. Bava Basra 55a. This decision is tempered by certain conditions: that the law does not contradict specific Torah observances; that it is uniformly enforced and not just selectively against Jews; and that it not be an onerous, unjust, and immoral law.
42. Ibid.
43. Bava Basra 35a.
44. See Rashi and Tosfos there, Bava Basra 35a, as to how wide the latitude is that the judges have in deciding the matter. Rabeinu Tam is of the opinion that the judges may decide for either party as they see fit and are not beholden to any sort of standard of preponderance of evidence or likelihood of circumstance. Rashi is more conservative in his opinion and states that the judges must take into consideration which "way the case is going" in reaching their decision. Both Rashi and Tosfos agree that the judges have ultimate discretion in deciding the case under consideration.
45. Bava Kama 46a. Mar Shmuel there annunciates the classic legal rule *hamotzi m'chavero alav harayah* – one who wishes to retrieve property from the possession of another must bring convincing proofs to support his claim.
46. Literally, the majority. In monetary matters, it would mean considering what is the normal intent of most people in the circumstances under question. Mar Shmuel states that the majority has no effect on the particular case under consideration, since this case may fit the minority of situations and intents. Rabi Meir, the great *Tanna* of the Mishnah rejects the concept of *rov* in almost all instances of Torah law, including ritual law and prohibitions. The Talmud, however, does not agree with Rav Meir's opinion.
47. Bava Kama 46a-b.
48. Ibid.
49. Kesubos 76b.
50. Kesubos 43b.
51. Bava Metzia 12b.
52. Yerushalmi Gittin, chapter 4, section 3.
53. Bava Basra 139b.
54. Bava Kama 37a. See Rashi there, that the *beis din* – rabbinical court - automatically represents the interests of the orphans. The *pruzbul* was a legal mechanism designed by Hillel to allow the assignment of private loans to a court of law, and that this assignment thus prevented the private loans from

being canceled on the *Shemittah* sabbatical year. See Gittin 36a. Mar Shmuel did away with the necessity of orphans formally obtaining this *pruzbul* in order to keep their loans owed to them viable and collectible.

55. Bava Basra 144a.

56. Kesubos 77a.

57. Yevamos 61b.

58. Bava Metzia 70b.

59. Avodah Zarah 76b.

60. Berachos 56a; Sanhedrin 46b and 98a.

61. Succah 53a.

62. Moed Katan 26a.

63. Pesachim 54a.

64. See Rashi there in Pesachim 54a.

65. Avodah Zarah 39a.

66. This was in line with the words that Rav said to him that he would not have living sons. See Shabbos 108b. Eliezer Shteinman, in *Be'er HaTalmud* (Tel Aviv: Masada Press, 1967), volume 3, p. 246, contends that Mar Shmuel had two sons who died during his lifetime. However, he cites no source for this.

67. The question of redeeming kidnapped Jews and at what cost appears numerous times in the Talmud. The main discussion regarding this matter is found in Gittin, beginning on folio 45a.

68. Had they been raped or seduced by their captors, they could no longer marry a *kohen* and their legitimacy to marry generally might be problematic.

69. This is in line with the Talmud's principle that *hapeh she'asar hu hapeh she'hiytir* – since the court would be unaware of the fact that they were once hostages, now freed, except by their own statement of that fact, they are also therefore believed to testify that they were not sexually violated when they were held captive. See Kesubos 23a.

70. Kesubos 23a.

71. Yerushalmi Kesubos, chapter 2, section 6.

72. Ibid. Naftal, volume 2, p. 202, is of the opinion that Mar Shmuel's attempt in Babylonia to regulate the calendar for a 60-year span (Chulin 95b) brought down the judgment of Heaven against his family. As to the objections of the rabbis of the Land of Israel to the establishment of the calendar by the rabbis living outside the Land of Israel, see Berachos 63a.

73. Bava Basra 149a. See Rashi there who apparently associates the story of Isur and Rachel with the incident of Shmuel's other daughters, as recorded in Kesubos 23a. However, from the Yerushalmi quoted in note 71 above, it appears that that incident and the story of Isur and Rachel are unrelated to the story of Mar Shmuel's other daughters. See also Rashi, Berachos 16a and Rashi, Bava Metzia 73b. The Talmud refers to Isur as Isur *giyura* – Isur the convert.

74. See Bava Basra 149a; Yevamos 45b; Bava Metzia 73b; Shabbos 124b; Chulin 112b; Taanis 24b; and Berachos 16a.

75. Isur is mentioned in connection with Rava of the fourth generation of *Amoraim* (Bava Basra 149a) and Rav Mari is mentioned with Rav Ashi of the fifth generation of *Amoraim* (Yevamos 92b).

76. Kiddushin 65b.

77. See Bechoros 39a.

78. Sanhedrin 28b.

79. Nedarim 81a.

80. Bava Metzia 107b. However, see Yerushalmi Shabbos, chapter 14, where Mar

Shmuel joins Rav Chanina in the opinion that 99% of people die from "cold."

81. Shabbos 108b.
82. Ibid.
83. Shabbos 133b.
84. Kesubos 110b; Sanhedrin 101a, and many other places in the Talmud and Midrash.
85. Shabbos 152b.
86. Berachos 62a.
87. Taanis 11a.
88. Nedarim 50b.
89. Shabbos 129a-b. Despite the accepted prevalence of bloodletting to purge the body of illnesses, the Talmud had a very low opinion of those who engaged in that profession as their livelihood. See Kiddushin 82a.
90. Shabbos 128b and 129; Avodah Zarah 28b. See also Shabbos 148a, where Mar Shmuel allows the setting of a broken bone on Shabbos, apparently in opposition to the opinion rendered in the *Mishnah* quoted in Shabbos 147a.
91. Bava Metzia 113b. See also Shabbos 41a.
92. For example, see Chulin 21a, 45b, 46a, 48a and many other places in Talmud.
93. Chulin 45b.
94. Chulin 76b.
95. Chulin 94b.
96. Kiddushin 70a.
97. Yoma 22b.
98. Kiddushin 70b. See Rashi there who states, "By exchanging regards and pleasantries through an intermediary, they may eventually come to develop a fond relationship one with the other."
99. Berachos 61a.
100. Bava Basra 133a.
101. Bava Basra 3b.
102. Shabbos 56b.
103. Berachos 34b. Rambam in *Mishneh Torah*, *Hilchos Melachim*, also subscribes to this view.
104. For example, see Beitzah 31a and many other places in the Talmud. Regarding the interpretation of *chisurei mechsara*, see Tosfos, Shabbos 102a that the phrase does not actually mean that there are words missing from the text of the Mishnah, but rather that it should be interpreted in this new fashion. However, see Rashbam, Pesachim 106a, where he implies that the phrase *chisurei mechsara* actually means that the text had words missing from it. This is also the opinion of Tosfos in Nazir 10a.
105. Midrash Rabah, Devarim, chapter 8, section 7.
106. Rosh Hashanah 20b, and see Rashi there.
107. Shabbos 156b. His statement *ein mazal l'Yisrael* – literally meaning that there is no constellation or sign of the zodiac that influences the events of the Jewish people – in later generations came to be a folk-saying meaning that the Jewish people, individually and collectively, have no good luck. This latter interpretation was certainly not the intent of Mar Shmuel's words, but rather a rueful comment upon the state of the Jewish people during the long exile. The Talmud in Shabbos 156a quotes an opinion that there is *mazal l'Yisrael* and also quotes other opinions, including that of Rav, that agree with Mar Shmuel that there is no *mazal l'Yisrael*.
108. Berachos 55a.

109. Pesachim 54a and other places in the Talmud.
110. See Rashi there in Pesachim 54a.
111. Shabbos 53a. Rashi there indicates that this is a title given to a king. It was granted to Mar Shmuel because of his expertise and authority in matters of monetary disputes and torts.
112. Kesubos 43b.
113. Rashi there in Kesubos 43b.
114. Iggeres Rav Sherira Gaon, Levin edition, p. 82. See footnote 124 in the chapter on Rav for a possible earlier date of death.
115. Ibid.
116. See their discussions in, for example, Berachos 56a and Sanhedrin 98a.
117. Bava Metzia 70b.
118. Avodah Zarah 76b.
119. Ibid.
120. Moed Katan 26a.
121. Ibid.
122. Kesubos 51b; Yerushalmi Trumos, chapter 8.
123. Tosefta Nazir, chapter 4, section 10; Niddah 56b; Yevamos 16a-b.
124. Midrash Rabah Bereshis, chapter 56, section 19.
125. Naftal, volume 2, p. 39, quotes early Church fathers who stated that the queen was of Jewish descent! See also Yerushalmi Trumos, chapter 8 regarding her sparing the life of a Jewish scholar.

SECTION II

Rabi Yochanan

1. See the commentary of Rabbi Yitzchak Alfasi (Rif) to the Babylonian Talmud at the end of Meseches Eiruvin. Nevertheless, Rambam, in his *Mishneh Torah*, sometimes follows the Jerusalem Talmud in his halachic rulings over the opinion of the Babylonian Talmud.
2. See Naftal, *HaTalmud V'yotzrav, Doros HaAmoraim*, (Tel Aviv: Yavneh Publishing House, 1972), volume 6, chapter 4 for a discussion of the differences between the two Aramaic dialects.
3. See Naftal, volume 6, p. 41 for examples of this.
4. Yerushalmi Beitzah, chapter 5, section 2. They characterized their own Torah stature as being significant due to their having once seen "Rabi's finger peeking out from under his sleeve."
5. Chulin 137b.
6. Chulin 54a.
7. Yoma 82b. See also Megillah 6a where Rabi Yochanan relates a teaching that found favor in the eyes of his teachers while he was yet a young child. Rabi Yochanan was born in Tzipori, the home of Rabi and of Rabi's yeshivah during the latter period of Rabi's life.
8. Kiddushin 31b.
9. Yerushalmi Maasros, chapter 1, section 2. Throughout the Talmud, Rabi Yochanan is known as *bar Nafcha*. See, for example, Sanhedrin 96a, Bava Metzia 85b and Kesubos 25b. At Sanhedrin 96a, Rashi interprets the name as meaning the son of a blacksmith (*nafcha* in Aramaic – a bellows operator). Rashi there

also offers an alternative explanation that *nafcha* was a term of description of Rabi Yochanan's unusual beauty.

10. Yitzchak Isaac Halevi, *Doros HaRishonim* (Warsaw, 1896) section two, p. 309.
11. Berachos 5b. There is an opinion that Rabi Yochanan had an eleventh son, Masna, whom he sent to Nehardea, Babylonia, to study in the yeshivah of Mar Shmuel. See the gloss to the Babylonian Talmud of Rav Nissim Gaon, there at Berachos 5b. It appears that Rabi Yochanan also had daughters. See Kiddushin 71b and Yerushalmi Gittin, chapter 7, section 6, where his daughters are mentioned.
12. Rashbam, Bava Basra 116a.
13. Berachos 5b.
14. Halevi, section 2, pp. 308-9.
15. Berachos 45b.
16. Chulin 54a.
17. Yoma 43b.
18. Bava Basra 57b.
19. Eiruvin 53a. He is not to be confused with Rav Oshiya who was of the next generation of *Amoraim* and was a student of Rav Huna, Rav Chisda and Rabi Yochanan. Our Rabi Hoshiyahu here taught Torah in Caesarea and Rav Ami was one of his students.
20. Chulin 141a-b. The *breisos* were a collection of opinions and laws, elucidations and discussions, all based on the Mishnah of Rabi.
21. Yerushalmi Kiddushin, chapter 1, section 3; Yerushalmi Bava Kama, chapter 4, section 6. Rabi Yochanan compared Rabi Oshiya to Rabi Meir of an earlier generation in that both were so great and deeply analytical in their thinking – and thus were able to argue for any given position on any matter, even when those positions contradicted each other. This very greatness precluded their colleagues from fully understanding them and thus the *halachah* was not established according to their opinions. See Eiruvin 53a.
22. Yerushalmi Kesubos, chapter 9, section 5.
23. Yerushalmi Kilayim, chapter 8, section 1.
24. Yerushalmi Horayos, chapter 3, section 4. See also Berachos 5b where it is related that Rabi Chanina "raised" Rabi Yochanan from a painful illness. See also Midrash Shir HaShirim Rabah, chapter 2, section 35, where apparently Rabi Yochanan is the one visiting Rabi Chanina, the latter being the one suffering the pain of the illness.
25. Eiruvin 53a.
26. Kiddushin 33a. He stated that, "What many experiences must have passed over him [in his many years of life!]" He also stated that one always should greet others with a smile. See Kesubos 111b.
27. Bava Metzia 84a, and see Tosfos there. He had long, beautiful eyelashes and perfect eyebrows.
28. Ibid.
29. Ibid.
30. Kesubos 62a.
31. Berachos 5a.
32. Midrash Rabah, Vayikra, chapter 30, section 1; Yalkut Shimoni, Parshas Mishpatim, section 333.
33. Yalkut Shimoni there.
34. Midrash Rabah there.
35. Kesubos 50a, and see Rashi there.

36. Taanis 21a.
37. Ibid.
38. Ibid. See the introduction to Rabbi Reuven Margoliyus' commentary to Sanhedrin, *Margoliyus HaYam,* where he advances the idea that due to the personality and attitudes of Ilfa, he did not wish to be appointed the head of the yeshivah and therefore willingly arranged for the appointment of Rabi Yochanan to that post. See Rashi in Taanis 21a that Ilfa was greater in Torah knowledge than Rabi Yochanan.
39. Yerushalmi Berachos, chapter 5, section 1.
40. Halevi, volume 2, p. 310.
41. Ibid. It is Halevi's opinion that Rabi Yochanan died in 289 CE. Our text of Iggeres Rav Sherira Gaon, Levin edition, p. 84, suggests 280 CE as his year of death.
42. Instances of this may be found in many places in the Talmud. See, for example, Bava Metzia 40a-b; Pesachim 55a; Bava Kama 41a; Shabbos 109a; Pesachim 49a.
43. Berachos 10a.
44. Berachos 6b.
45. Berachos 7b. The "war of Gog and Magog" is the fearsome struggle between nations predicted in prophecy as being the onset of the "end of days." See also Rabi Yochanan's statement at Pesachim 118a regarding the war of Gog and Magog.
46. Ibid.
47. Berachos 34b. However, see there Rabi Abahu's opinion that the penitent is held to be greater than the one who was pious all of one's life. This view stands in disagreement with the view of Rabi Yochanan.
48. Ibid.
49. Berachos 43b.
50. Pesachim 53b.
51. Pesachim 113a.
52. Pesachim 87b.
53. Yoma 9b.
54. Ibid.
55. Sanhedrin 90b.
56. Yevamos 79a.
57. Yerushalmi Berachos, chapter 5, section 1.
58. Eiruvin 100b.
59. Niddah 16b.
60. Bava Basra 12b.
61. Rosh Hashanah 23a.
62. Bava Metzia 59a.
63. Succah 53a.
64. Yerushalmi Kesubos, chapter 11, section 3.
65. Yerushalmi Peah, chapter 1, section 1.
66. Sanhedrin 98b. Many other scholars of the Talmud echoed this sentiment.
67. Sanhedrin 42a. See also Yerushalmi Peah, chapter 2, section 4.
68. Shabbos 114a.
69. Ibid.
70. Sanhedrin 99b.
71. Menachos 99b.
72. Eiruvin 55a.
73. Megillah 32a.

74. Nedarim 62a.
75. Sanhedrin 99b.
76. Berachos 11b, 16b, 59a.
77. Avodah Zarah 39a. This is probably the origin of the famous Yiddish expression that even the non-Jewish maid who works in the house of the rabbi is competent to decide questions of Jewish law.
78. Yerushalmi Kesubos, chapter 5, section 5.
79. Midrash Bereshis Rabah, chapter 96, section 9.
80. Bava Metzia 30b.
81. Yoma 86a.
82. Chagigah 15b.
83. Megillah 16a.
84. See his statement in Bava Basra 145b that a person who is overly soft and merciful is condemned to a life of "bad days."
85. Bava Kama 117a-b.
86. Ibid.
87. The halachic opinions of Rabi Yochanan supersede those of Rabi Shimon ben Lakish (Megillah 7a) and of Rav (Beitzah 4a.)
88. Eiruvin 46a. See Shabbos 112b and Sanhedrin 34b where Rabi Yochanan establishes the supremacy of a *stam mishnah* to determine the halachah – the law and practice of Israel. *Stam mishnah* is a *mishnah* where there is no dispute within it as to the law and it is not specifically attributed to the opinion of any one scholar.
89. Pesachim 113a.
90. Chulin 98a. The Talmud infers there that Mar Shmuel's sudden passing was ordained in Heaven in order to spare Rabi Yochanan this burdensome journey!
91. Sanhedrin 104b.
92. For example, see Sanhedrin 111a, that Jews can be saved from judgment in the grave if they studied and observed even one law of the Torah. See also there his interpretation that one or two righteous people in a family or city can save the entire family and city. His colleague, Rabi Shimon ben Lakish, has a less lenient interpretation of these verses.
93. After Rabi Meir died, an apparition of fire and smoke continually arose from the grave of Elisha ben Avuyah. When Rabi Yochanan died, the fire and smoke from the grave of Elisha ben Avuyah abated. See Chagigah 15b. Even "the keeper of the gate of Hell" had to honor the wishes of Rabi Yochanan.
94. See Shabbos 112b for another opinion that Rabi Yochanan is the perfect example of what a human being should be. If Rabi Yochanan is a "human being," then what is everyone else?
95. Bava Metzia 84a.
96. Moed Katan 25b.
97. Sanhedrin 96a.
98. Yerushalmi Avodah Zarah, chapter 3, section 1.
99. Moed Katan 25b.
100. Ibid.
101. Naftal, volume 6, p. 251. There is other opinion that Rabi Yochanan died c. 280 CE. See also footnote 10 and footnote 41 above.
102. See Chagigah 10a and the comments of Rabeinu Chananel there.
103. Berachos 7a.

Rabi Shimon Ben Lakish

1. See their common statements quoted in many places in the Talmud. For example, Berachos 33a; Shabbos 75b; Kesubos 84b.
2. Bava Metzia 84a.
3. Megillah 28b.
4. See Avraham Moshe Naftal, *HaTalmud V'yotzrav*, (Tel Aviv: Yavneh Publishing House, 1972), volume 6, p. 255.
5. See Shabbos 119b where he quotes Torah learned from his father's house.
6. Yerushalmi Beitzah, chapter 5, section 2.
7. Chulin 54a.
8. Naftal, volume 6, p. 256, states that we do not find Rabi Shimon ben Lakish quoting a teaching that he attributed to Rabi anywhere in the Talmud and concludes therefore that he cannot be reckoned as a true student of Rabi. He is of the opinion that the *halachah* that Reish Lakish attributed in our printed version of the Talmud to Rabi Yehudah HaNasi in Shabbos 130b refers to Rabi Yehudah Nesiah I, Rabi's grandson, and not to Rabi himself.
9. Rabeinu Tam in Tosfos, Bava Metzia 84a. See also Tosfos, Eiruvin 65b and Tosfos, Yevamos 57a to this effect, namely that Reish Lakish was already a Torah scholar before he changed his lifestyle and left the study of Torah.
10. Gittin 47a. Rashi there intimates that they were possibly cannibals as well.
11. Ibid.
12. Bava Metzia 84a.
13. Sanhedrin 26b. Nevertheless, we find in the Talmud that even later in life, Rabi Shimon ben Lakish was strong physically and bold in his behavior. See Yerushalmi Moed Katan, chapter 3, section 7, where he smites a Samaritan blasphemer, and Yerushalmi Trumos at the conclusion of chapter 8, where he frees Rav Iymi (Ami) from his kidnappers.
14. Bava Metzia 84a. See, for example, Bava Basra 154b, where Reish Lakish asks Rabi Yochanan to help in explaining to him a statement of Bar Kapara. Reish Lakish's asking Rabi Yochanan's for explanations and opinions is repeated many times in the Talmud.
15. Eiruvin 65b.
16. Pesachim 15a and other places in the Talmud.
17. See Reish Lakish's acceptance of condolences on the death of his teacher, Rabi Chiya bar Ada, Yerushalmi Berachos, chapter 2, section 5. See also Kesubos 111b, where Rabi Chiya bar Ada is mentioned as the teacher of Reish Lakish.
18. Eiruvin 65b.
19. Yerushalmi Moed Katan, chapter 2, section 4.
20. Bava Kama 9b-10a.
21. Eiruvin 11a-b.
22. Bava Metzia 10b.
23. Nazir 20b.
24. Pesachim 34b. Reish Lakish considered him the "father of the Mishnah." Yerushalmi Bava Kama, chapter 4, section 6.
25. Eiruvin 80a.
26. Succah 17b.
27. See Berachos 33a; Shabbos 75b; Kesubos 84b and numerous other places in the Talmud.
28. Yerushalmi Berachos, chapter 8, section 6.

29. Midrash Rabah Eichah, chapter 1, section 39.
30. Yoma 9a.
31. Kesubos 54b.
32. Bava Kama 117a, and see Rashi there.
33. Chagigah 16a. The name of the *meturgeman* appears to be Rabi Yehudah bar Nachmani. See Kesubos 8b.
34. Gittin 47a.
35. Kesubos 8b. See also Taanis 9a.
36. Taanis 9a. See Rashi there that Rabi Yochanan was impressed by the genius of the child. The child's mother was afraid of Rabi Yochanan's gaze after the incident that happened with her husband and Rabi Yochanan as related immediately below in this paragraph.
37. See Yerushalmi Berachos, chapter 2, section 8.
38. Kesubos 111b.
39. Yerushalmi Megillah, chapter 1, section 11.
40. Bava Metzia 84a.
41. See note 30 above that he was called "the strong person in the Land of Israel."
42. Yoma 9b. See also Shabbos 113b for his opinion that all of the corpses from the great flood were deposited in Babylonia.
43. Sanhedrin 26a. See Maharsha there that it was the custom of the great rabbis to sometimes use strong language to others when they felt that the situation needed such emphasis.
44. Yerushalmi Rosh Hashanah, chapter 2, section 5.
45. Yerushalmi Sanhedrin, chapter 2, section 1; Yerushalmi Horayos, chapter 3, section 1.
46. Niddah 41b; Shabbos 119b; Yerushalmi Pesachim, chapter 4, section 5.
47. Avodah Zarah 6b.
48. See Shabbos 119b; Yerushalmi Chagigah, chapter 1, section 7.
49. Shabbos 119b.
50. Yoma 72b.
51. Chulin 60b and Rashi there.
52. Menachos 99a-b and Rashi there.
53. Berachos 19a.
54. Bava Basra 16a.
55. Berachos 5a.
56. Eiruvin 19a; Chagigah 27a.
57. Sotah 47b.
58. Midrash Rabah Bereshis, chapter 34, section 15.
59. Kiddushin 44a.
60. Yerushalmi Berachos, chapter 5, section 1.
61. Taanis 8a.
62. Sanhedrin 24a.
63. Bava Metzia 84a.
64. Berachos 63b.
65. Eiruvin 65a.
66. Chagigah 12b.
67. Taanis 11b.
68. Midrash Rabah Shemos, chapter 35, section 1.
69. Eiruvin 18a.
70. Taanis 8a.
71. Yoma 9b.

72. Moed Katan 17a.
73. Gittin 47a.
74. Ibid.
75. Ibid.
76. Ibid. See Rashi there.
77. Megillah 28b.
78. Midrash Rabah Shir HaShirim, chapter 4, section 22.
79. Shabbos 63a.
80. Yoma 9b.
81. Shabbos 97a.
82. Pesachim 66b.
83. Sanhedrin 58a.
84. Eiruvin 19a.
85. Bava Metzia 107b.
86. Sotah 3a.
87. Shabbos 104a.
88. Menachos 99a.
89. Beitzah 16a.
90. Sanhedrin 99b.
91. Yerushalmi Berachos, chapter 9, section 5.
92. Yoma 86b.
93. Shabbos 88a.

Scholars of Caesarea

1. See Eiruvin 76b.
2. Megillah 6a.
3. Sanhedrin 30b
4. Kesubos 110b.
5. Taanis 13a.
6. Shabbos 97a.
7. See Berachos 10b: "A woman is a better judge of guests than a man." See also Sanhedrin 105b: "People are always jealous of others, except for the achievements of one's own child and/or student." Arachin 16b: "A traveler should not change his accustomed places of lodging." There are many more examples of Rabi Yosi bar Chanina's wisdom scattered throughout the Talmud.
8. See Berachos 5b.
9. Berachos 63b.
10. Bava Metzia 85b.
11. See Pesachim 100a, Shabbos 94b and dozens of places in Talmud Yerushalmi where Rabi Abahu quotes Rabi Yosi ben Chanina's opinions and teachings.
12. Yerushalmi Peah, chapter 1, section 1.
13. Sotah 40a.
14. Bava Metzia 84a.
15. See Kesubos 17a.
16. See Chagigah 14a.
17. For example, see Yerushalmi Megillah, chapter 3, section 2. He became the classic *shtadlan* – lobbyist – on behalf of Jewish interests.
18. Midrash Rabah, Shemos, chapter 29, section 4 (in some editions, section 5.] See

also other debates of his with Christians and apostate Jews in Shabbos 152b, Sanhedrin 39a and 99a, and Succah 48b.

19. Yerushalmi Yevamos, chapter 4, section 2.
20. Yerushalmi Peah, chapter 1, section 1.
21. Midrash Rabah, Koheles, chapter 7, section 35.
22. See this beautiful story in Yerushalmi Taanis, chapter 1, section 4.
23. See his statement regarding humility in Chulin 89a.
24. Bava Kama 93a.
25. Gittin 7a.
26. See Eiruvin 53b, for example.
27. Midrash Rabah, Koheles, chapter 10, section 23.
28. Yerushalmi Pesachim, chapter 3, section 7.
29. Kiddushin 33b. He is quoted numerous times in Talmud Yerushalmi.
30. Midrash Rabah, Bereshis, chapter 3, section 7; Yerushalmi Berachos, chapter 9, section 1.
31. Kesubos 85a.
32. Sanhedrin 99a; Avodah Zarah 34b; Chulin 63b.
33. Kiddushin 31b.
34. Ibid.
35. Yerushalmi Avodah Zarah, chapter 3, section 1.
36. Moed Katan 25b.
37. He was more of a colleague than an actual student. See Berachos 46a; Yerushalmi Beitzah, chapter 1, section 9.
38. A beloved student of Rabi Abahu, see Bava Metzia 16b. Also see Bava Basra 140a, Shavuos 21a.
39. He was also a disciple of Rabi Yirmiyahu. See Yerushalmi Berachos, chapter 2, section 3; Beitzah, chapter 5, section 2; Yoma, chapter 2, section 2.
40. Yerushalmi Sanhedrin, chapter 6, section 6.
41. Midrash Rabah, Bereshis, chapter 68, section 3.
42. Yerushalmi Sanhedrin, chapter 6, section 6.
43. Yoma 73a; Yevamos 65b.
44. Sotah 40a; Bava Basra 39a.
45. Sanhedrin 110a.
46. Berachos 34b.
47. Sanhedrin 99b.
48. Moed Katan 16b.

SECTION III

Rav Huna

1. Yerushalmi Succah, chapter 4, section 2.
2. Ibid. See also Yerushalmi Berachos, chapter 1, section 5.
3. Berachos 12a.
4. Yerushalmi Berachos, chapter 1, section 5. See also Kesubos 21a.
5. Succah 9a; Chulin 30a, and many other places in the Talmud. After the death of Rav, Rav Yehudah went to study with Rav Assi, who also passed away. He then came to study with Mar Shmuel. See Yevamos 16b-17a and Rashi there.
6. Rosh Hashanah 32a; Arachin 16b and many other places in the Talmud.

7. Chulin 127b.

8. Even Rav Yehudah bar Yechezkel, the *Rosh Yeshivah* of Pumbedisa, traveled to Sura to study with Rav Huna. See Chulin 111b. Another great sage of that generation, Rav Nachman bar Yaakov, also came to Sura periodically to study there with Rav Huna. See Niddah 28a. This was true as well for Rav Yirmiyahu bar Abba, another second-generation *Amora* who also journeyed to see and learn from Rav Huna. See Bava Basra 65b and 170b.

9. See Sanhedrin 5a, where Rav Huna's son, Rabah, traces his Torah tradition from his father through Rav, through Rav Chiya, and then back through Rabi. See also Shabbos 66b.

10. Sanhedrin 17b; also see Rashi, Yevamos 83b.

11. Iggeres Rav Sherira Gaon, Levin edition, p. 84.

12. Kesubos 106a.

13. Yevamos 64b and see Rashi there.

14. Kesubos 106a.

15. Ibid.

16. Megillah 27b.

17. Ibid.

18. Ibid.

19. Ibid.

20. Yerushalmi Sanhedrin, chapter 1, section 1.

21. Kesubos 105a.

22. Yerushalmi Sanhedrin, chapter 1, section 1.

23. See notes 20-22 directly above.

24. Under ideal circumstances, when these officials were able to support themselves without receiving a salary from the community, no payment was to be made to them. This is in accord with the statement of the Talmud in Bechoros 29a that we are to emulate Moshe who taught Torah to Israel without receiving any monetary compensation. Therefore, most of the scholars and teachers of the times of the Talmud, and later times as well (in fact, until the later Middle Ages,) supported themselves independently of their public and educational duties. As the long exile of Israel deepened, the situation changed, and by the fifteenth century, it was common for all public functionaries of the Jewish community to receive a salary for their services – *schar batala* – from the community's coffers.

25. Yerushalmi Moed Katan, chapter 1, section 8. See also Bava Basra 125b, where Rav Huna is called "great" in comparison to other scholars of the time. See also Gittin 59b where it is stated that Rav Ami and Rav Assi, the leading scholars of the Land of Israel at that time, deferred to Rav Huna in halachic matters.

26. Sanhedrin 17b.

27. Taanis 23b.

28. Berachos 57a.

29. Moed Katan 25a.

30. Berachos 5b; Taanis 20b.

31. He always ate with his house door open so that anyone hungry could enter and share his meal. See Taanis 20b. He also stated that one who only studies and does not engage in any charitable acts at all is comparable to "one who has no God!" See Avodah Zarah 17b.

32. Again, see Taanis 20b, that Rav Huna would pay for public repairs out of his own pocket and that he would buy the leftover market vegetables on Friday afternoon so that the vegetable vendors would not hesitate to continue bringing

sufficient stock on Fridays to sell for Shabbos use.

33. Yerushalmi Maaser Sheini, chapter 5, section 3 and see Pnei Moshe there.
34. Megillah 27a-b.
35. Shabbos 151b. This seems to be directed towards students of yeshivos who are lax in their studies and pursue other activities.
36. Shabbos 63b.
37. Yerushalmi Chagigah, chapter 1, section 7.
38. Menachos 110a.
39. Gittin 6a.
40. For example, see Eiruvin 79a; Yoma 14b and 16a; Yerushalmi Gittin, chapter 8, section 5. In this, he continued the example of his mentor, Rav, who also sought to attribute statements in the Mishnah to their original authors. See Arachin 20b; Horayos 5a; Shabbos 107b; Kesubos 29a and many other places in the Talmud.
41. For example, "A person who has fear of Heaven will have his opinions heard here on earth" (Berachos 6b); "When one becomes accustomed to committing a sin on a regular basis, then one no longer deems the act to be a sin at all" (Yoma 87a); "The Lord allows one to go on the path that one chooses" (Makkos 10b); "One who eats from a wedding feast and does not participate in helping make the bride and groom joyful transgresses the five 'sounds' [that appear in the prophet Yirmiyahu]" (Berachos 6b); "He who is stringent for others, but lenient regarding himself is piously foolish (Sotah 21b) or cunningly wicked"(Yerushalmi Sotah, chapter 3, section 4); and, "One should never walk away from the synagogue hurriedly." (Berachos 6b) Rav Huna's many sayings are scattered over hundreds of pages throughout the Talmud.
42. Kiddushin 29b.
43. Gittin 86b; Moed Katan 25a and 28a.
44. Moed Katan 25a.
45. Ibid.
46. Ibid.
47. Nazir 57b; Bava Kama 80a.
48. Avodah Zarah 89a.
49. Shevuos 30b.
50. Megillah 27b.
51. For example, see Kiddushin 30a; Sotah 49b; Shabbos 10a and Gittin 36a. He was especially noted for his pure modesty. See Moed Katan 28a.
52. See Shabbos 150a.
53. Niddah 31b, and other places in the Talmud.

Rav Chisda

1. Iggeres Rav Sherira Gaon, Levin edition, p. 85.
2. Moed Katan 28a.
3. Berachos 44a.
4. Yevamos 21b.
5. Shabbos 140b; Bava Kama 91b.
6. Pesachim 113a; Moed Katan 28a; Shabbos 62b.
7. Shabbos 140b.
8. Ibid.

9. Pesachim 113a.

10. Pesachim 88a and 107a.

11. Kiddushin 29b.

12. Nedarim 41a.

13. Shabbos 152a.

14. Yoma 75b; Moed Katan 28a.

15. Shabbos 119a.

16. Moed Katan 28a.

17. Berachos 38b.

18. Succah 33a; Taanis 12b.

19. See Eiruvin 16b, where Rav Chisda calls Mar Shmuel *rabeinu,* our teacher.

20. Berachos 55b; Taanis 12b.

21. Berachos 43a; Sanhedrin 69b.

22. Menachos 78a.

23. Chulin 63a.

24. Eiruvin 62b: Bava Metzia 6b.

25. Berachos 29b; Shabbos 116b.

26. Succah 16b; Kesubos 71b, 72b and other places in the Talmud. He is not to be confused with Avimei, the son of Rabi Abahu, nor with a later Avimei who was a student of Abaye and Rava.

27. Arachin 22a; Menachos 7a.

28. Menachos 7a.

29. Pesachim 117a; Yevamos 25b; Avodah Zarah 27b and other places in the Talmud.

30. These were the *rabanan nechosei* (Berachos 38b) – the scholars who "went down" from the Land of Israel to Babylonia, transmitting the Torah insights of the yeshivos located in the Land of Israel to those of Babylonia. See Avraham Moshe Naftal, *HaTalmud V'yotzrav,* (Tel Aviv: Yavneh Publishing House, 1972), volume 3, p. 85 and also p. 269 and 273.

31. Shabbos 10b.

32. Makkos 10a. See Shabbos 30b where a similar incident regarding King David is recorded.

33. Gittin 7a.

34. Shabbos 82a.

35. Bava Metzia 33a.

36. Ibid. See Maharsha there, where he explains that they were separated for 40 years because of this misunderstanding and therefore they each fasted for 40 days – a day per year of separation. See also Rabeinu Chananel there in Bava Metzia that the 40-day period was in itself symbolic of the fact that a student does not really appreciate the lessons of his teacher until 40 years have passed. (Avodah Zarah 5b.)

37. A detailed description regarding him will follow in this section of the book.

38. Iggeres Rav Sherira Gaon, Levin edition, p. 85.

39. Ibid.

40. Yoma 71b.

41. Eiruvin 21b.

42. Chulin 44a, and see Rashi there.

43. Eiruvin 65a.

44. Eiruvin 54b.

45. Gittin 36a.

46. Avodah Zarah 17a.

47. Megillah 15b.

48. Rosh Hashanah 17a.
49. Gittin 6b.
50. Sanhedrin 103a.
51. Shabbos 33a.
52. Bava Metzia 59a.
53. Berachos 55a.
54. Bava Basra 3b. This is a good rule in life for all matters, not only synagogue buildings.
55. Moed Katan 9b.
56. Bava Basra 141a.
57. Bava Basra 141a.
58. Berachos 44a.
59. Bava Basra 12b. See Maharsha there.
60. Shabbos 140b.
61. He is called this throughout the Talmud, always with his patrimony. When the Talmud refers to a Rav Nachman without indicating who his father was, it is almost always referring to Rav Nachman bar Yaakov, the *Rosh Yeshivah* and judge in Pumbedisa in the fourth century. Rav Nachman bar Rav Chisda studied with that Rav Nachman bar Yaakov after the death of his father, and considered him one of his main mentors. See Kesubos 104b; Bava Basra 46b. He also was in contact with Rabah bar Nachmani, also a *Rosh Yeshivah* in fourth century Pumbedisa. See Gittin 80b. Rav Nachman bar Rav Chisda's sayings and teachings appear throughout the Talmud. For examples, see Berachos 61a, Succah 56a and other places in the Talmud.
62. Apparently he was named after his grandfather, Rav Chisda's father-in-law, Rav Chanan bar Rava, who was Rav's son-in-law.
63. Shabbos 45a; Avodah Zarah 11b.
64. Gittin 31b.
65. Kiddushin 32b; Kesubos 61a.
66. Kesubos 89b. Rashi there is of the opinion that Rav Chisda had two sons who had similar names and therefore one was called "*yenuka*" – the younger, and the other was called "*kashisha*" – the elder one, to differentiate between them. However, Tosfos there is of the opinion that Mar Yenuka was the older one, born while Rav Chisda was younger and Mar Kashisha was the younger one, born when Rav Chisda was older. Thus, according to Tosfos, the names "*yenuka*" – younger, and "*kashisha*" – older, refer to Rav Chisda's age at the times of the birth of these two sons and do not refer to the sons themselves.
67. Bava Basra 7b; Kesubos 89b.
68. Bava Kama 117a.
69. See Kesubos 21b; Beitzah 29b.
70. Sotah 3b.
71. Bava Basra 25b.
72. Sanhedrin 38a.
73. Taanis 7b.
74. Berachos 29b.
75. Shabbos 119b.
76. Berachos 8a.
77. Shabbos 152a.
78. Chulin 44b. This concept of being able to see and decide against one's own self-interest has been expanded by the ethical teachers of Israel to include the ability to recognize one's own "non-kosher" personal faults and behavior

characteristics, and to attempt to correct them.
79. As mentioned, Rav Chisda lived 92 years. See Moed Katan 28a.
80. Moed Katan 25a.

Rav Yehudah Bar Yechezkel

1. Kiddushin 72b.
2. Ibid.
3. Kiddushin 33b.
4. See Yerushalmi Taanis, chapter 1, section 3.
5. For example, see Shabbos 22a; Bava Kama 39a; Kesubos 105a, and other places in the Talmud.
6. Kiddushin 81a.
7. Eiruvin 2b.
8. Rashi, Chulin 44a.
9. See Avraham Moshe Naftal, *HaTalmud V'yotzrav*, (Tel Aviv: Yavneh Publishing House, 1972) volume 3, p. 123.
10. See Niddah 36b.
11. Niddah 13a.
12. Chagigah 15b, and many other places in the Talmud. An alternative explanation of the word *shinanah*, relating to the prominent teeth of Rav Yehudah, quoting Rav Hai Gaon, is found in Iggeres Rav Sherira Gaon, Levin edition, p. 78, note 1. See also *Aruch HaShalem*, in the section devoted to the word *"shen."*
13. Bava Metzia 40a.
14. Iggeres Rav Sherira Gaon, Levin edition, p. 85. Among them were Rav Abba, Rav Zeira, Rav Kahana, Rabah bar Nachmani, and Rav Yosef, all prime disciples of Rav Huna at Sura. See Naftal, volume 3, p. 129.
15. Rashi, Gittin 19b.
16. See Chulin 110a-b.
17. Bava Metzia 38b.
18. Pesachim 66b. See also Berachos 55a.
19. See Kesubos 21a, Chulin 44a, and other places in the Talmud.
20. Chulin 18b.
21. For example, see Bava Basra 21a; Shabbos 13b; Sanhedrin 13b; Chagigah 23a; Gittin 58a; Avodah Zarah 32a; and many other places in the Talmud.
22. Berachos 20a. See also Rashi, Taanis 24b.
23. Bava Kama 30a.
24. See for example Beitzah 33b, Nedarim 20a, and many other places in the Talmud.
25. He often uses the phrase *hachei kaamar* – "this is what the Mishnah really means" – or *hacha katani* – "this is the way the Mishnah is to be learned" – and like his teacher Mar Shmuel, the phrase *chisurei mechsara* – "there are words missing in our text of the Mishnah" (See note 104 in the chapter on Mar Shmuel for a more detailed discussion of this phrase.) For examples, see Kiddushin 29a; Bava Basra 139a; Sanhedrin 26a; Nedarim 20a; Beitzah 31b, and many other places in the Talmud.
26. Nazir 23b.
27. Shabbos 64b.
28. Yoma 22b.

29. Eiruvin 65a. The other opinion there is that night was created for Torah study. However, this latter opinion literally states that the moon was created in order to allow for Torah study at night and thus these two opinions may not really be contradictory to each the other.
30. Bava Basra 89b.
31. Bava Basra 165a.
32. Bava Metzia 59a.
33. Shabbos 118b.
34. Rosh Hashanah 35a.
35. Berachos 30b.
36. Shabbos 118b.
37. See Yevamos 63b and Taanis 13b.
38. See the later chapter regarding Abayei for more information on Isai and his family.
39. A student of Rav and a teacher of Rav Chisda. See Menachos 7a, Arachin 22a. See the earlier section on Rav Chisda in this work.
40. Yevamos 83b.
41. A disciple of both Rav and Mar Shmuel. See Berachos 42b and Avodah Zarah 40a. He is not to be confused with Rav Ada bar Ahava II who was a student of Rava and a member of the fourth generation of *Amoraim*.
42. Also a disciple of Rav. See Shabbos 119a. Again, he is also is not to be confused with Rav Ada bar Masna II who was a student of Abayei and Rava and a member of the fourth generation of *Amoraim*. Rav Ada bar Masna II lived a long life and thus was also a colleague of Rav Papa and Ravina in the fifth generation of *Amoraim*.
43. Succah 26a.
44. A disciple of Rav and later of Rav Huna. See Kiddushin 59a and Yevamos 64b.
45. Another disciple of Rav. See Pesachim 103a.
46. Rav treated him as an equal. See Yerushalmi Avodah Zarah, chapter 2, section 8. He was a man of wealth and influence, but he engaged in a bitter dispute with Mar Ukva, the *Reish Galusa*/Exilarch, and as a result was arrested by the governmental authorities and executed. See Gittin 7a.
47. Zevachim 36b. Another scholar by the same name flourished two generations later in the time of Rava. See Bava Basra 13b.
48. A disciple mainly of Mar Shmuel. Kesubos 60a, Niddah 66a. See Berachos 45b where he quotes a teaching of Rav.
49. A disciple of Rav. See Bava Kama 106a.
50. Another disciple of Rav. See Yevamos 21a. He originally studied in the Land of Israel under Rav Chanina bar Chama before coming to Babylonia to study under Rav. See Shabbos 17a, Kesubos 16a.
51. See Kiddushin 81a.
52. See Midrash Rabah, Bamidbar, chapter 9, section 38, regarding his efforts to ransom female Jewish captives.
53. Rav's son. See the earlier chapter on Rav regarding further details about him.
54. A premier student of Rav, as well as a sometimes teacher of Rav Chisda. See Menachos 78a; Bava Metzia 65a; Midrash Rabah, Bereshis, chapter 92, section 1.
55. A famed philanthropist, whose home was always open to all guests and wayfarers. See Berachos 58b. He was a student of Rav Huna, who regarded him highly. See Megillah 28a.
56. A disciple of Rav. See Yoma 41b, Nedarim 7b.
57. Nedarim 61b, Bava Kama 96b.

58. A son-in-law of Rav. See Rosh Hashanah 22a; Chulin 95b; Shabbos 66a.
59. Rav's faithful student. See Pesachim 103a; Chulin 86b; Menachos 31b. He was a scribe. See Megillah 18b, Moed Katan 19a.
60. A disciple of Rav. See Bava Metzia 94a, Yerushalmi Eiruvin, chapter 8, section 6.
61. A disciple of Mar Shmuel. See Shabbos 13a; Kesubos 6a; Gittin 52b.
62. Also a disciple of Mar Shmuel. See Yevamos 40b; Kesubos 64a; Nedarim 12b.
63. Studied under Rav Brona and Rav Chananel, who were disciples of Rav. See Pesachim 103a.
64. A student and colleague of Rav. See Berachos 27b. Later a colleague and teacher of Rav Yehudah bar Yechezkel (Shabbos 150a) and Rav Chisda (Berachos 55b). Tosfos, Kiddushin 46a, states that there is a second scholar in the next generation of *Amoraim*, a student of Rav Huna, also named Rav Yirmiyahu bar Abba.
65. One of the primary students of Rav. See Bava Metzia 64a. Naftal, volume 3, p. 168, points out that there are at least 50 scholars throughout the times of the Talmud who were called Kahana! It was undoubtedly a common name for *kohanim*, descendants of the priestly family of Aharon, analogous to the name Cohen in more modern times. For information on Rav Kahana I, see the earlier chapter on Rabi Yehudah HaNasi and his students in the first section of the book dealing with the *Tannaim*, as discussed in Oral Law of Sinai, the companion volume to this work
66. A student of Rav and later of Rav Huna. See Shevuos 45b; Menachos 108b; Yevamos 19b.
67. A student of Rav. See Pesachim 68a.
68. The Exilarch during the time of Rav, Mar Shmuel and later Rav Huna. He was a person of strong character and great erudition and was well respected by the rabbis of his time. See Kesubos 69a.
69. Tosfos, Gittin 31b, states that he is the Rav Nachman who is referred to throughout the Talmud. He was famed as the expert in commercial and monetary matters in the Talmud. See Kesubos 13a. His main sphere of activity was during the next (third) generation of *Amoraim*.
70. A student of Rav. See Bava Metzia 41a, Beitzah 32b.
71. A student of Rabi Yochanan in Tiberias. See Shabbos 102b. Later moved to Babylonia and is recorded in discussions with Rav Yehudah bar Yechezkel (Kiddushin 32a) and Rav Chisda (Yevamos 89a).
72. Also a disciple of Rabi Yochanan in Tiberias. See Chagigah 19a, Nedarim, 22a, and other places in the Talmud. He was one of the *rabanan nechusei* – a number of scholars from the Land of Israel who regularly traveled between the Land of Israel and Babylonia, cross-pollinating the yeshivos of both countries with teachings from the other country. See Berachos 38b. He was buried in Babylonia. See Yerushalmi Kilayim, chapter 9, at the end of section 3.
73. One of the elders of Pumbedisa with Rav Yehudah bar Yechezkel. See Sanhedrin 17b.
74. A student of Rav. See Pesachim 105a; Moed Katan 19b; Nedarim 28a. A later *Amora* has the same name.
75. A disciple of Mar Shmuel. See Eiruvin 95a; Gittin 44b; Chulin 4b. He was also one of the judges on the *beis din* of Nehardea. See Kesubos 105b.
76. A student of Mar Shmuel. See Pesachim 101a.
77. A student of Rav. See Kiddushin 71b, Menachos 33b.
78. He was a disciple of Rav Yochanan and one of the *rabanan nechusei* mentioned in footnote 72. He is not to be confused with Rabah bar Chana, the colleague

of Rav in the previous generation. See Naftal, volume 3, p. 170, that there is an opinion that Rabah bar bar Chana was actually the son of Rabah bar Chana. There are numerous stories regarding him in the Talmud. See Berachos 44a; Gittin 16b; Bava Metzia 83a; Pesachim 51a; Shabbos 148a. He is also well known for his fantastic stories, which contained within them hidden meanings. See Bava Basra 73a.

79. Berachos 59a.

80. The son of the great Rav Huna.

81. Avodah Zarah 16b; Pesachim 36a; Gittin 74a.

82. The younger brother of Rav Yehudah bar Yechezkel. See Sanhedrin 80b. In the Talmud Yerushalmi, he is called Ami bar Yechezkel. See Yerushalmi Eiruvin, chapter 5, section 1. He studied with Rav Huna (Shabbos 138b) and Rav Amram (Eiruvin 102a).

83. A colleague of Rav Chisda and Rav Nachman and a primary student of Rav Huna. See Kesubos 69a, Bava Basra 85b. He was erudite in all of the works of Torah. See Shevuos 41b. He was "iron" – hard and sharp in his ability to decide halachic questions. See Rashi, Menachos 95b. Rav Sheishes and Rav Chisda complemented each other while learning Torah, with Rav Sheishes being the one with encyclopedic knowledge of the sources and texts, while Rav Chisda was the innovative and creative sharp interpreter of those texts. See Eiruvin 67a. Rav Sheishes was sightless in his later years, but nevertheless continued teaching. See Berachos 58b. He reviewed all of the texts that he had committed to memory every 30 days. See Pesachim 68b. Though he never officially headed a yeshivah, he had many students and disciples. He praised work, and was engaged in the timber trade. See Gittin14a and 67b. He was of delicate physique and character. See Pesachim 108a. His senses were so sharp that he could test the ritual knife of a *shochet* for minute imperfections of smoothness of the blade with his tongue. See Chulin 17b. He experienced the holy spirit of God (Megillah 29a) and identified the Angel of Death while walking in the marketplace (Moed Katan 29a). His discussions and wisdom appear throughout the Talmud. In matters of ritual and things which are allowed or forbidden to eat, the law is according to Rav Sheishes. In matters pertaining to commerce and money, the law follows the opinion of Rav Nachman. See Tosfos, Eiruvin 32a.

84. A disciple of Mar Shmuel. See Chulin 107b; Pesachim 107a; Avodah Zarah 6a; Bava Basra 8b.

SECTION IV

Rabah Bar Nachmani

1. Berachos 64a.

2. Bava Metzia 86a.

3. Berachos 64a. However, both Rav Yosef and Rabah agreed on the necessity for constant new insights in Torah and prayer. See Berachos 29a. They differed in their approach and methodology, but not in purpose. Torah without *chidush* – new insights and understandings – is simply not the living Torah.

4. Ibid.

5. Ibid.

6. Ibid. See also Yitzchak Isaac Halevi, *Doros HaRishonim* (Warsaw, 1896), section

2, p. 435 onwards.

7. Ibid.

8. Rosh Hashana 18a.

9. Shmuel I, 2:31 and 2:33.

10. Rosh Hashana 18a.

11. See Halevi, section 2, p. 435 onwards. See also Eliezer Shteinman *Be'er HaTalmud* (Tel Aviv: Masada Press, 1967) volume 4, pp. 68-9. Rabah apparently died in the year 321 CE. See Avraham Moshe Naftal, *HaTalmud V'yotzrav*, (Tel Aviv:Yavneh Publishing House,1972) volume 3, pp. 203-7. See also Iggeres Rav Sherira Gaon, Levin edition, pp. 85-7.

12. One of his brothers who died young was Baylil (Kaylil), the father of the great Abayei. See Rashi, Zevachim 118b. His other brothers were Rabi Oshiya and Rabi Chanina. See Maharsha, Sanhedrin 14a.

13. See Kesubos 111a. See Tosfos, Eiruvin, 22b that Rabah did, in fact, journey to the Land of Israel and there studied Torah at the feet of Rabi Yochanan. See also Tosfos, Bava Basra 155a.

14. See especially Sanhedrin 104a-b. See also Bava Basra 75b; Makkos 16b; and Avodah Zarah 27b.

15. As did his colleague, Rabi Zeira who stayed in the Land of Israel for the rest of his life. See the coming chapter regarding him. Rabah may have been influenced in his decision to return to Babylonia by the strong opinion of his teacher, Rav Yehudah bar Yechezkel, that one must stay in Babylonia and not leave for the Land of Israel. The large Jewish community of Babylonia, greater in number than the Jewish community of the Land of Israel at that time, required rabbis, teachers, spiritual leaders and Torah scholars to maintain itself. If all of these worthies would have left to settle in the Land of Israel, the Jewish community of Babylonia would have been in danger of withering away. In a sense, this is a problem in present day Jewish life as well: when rabbis and scholars living in the Diaspora long to leave to settle in the Land of Israel, they are torn between their personal fulfillment and their sense of overall communal duties to the Jewish people and their local constituencies.

16. See Bechoros 17a; Yevamos 61b; Gittin 27a.

17. Bava Basra 172b.

18. Shteinman, volume 4, p. 67.

19. Eiruvin 40b.

20. Yevamos 66b. See the previous chapter regarding Rav Nachman.

21. Pesachim 40a, and see Rashi there.

22. Eiruvin 65b. See the previous chapter regarding Rav Sheishes.

23. Bava Metzia 6b. Naftal, volume 3, p. 180, is of the opinion that even when Rabah was already the head of the yeshivah in Pumbedisa, he visited Rav Chisda often in Sura to discuss halachic issues with him, and he did so as a sign of respect to Rav Chisda who was the elder scholar of the generation.

24. Menachos 68b; Berachos 39b; Shabbos 133b; Kesubos 50a, and numerous other places in the Talmud.

25. Avodah Zarah 49b.

26. Shabbos 123a, Yevamos 76a.

27. Succah 26b.

28. Shabbos 40a.

29. Shabbos 156a.

30. Ibid.

31. Perhaps Rabah was comparing his situation in Pumbedisa with that of the

prophet Yirmiyahu and his opponents in his home town of Anasos. See Bava Basra 9b. Rabah also attributed the fact that his prayers for rain were not immediately answered – even though he felt that the level of Torah study of his time was even greater, in some respects, than that of some previous generations – to the improper behavior and dishonesty of the masses in his generation. See Taanis 24a-b.

32. Shabbos 30b.
33. Sanhedrin 98b.
34. See Kesubos 106a as well as Bava Kama 66b.
35. Rav Ami was actually the head of the yeshivah, but he and Rav Assi worked and studied in tandem all of their lives. Rav Assi generally refused to take any public position or even to judge monetary cases when he could avoid doing so, due to his great modesty. See Midrash Tanchuma, Shemos, Parshas Mishpatim.
36. See Shabbos 119a.
37. Megillah 22a.
38. Sanhedrin 17a.
39. Shteinman, volume 4, p. 54 is of the opinion that they also studied for a period of time in the yeshivah of Rav in Sura, Babylonia.
40. Berachos 62a and Rashi there.
41. Kesubos 106a.
42. Bava Metzia 86a.
43. See Bechoros 31a.
44. Iggeres Rav Sherira Gaon, Levin edition, p. 86.
45. See Sanhedrin 25b.
46. The entire story is related in Bechoros 31a.
47. Iggeres Rav Sherira Gaon, Levin edition, p. 86.
48. Shabbos 153a and Rashi there.
49. Ibid.
50. Moed Katan 28a
51. Ibid.
52. Ibid.
53. Eiruvin 68a.
54. See Bechoros 29a. See also the commentary of Rambam, *Perush Hamishnayos, Avos,* chapter 4, section 7.
55. See Chulin 127a and Rashi, Shabbos 153b.
56. This entire story appears in Bava Metzia 85b.
57. Ibid.

Rav Yosef

1. Berachos 64a.
2. Bava Basra 114b and Rashbam there. The implication is that the law is according to Rabah in all other instances of their differing halachic opinions. See Tosfos, Bava Basra 114b. This is in spite of the opinion of the rabbis that a *Sinai* – Rav Yosef – is better than an *okeir harim* – Rabah bar Nachmani. Perhaps this opinion of the rabbis refers only to matters of education and teaching, but not to the actual determination of the law.
3. See Naftal, *HaTalmud V'yotzrav, Doros HaAmoraim,* (Tel Aviv: Yavneh Publishing House,1972), volume 3, p. 244 for possible explanations.

4. Berachos 45a.
5. See the information regarding this in the previous chapter on Rabah bar Nachmani. Rav Yosef died in c.323 CE.
6. Shabbos 119b; Eiruvin 7a; Succah 11a; Chulin 74a.
7. Bava Metzia 8a-b; Yevamos 17a.
8. Yevamos 66b; Kiddushin 20b.
9. See Kiddushin 59b.
10. Kesubos 50b. Rav Hamnuna I was a disciple of Rav and a colleague/student of Rav Huna.
11. Nedarim 81a. And see the commentary of Rosh (Rabbi Asher ben Yechiel) there.
12. Bava Metzia 85a.
13. Ibid.
14. Pesachim 68b.
15. Eiruvin 29a; Sanhedrin 99a, and other places in the Talmud.
16. Kiddushin 39a; Sanhedrin 61a, and other places in the Talmud.
17. Berachos 14b.
18. Megillah 16b.
19. Shabbos 145b.
20. Sanhedrin 99b. He equated those that denigrated the value of a Torah scholar to the Jewish world as being the equivalent of an *apikores* – a heretic and non-believer.
21. Kiddushin 30a.
22. See Tosfos, Bava Kama 3b. The phrase "as Rav Yosef translated" is found very often in the Talmud. For example, see Berachos 28a, Yoma 32b, and many other places in the Talmud.
23. Shabbos 119a; Eiruvin 54a; Pesachim 116b.
24. See Ran (Rabeinu Nissim ben Reuven, 15th century Spain) in his commentary to Kiddushin 31a. There are various accounts as to how his blindness arose. Some say, and this is what Ran is most probably referring to, that he sat in total darkness for 40 days in order to train himself not to look outside of the study hall and be distracted from his Torah studies. Others attribute his blindness to having spent long periods of time staring at bright white marble in the sunlight while preoccupied fully on a matter of Torah scholarship. See Eliezer Shteinman, in *Be'er HaTalmud* (Tel Aviv: Masada Press, 1967), volume 4, p. 73.
25. Kiddushin 31a.
26. Ibid.
27. Nedarim 31a. See Rashi, Kesubos 2a.
28. Nedarim 41a; Pesachim 13b.
29. Menachos 99a. See also Nedarim 41a.
30. Sanhedrin 102b.
31. Shabbos 151b.
32. Chagigah 9b. See the commentary of Rabeinu Chananel there that Jews find it hard to handle prosperity well, regarding Torah values and observance.
33. See Bava Basra 22b-23a; Bava Basra 26a; and Menachos 87a.
34. Pesachim 107a.
35. Bava Kama 36b.
36. Bava Kama 93a.
37. Bava Basra 8a.
38. Pesachim 113b. See also Succah 29a and Bava Basra 23a in reference to his delicate nature.
39. Sotah 5a. See also his statement regarding his personal trait of humility in Sotah

49a. There have been countless explanations given throughout the ages to interpret Rav Yosef's true meaning there.

40. Shabbos 119a. This was also the practice of Rabah bar Nachmani, the colleague of Rav Yosef.

41. Kiddushin 31b.

42. Gittin 45a.

43. Chagigah 4a.

44. Sanhedrin 98a.

45. Nedarim 39b.

46. Moed Katan 28a.

47. Berachos 19a.

48. Beitzah 28a; Moed Katan 19b; Kesubos 65a.

49. There were a number of people named Rav Dimi. Rav Dimi I was a colleague of Rav Yosef and will be discussed presently in this book. Two generations later, there was Rav Dimi of Nehardea. Neither of these two scholars is the Rav Dimi who was the grandson of Rav Yosef.

50. Sanhedrin 23b – 24a.

51. Rav Zeira I is not to be confused with Zeirei I who lived at the time of Rav and Mar Shmuel or with Rav Zeira II who lived at the time of Abayei and Rava in the fourth generation of *Amoraim*. These are three different people. See Pesachim 37b, that Rava, Rav Yosef, and Rav Zeira I studied together at the yeshivah of Ulla bar Yishmael.

52. Taanis 26b. See Moed Katan 20b that his given name was Isay. There is an opinion there that Isay was really the name of Rabi Zeira I's brother.

53. Shabbos 121b –122a. See Rashi and Tosfos there. See also Naftal, volume 3, p. 280.

54. Sanhedrin 25b –26a.

55. Ibid.

56. Ibid.

57. Berachos 39a and 49a; Bava Kama 9a.

58. Berachos 39a. See Shabbos 77b for a lengthy conversation and questions raised by Rav Zeira I when he met Rav Yehudah bar Yechezkel at the door of the home of Rav Yehudah's father-in-law.

59. Pesachim 37b; Yerushalmi Maaser Sheini, chapter 2, section 3. Regarding Ulla bar Yishmael, see footnote 72 in the chapter above regarding Rav Yehudah bar Yechezkel.

60. Berachos 23b; Zevachim 105b. Regarding Rav Hamnuna see footnote 49 in the chapter above regarding Rav Yehudah bar Yechezkel.

61. Kesubos 43b; Shabbos 21b. Rav Masna was a student of Rav and Mar Shmuel.

62. Pesachim 36a; Gittin 74a. Rabah bar Yirmiyahu was also a student of Rav and Mar Shmuel.

63. Bava Metzia 43b; Eiruvin 80a.

64. Shabbos 77b.

65. Shabbos 41a and see Rashi there.

66. Berachos 57a.

67. Kesubos 112a.

68. Yerushalmi Sheviis, chapter 4, section 7.

69. Kesubos 112a.

70. Midrash Rabah, Shir HaShirim, chapter 8, section 11.

71. Yerushalmi Berachos, chapter 2, section 5.

72. Ibid. Midrash Rabah, Shir HaShirim.

73. See Kiddushin 52a; Gittin 40a; Berachos 47b, and other places in the Talmud.
74. See Kiddushin 44a; Pesachim 72b, and other places in the Talmud.
75. Nedarim 8b; Niddah 48a; Yerushalmi Terumos, chapter 11, section 3, and see the commentary of *Pnei Moshe* there.
76. Chulin 21a; Yerushalmi Dmei, chapter 6, section 1.
77. Bava Basra 84b; Shabbos 71a; Chulin 70a, and other places in the Talmud.
78. Bava Metzia 85a. See Rashi there that the style of learning in the Land of Israel was not the question and answer, give and take, pointed discussion format that was common in Babylonia, but rather it was one of consensus and cooperative reconciliation of views between the scholars.
79. Chagigah 10a, and see Tosfos there.
80. Sanhedrin 14a. Rav Zeira I was afraid that Rabi Elazar ben Pedas, who was Rabi Yochanan's successor at Tiberias, would pass away before him and that the public responsibility of leading the community would devolve upon him. He fasted 100 times that Rabi Elazar ben Pedas should survive him. See Bava Metzia 85a.
81. Ibid.
82. Kesubos 17a.
83. Ibid.
84. See Rashi, Kesubos 43b.
85. Bava Metzia 85a.
86. Rashi, Bava Metzia 85a.
87. Naftal, volume 3, p. 279, quoting the book *Eshkol* in the name of Rav Hai Gaon.
88. Chulin 122a.
89. Bava Metzia 85a.
90. Sanhedrin 37a.
91. Yoma 87a.
92. Yerushalmi Shabbos, chapter 1, section 2.
93. Yerushalmi Maasros, chapter 3, section 4.
94. Ibid.
95. Yerushalmi Kilayim, chapter 5, section 1. See also Sanhedrin 97a; Taanis 16a; Berachos 38a, and many other places in the Talmud.
96. Bava Kama 117a.
97. Yerushalmi Kiddushin, chapter 1, section 7.
98. Yerushalmi Berachos, chapter 3, section 1.
99. Rosh Hashanah 29a; Nedarim 32a.
100. Megillah 28a.
101. Ibid.
102. Moed Katan 25b.
103. Bechoros 37b.
104. Gittin 25a; Bava Metzia 43b.
105. Bechoros 17a; Bava Metzia 6b. See Maharsha, Sanhedrin,14a quoting *Sefer Yuchsin* that Rabah bar Nachmani and Rav Oshiya were brothers.
106. Bechoros 17a; Bava Metzia 6b.
107. Chulin 124a; Pesachim 63b.
108. Menachos 3b; Shabbos 18a.
109. Yerushalmi Terumos, chapter 8, section 3; Shabbos, chapter 3, section 1, and other places.
110. Sanhedrin 14a. See there that Rabi Oshiya consoled himself and Rabi Yochanan on the failure of the ordination by stating that he was descended from the house of Eli the High Priest, and it was known that the family of Eli would not be

privileged to be ordained.

111. Yerushalmi Sanhedrin, chapter 1, section 2.
112. Shabbos 19b; Beitzah 26b; Yerushalmi Shevuos, chapter 5, section 2; Yoma, chapter 1, section 1.
113. See, for example, Sanhedrin 65b.
114. Pesachim 113b.
115. Ibid.
116. Yerushalmi Avodah Zarah, chapter 3, section 1.
117. Naftal, volume 3, p. 257, lists 66 of them.
118. See Tosfos, Eiruvin 63a that he is not to be confused with Rav Hamnuna I who was a member of the second generation of *Amoraim*. See footnote 49 in the previous chapter on Rav Yehudah bar Yechezkel.
119. Kiddushin 29b.
120. Kiddushin 25a.
121. Kiddushin 29b.
122. Shabbos 119a.
123. Taanis 7b.
124. Berachos 31a.
125. Yoma 87b.
126. Moed Katan 25a-b.
127. Ibid.
128. Berachos 29b; Kiddushin 65a; Avodah Zarah 19b.
129. Succah 26a: Bava Basra 167a.
130. Eiruvin 77b.
131. Sanhedrin 90b.
132. Succah 21b.
133. Shabbos 140a.
134. Bava Metzia 87a; Chulin 105a.
135. Shabbos 140a.
136. Shabbos 110b and 140a.
137. Yevamos 64b.
138. Eiruvin 63a; Bava Basra 16a; Kiddushin 29b.
139. Chulin 10b; Horayos 6b.
140. Kiddushin 35a; Bava Kama 54b.
141. Kiddushin 29b.
142. Sotah 49a.
143. Chulin 33a.
144. Kesubos 74a.
145. Sanhedrin 55a.
146. Bava Basra 9b.
147. Rashi there in Bava Basra 9b, is of the opinion that it was the mother of Rav Sheishes that intervened with her son to heal Rav Achdvoi. Tosfos is of the opinion that it was the mother of Rav Achdvoi who at one time had been the wet nurse of Rav Sheishes himself.
148. Bava Basra 9b.
149. Yevamos 83b. He is not Rav Abba bar Zavda, who lived in the Land of Israel at the same time, came to Babylonia to study with Rav Huna, and then returned to the Land of Israel.
150. Beitzah 33b.
151. Ibid. Both he and Rava bar Rav Ada were students of Rav Yehudah bar Yechezkel.

152. Bava Metzia 107a. He was also a student of Rav Yehudah bar Yechezkel.
153. Pesachim 49a.
154. Kiddushin 44a. He is not the better known Rav Assi, the compatriot of Rav Ami, in the yeshivah of Tiberias in the Land of Israel.
155. Kiddushin 76b. He was held to be a great man in Torah knowledge by his peers and teacher, Rav Yosef. He is not to be confused with Rav Bibi bar Abayei.
156. Bava Metzia 64b. He was the father of the famed Rava of the fourth generation of Babylonian *Amoraim*.
157. Kiddushin 8a. See Tosfos there that there were a number of *Amoraim* named Rav Kahana.
158. Megillah 31b. He was yet another student of Rav Huna.
159. Makkos 21a.
160. Avodah Zarah 26a.
161. Shabbos 147b; Bava Kama 38a.
162. Shabbos 10a.
163. In a world of self-aggrandizing publicity, advertisements, and public relations, it is difficult for us truly to appreciate how the great rabbis of the Talmud treasured their privacy and their anonymity.

SECTION V

Rav Ami and Rav Assi

1. Chulin 111b.
2. Gittin 44a.
3. Gittin 44a; Gittin 63b.
4. Gittin 59b; Megillah 22a.
5. Nedarim 40b.
6. See Kesubos 62a about the close relationship between the two.
7. Bava Kama 105b.
8. Chagigah 24b; Yevamos 95a. See also Yerushalmi Terumos, chapter 8, section 11 that Rabi Shimon ben Lakish risked his own life in order to save Rav Ami from kidnappers. According to some texts, it was Rav Assi who was saved. See the Zusman edition of the Talmud Yerushalmi text.
9. Zevachim 25b.
10. Yerushalmi Shabbos, chapter 3, section 1.
11. Moed Katan 25a.
12. Iggeres Rav Sherira Gaon, Levin edition, p. 84.
13. Gittin 59; Megillah 22a. See also Shabbos 119a.
14. Kesubos 17a.
15. Shabbos 63a.
16. Berachos 8a.
17. Chulin 86b.
18. Eliezer Shteinman *Be'er HaTalmud* (Tel Aviv: Masada Press, 1967), volume 4, p. 55 estimates that he was over 90 years old at his passing.
19. Yevamos 96b; Berachos 6b; Sanhedrin 100b; Berachos 62a, and many other places in the Talmud.
20. Chulin 106b.
21. Kesubos 17a.

22. Sanhedrin 17b.
23. Yerushalmi Chagigah, chapter 1, section 7.
24. Midrash Tanchuma, Shemos, Parshas Mishpatim.
25. Chulin 103b.
26. Moed Katan 25b.
27. Yerushalmi Avodah Zarah, chapter 3, section 1.
28. See Berachos 24b.
29. Chulin 79a.
30. Bava Basra 170a and 171b; Kiddushin 59a; Bava Kama 88a.
31. Kesubos 67b.
32. Kesubos 112a.
33. Sanhedrin 17a.
34. Beitzah 31a. As discussed earlier, the methodology and pedagogical style of the Torah scholars in the Land of Israel differed markedly from their colleagues in Babylonia; hence, the special significance of Rabi Abba's prayer.
35. Taanis 4a.
36. Ibid.
37. Shabbos 105b.
38. Bava Kama 60b.
39. Ibid.
40. Ibid.
41. Sanhedrin 96a.
42. Arachin 22b.
43. Moed Katan 24b.
44. Midrash Rabah, Koheles, chapter 1, section 34.
45. Kesubos 111b.
46. Sanhedrin 94b.
47. Shabbos 124a.
48. Berachos 63a.
49. Berachos 62b.
50. Berachos 47a.
51. Berachos 17a.
52. Ibid.
53. Bava Basra 144a.
54. Avodah Zarah 4a.
55. Makkos 24a. See Rashi there.
56. Bava Kama 116a.
57. Moed Katan 25a. They had initially refused to do so, stating that they had not learned any Torah from him. Abayei rejected this claim.
58. Kiddushin 81a. His piety is exalted there.
59. Sanhedrin 81a.
60. Berachos 10a.
61. Yerushalmi Challah, chapter 1, section 6 (7). It is related there that Rabi Yochanan visited Rabi Oshiya Rabah in Caesarea.
62. Midrash Rabah, Bereshis, chapter 22, section 27.
63. Midrash Rabah, Koheles, chapter 10, section 23. He was the father-in-law of Rabi Abahu.
64. Taanis 23b.
65. Sanhedrin 44a. He was a grandson of Rabi Levi ben Sisas (Levi).
66. Bava Basra 39b.
67. Chulin 84b. He was a student of Rav Ami and Rav Assi.

68. Taanis 23b.
69. Midrash Tanchuma, Behaaloscha, chapter 16.
70. Midrash Rabah, Bereshis, chapter 3 and chapter 9, section 9; Vayikra, chapter 31, section 1; Sanhedrin 22a. He was famed as a master of Aggadah and as an orator of note.
71. He was known as Rachva of Pumbedisa. He was recognized for his exactitude in transmitting teachings and sayings of his teachers. See Pesachim 52b; Chulin 18b. He was married to Choma, who after being widowed married Rabi Yitzchak breih d'Rabah bar bar Chanah; widowed again, she eventually married Abayei. Rachva fathered two sons who are mentioned in the Talmud, Avimei and Eifah (Cheifah). See Shavuos 28b; Yerushalmi Nedarim, chapter 2, section 3. They are usually referred to simply as "the sons of Rachva." See Shabbos 103a.
72. Berachos 55a; Taanis 4a. He was also a noted master of Aggadah and a renowned orator.

SECTION VI

Abayei

1. Succah 28b.
2. Iggeres Rav Sherira Gaon, Levin edition, p. 87 makes the date as 289 CE. However, see Naftal, *HaTalmud V'yotzrav, Doros HaAmoraim,* (Tel Aviv: Yavneh Publishing House, 1972) volume 4, p. 19 in the footnotes where he states according to the Talmud in Rosh Hashanah 18a, that Abayei lived 60 years and all agree that he died in 339 CE. Therefore, he had to have been born in 279 CE.
3. Rosh Hashanah 18a.
4. Kiddushin 31b.
5. Ibid.
6. Shabbos 33a; Nedarim 54b; Kesubos 82a, and many other places in the Talmud.
7. *Aruch HaShalem,* section "Abayei" in the name of Rav Sherira Gaon.
8. Rashi, Gittin 34b; Rashbam, Pesachim 112b; Ran, Nedarim 54b.
9. Maharsha, Kiddushin 31b in the name of *Sefer Yuchsin.*
10. See Rashi, Zevachim 118b.
11. Yoma 88b; Pesachim 110a; Gittin 70a, and many other places in the Talmud.
12. Eiruvin 68a.
13. Berachos 48a; Pesachim 115b. The Talmud there in Berachos 48a records that, as a child, Rava also sat together with Abayei in the study chamber of Rabah bar Nachmani. Most commentators accepted it as fact that the Rava that is mentioned there is Rava bar Rav Yosef bar Chama, Abayei's companion in the Talmud. However, see the gloss of Rabbi Akiva Eiger, *Gilyon HaShas,* in Berachos 48a that the correct text in the Talmud refers to Rava bar Rav Chanan, a different Rava. See Naftal, volume 4, p. 21, who confirms that this is the correct text. As such, many of the numerous essays comparing the different temperaments and world outlook of Abayei and Rava based on that story in the Talmud (such as Shteinman, *Be'er HaTalmud* (Tel Aviv: Masada Press, 1967), volume 4, pp. 133 onwards) are unfortunately without basis.
14. Pesachim 104b; Sanhedrin 30b.
15. See Naftal, volume 4, p. 23.
16. Berachos 33b; Chulin 43b, and other places in the Talmud.

17. Chulin 43b; Sanhedrin 98b; Shabbos 156a; Eiruvin 68a, and other places in the Talmud.
18. For example, see Megillah 7b.
19. Berachos 30b.
20. Berachos 48a.
21. Pesachim 45b; Shevuos 35a.
22. Shevuos 17b.
23. Berachos 14b.
24. Kiddushin 16b.
25. Taanis 12a.
26. Nedarim 41a.
27. Kiddushin 33a.
28. Zevachim 62a
29. Eiruvin 60a.
30. For example, see Eiruvin 50a; Succah 7a; Gittin 28a, and many other places in the Talmud.
31. Nedarim 55a; Shabbos 38b and 77a; Arachin 11b, and many other places in the Talmud.
32. For example, see Shabbos 13b and 49b.
33. For example, see Eiruvin 10a and 89b. See also Rashi, Niddah 39a.
34. Succah 26b.
35. See Pesachim 108a.
36. Yehudah Leib (Fishman) Maimon, *Abayei V'Rava* (Jerusalem: Mosad Harav Kook, 1965) p. 18.
37. Chulin 124a; Niddah 10b.
38. Rashi, Berachos 47a; Iggeres Rav Sherira Gaon, Levin edition, p. 61.
39. Nazir 37a; Bava Kama 43a; Bava Metzia 58a; Bava Basra 170a; T'murah 4a, and many other places in the Talmud.
40. Shabbos 20b; Kiddushin 12a; Bava Basra 129a, and other places in the Talmud.
41. Berachos 47a.
42. Kesubos 105a.
43. Yevamos 45a and 64b. See Rashi there at Yevamos 64b. See also Kiddushin 44a regarding Ravin's extreme reliability in transmitting teachings and traditions.
44. Chulin 110b; Bava Basra 167b, and many other places in the Talmud. See, in particular, Bava Metzia 31b – 32a.
45. Horayos 14a.
46. Iggeres Rav Sherira Gaon, Levin edition, p. 87.
47. Horayos 14a.
48. Ibid. See Rashi and Tosfos HaRash there.
49. Sanhedrin 27a.
50. Sotah 45a. As noted in other places in this book, this phrase also was used by other scholars to describe their abilities in Torah knowledge and teachings.
51. Maimon (Fishman), p. 20.
52. Eiruvin 25b and Rashi there; Shabbos 4a; Sanhedrin 66b, and other places in the Talmud.
53. Kesubos 60a.
54. Nedarim 23a.
55. Yevamos 64b.
56. Kesubos 65a.
57. Yevamos 64b.
58. In 339 CE, at the age of 60. See Rosh Hashanah 18a and Iggeres Rav Sherira

Gaon, Levin Edition, p. 87.
59. Kesubos 65a.
60. Megillah 7b.
61. Gittin 60b.
62. See Rashi, Berachos 56a.
63. Berachos 45b.
64. Kesubos 60b.
65. Chulin 105a.
66. Shabbos 118b, and many other places in the Talmud.
67. Moed Katan 16a.
68. Berachos 42a.
69. Kesubos 106a.
70. So much so that he did not participate in *Birkas Kohanim* on a regular basis. See Rif, Rabbi Yitzchak Alfasi's commentary to the Talmud; Chulin 133a.
71. Yoma 84a. See Rashi there regarding this illness which causes the loss of one's teeth. Rashi associates it with digestive problems as well, and ranks it as a most dangerous disease.
72. Nedarim 39b.
73. Bava Basra 7b. He called this a *mitzvah rabah* – a great and overriding commandment.
74. Berachos 17a.
75. Kiddushin 33a.
76. Berachos 35b.
77. Berachos 17a.
78. Gittin 59b.
79. Gittin 45a.
80. Rosh Hashanah 18a.
81. Taanis 21b.
82. Bava Basra 167a; Chulin 105a.
83. Kesubos 105b.
84. Yoma 86a.
85. Eiruvin 65a. See also Kiddushin 81b.
86. Succah 52a.

Rava

1. Eiruvin 54a; Beitzah 8a; Bava Kama 104b, and many other places in the Talmud.
2. He was a person of great wealth. See Bava Kama 97a; Gittin 14a.
3. Bava Kama 30a.
4. From many references in the Talmud, it is clear that he was extremely well acquainted with the city, its community, and its practices. Both Avraham Moshe Naftal, *HaTalmud V'yotzrav*, (Tel Aviv: Yavneh Publishing House, 1972) and Yehudah Leib (Fishman) Maimon, *Abayei V'Rava* (Jerusalem: Mosad Harav Kook, 1965) are of the opinion that Rava was a native son of Mechoza.
5. Shabbos 47a; Chulin 49b; Berachos 34b; Moed Katan 28a.
6. Temurah 31a; Megillah 8b.
7. For example, see Pesachim 114b.
8. Shabbos 129a; Bava Kama 97a.
9. Succah 29a. Later in life, after both Rava and Rav Chisda's daughter had been

widowed, they married, and thus Rava was a son-in-law of Rav Chisda, as well as his student. Rava attributed the fact that Rav Chisda was his father-in-law to supernatural help. See Yoma 75b. See also Bava Basra 12b for the story that Rav Chisda's daughter, while yet a small child, predicted that she would be married one day to Rava. See also Tosfos, Yevamos 34b regarding her intent to marry Rava after she became a widow.

10. Berachos 23b and 34b; Yevamos 55b.
11. Bava Metzia 16a.
12. Chulin 133a.
13. Yoma 53b.
14. Ibid.
15. Eiruvin 54a; Nedarim 25a.
16. Yoma 53b.
17. Kesubos 63a.
18. Eiruvin 82b; Berachos 13b.
19. Moed Katan 28a; Yoma 87a.
20. Nedarim 55a; Bava Basra 149b.
21. See Bava Metzia 73a and Rashi, Berachos 16a.
22. Berachos 56a; Eiruvin 44b.
23. See Bava Basra 153a. Rava was known for miracles that occurred to him while on board ships on the Tigris. See Berachos 56a.
24. Berachos 50a; Pesachim 74b; Moed Katan 11a, and other places in the Talmud.
25. Bava Basra 22a.
26. Gittin 31b.
27. Shabbos 4a and 47a; Pesachim 30a and 72b; Berachos 23b, Gittin 63b; Avodah Zarah 37b, and many other places in the Talmud.
28. Gittin 31b.
29. See Zevachim 116b; Bava Basra 10b; Niddah 20b.
30. Taanis 24b.
31. Ibid.
32. See Avodah Zarah 65a.
33. Ibid.
34. As noted earlier, examples of his influence and closeness with the Exilarch can be found in Moed Katan 11a; Pesachim 74b; Berachos 50a and Bava Basra 22a.
35. Moed Katan 28a.
36. Berachos 61b.
37. Ibid and see Rashi there.
38. Yoma 87a.
39. Berachos 17a. It appears in our prayer service for *Neilah* on Yom Kippur and begins: "My Lord, until I was created I was but nothing…" This was also the prayer of Rav Hamnuna Zuta. See footnote 105 below.
40. Sotah 5a and see Rashi there.
41. See, for instance, Nedarim 90a; Yevamos 113a; Bava Basra 174a; Bava Kama 40a, and other places in the Talmud. See Makkos 22a, where he complains that people stand before an inanimate scroll, the Torah, and do not give proper respect to living scholars of the Torah who interpret its words to benefit humanity.
42. Shabbos 111b; Kiddushin 48b; Sanhedrin 8b.
43. Eiruvin 104a; Bava Basra 127a; Zevachim 94b. See also Shabbos 27a; Bava Basra 24a; Makkos 8a; Yevamos 20b for examples of cases where Rava later rejected previous interpretations and decisions that he had made.

44. Berachos 17a.
45. Ibid.
46. Succah 26a.
47. See Nedarim 27a (someone who acts out of coercion is not held liable); Avodah
    Zarah 54a (one must live by the Torah, but one is not commanded to die by it)
    and Sanhedrin 25a (a person is not believed to incriminate himself in capital
    cases).
48. Sanhedrin 97a. See also Shabbos 119b, where Rava states that Jerusalem was
    destroyed because of the lack of honest people in its midst.
49. Berachos 25b.
50. For example, see Makkos 22a and Shabbos 23b.
51. Shabbos 88a.
52. Sotah 21a.
53. Bava Basra 16a.
54. Menachos 110a.
55. Shabbos 119a.
56. Nedarim 62a.
57. Chagigah 15a.
58. Berachos 5a
59. Shabbos 10a.
60. Shabbos 31a.
61. Ibid.
62. Yoma 23a.
63. Chulin 141b.
64. Ibid and see also Chulin 30b.
65. Bava Basra 16a.
66. Ibid.
67. Chulin 49a.
68. Bava Metzia 59a.
69. Yevamos 63b.
70. See Tosfos, Yevamos 34b.
71. Yevamos 34b.
72. Kesubos 85a.
73. See for example, Yevamos 64b; Bava Metzia 83a; Menachos 33b, and other
    places in the Talmud.
74. Chulin 50a.
75. See Chulin 28b and 50a.
76. Yevamos 66b; Bava Basra 143b; Chulin 141a, and other places in the Talmud.
77. See Berachos 62a; Shabbos 129a; Chagigah 5a.
78. Bava Basra 22a.
79. Iggeres Rav Sherira Gaon, Levin edition, p. 88.
80. Gittin 6a.
81. See Kiddushin 73a.
82. Rosh Hashanah 17a; Shabbos 32b and 109a.
83. See Kesubos 105b and Kiddushin 73a.
84. Iggeres Rav Sherira Gaon, Levin edition, p. 88.
85. Ibid. p. 89.
86. Ibid.
87. Moed Katan 28a. Compare this to the description of the complete lack of pain
    of death (like a hair pulled out of milk) stated by Rav Nachman bar Yaakov also
    there in Moed Katan 28a. Nevertheless, even Rav Nachman stated that he did

not want to return to this world – even if afforded that opportunity – because of the terror of death that afflicts all humans. Ibid.

88. Moed Katan 25b.

89. Because of copyist errors over the centuries in recording the manuscripts of the Talmud, much confusion has arisen over hundreds of passages in the Talmud attributed to either Rabah (bar Nachmani) or to Rava. The great latter day scholars of Israel have made hundreds of corrections in the manuscripts and printed editions of the Talmud in the attempt to attribute those passages to the correct author, be it Rabah or Rava. This process is still ongoing in our time, as our treasure trove of newly-discovered manuscripts yield results.

90. See Yitzchak Isaac Halevi, *Doros HaRishonim* (Warsaw, 1896) volume 2, p. 480 and onwards.

91. See for example, Niddah 11b, where the opinions of Rav Gidel, Rav Yonah and Rava are recorded as though they were conducting a three-way face-to-face discussion, when in reality Rav Yonah lived in the Land of Israel, Rava lived all of his life in Babylonia, and Rav Gidel died before Rava and Rav Yonah were born.

92. See Naftal, volume 4, pp. 297-8 for a partial list of these *Amoraim*. I am especially indebted to his work and research for this section of my book.

93. The scholars disagree on whether this name – Marta – is a woman's name or a man's name. See Bava Basra 52a and the commentaries of Rashbam and Rabeinu Gershom there for the differing opinions.

94. Shabbos 121b; Yoma 84a. He is known as a highly respected scholar. See Gittin 37b for an incident between him and Rabah bar Nachmani regarding a loan that apparently was subject to cancellation on the sabbatical year of *Shemittah*.

95. He is usually paired in his statements in the Talmud with his friend and colleague (who was also probably his brother), Rabi Chanina bar Avin. See Berachos 29b; Pesachim 34a; Yevamos 119b; Shabbos 86b; Megillah 7b, and other places in the Talmud. He was a student/colleague of Abayei, the head of the yeshiva of Pumbedisa. See Eiruvin 62a.

96. They were known as *charifei d'Pumbedisa* – the "sharp" geniuses of Pumbedisa. See Sanhedrin 17b. They are also quoted as such at Menachos, 17a and Kiddushin 39a. They were students of Rabah bar Nachmani. See Shevuos 28b.

97. Chulin 68b and Niddah 5b. He was a colleague of Rava and of Rav Nachman bar Yitzchak. Chozai was the name of his hometown.

98. Chulin 48a and 86a. He was a colleague of Rava.

99. The first Rav Ada bar Ahava was a second generation *Amora*, a student of Rav. Rav Ada bar Ahava II was a student of Rava. He was beloved by Rava, who called him "my son." See Sanhedrin 81b. See also Shabbos 94a; Pesachim 60b; Bava Metzia 63b; Yoma 14a, and many other places in the Talmud where Rava and Rav Ada bar Ahava II engage in halachic discussions. He was a confidant of Rava (see Bava Basra 22a) and reviewed Rava's teachings most diligently – 24 times. See Taanis 8a. He was a partisan of Rava over Abayei. See Bava Basra 22a and Chulin 77a in Dikdukei Sofrim there, note ten, that the correct text in the Talmud should read Rav Ada bar Ahava. See also Rashi there. Nevertheless, he also was known to praise Abayei, and apparently studied with him for a period of time. See Kiddushin 76b. He died suddenly, much to the consternation and grief of his colleagues. See Bava Basra 22a and Tosfos there.

100. Zevachim 38a; Niddah 54a; Yoma 17a, and other places in the Talmud.

101. Shabbos 66b; Moed Katan 16a.

102. He was a student of Rav Yosef. See Shabbos 148a. He was a colleague of

Rava. See Shabbos 46a. He is mentioned numerous times in the Talmud. See Menachos 88a; Gittin 65a; Bava Basra 143a; Chulin 43b, for some examples out of many. He also studied under Rav Ami in the Land of Israel. See Chulin 50a. His sons, Rav Acha and Rav Chilkiyah were scholars of the fifth generation of *Amoraim* in Babylonia. See Eiruvin 48b; Pesachim 44b; Bava Metzia 96b.

103. He was mainly a disciple of Rav Sheishes. See Bava Basra 70a; Sanhedrin 43a and 82b. He is the author (in the name of his mentor, Rav Sheishes) of the famous words of caution: "An overly full stomach leads to many illnesses." See Berachos 32a. He also studied with Rabah bar Nachmani. See Shevuos 36b. Rav Chisda sent him as a messenger to Rabah numerous times. See Yevamos 89b and Pesachim 47a. He also studied with Rav Yosef (Kiddushin 12b), Rav Nachman (Chulin 76b), Abayei (Bava Basra 167b), and Rava (Kiddushin 50b and Shabbos 150a). Rav Acha had a son, Rava bar Rav Acha, a noted scholar, who is mentioned in the Talmud. See Niddah 31b.

104. Not to be confused with Rav Dimi of the third generation of *Amoraim* who was one of the scholars that traveled back and forth between the yeshivos of the Land of Israel and Babylonia. See Avodah Zarah 11b. Rav Dimi of Nehardea was engaged in commerce, supplying dried figs for the markets. See Bava Basra 22a for the details of his encounter with Rav Ada bar Abba (Ahava) while delivering dried figs to Mechoza. Thirty years after the death of Rava, Rav Dimi became the head of the yeshivah of Pumbedisa for three years, from 385 to 388 CE. He studied with Abayei (Menachos 35a); Rava (Bava Basra 21a); Mar Shmuel (Moed Katan 12a and Horayos 2a) and Ameimar (Chulin 51b). From all of the above, it is apparent that he lived a very long life, spanning a number of generations of *Amoraim*. Rav Dimi favored a meritocracy in choosing teachers of Torah. See Bava Basra 21a.

105. A scholar of great humility and piety. His prayer at the end of Yom Kippur has been adopted by all of Israel. See Berachos 17a and Yoma 87b. The prayer was adopted by Rava to be said daily (Yoma 87b). See note 39 above. He is recorded as having sung a sad song at the wedding of Ravina's son. See Berachos 31a.

106. A student/colleague of Abayei who would later serve as the head of the yeshivah of Pumbedisa for eight years. He was a teacher of Ameimar and Rav Chanan bar Nosson. See Bava Metzia 73b; Yevamos 18a. For the eulogy over Rav Zvid delivered by Rav Kahana IV, see Moed Katan 27b. There was another *Amora* named Zavdi who flourished in the Land of Israel in the third century and is also mentioned in the Talmud. See Zevachim 28b; Krisus 5a.

107. Famed for his piety and his conversations with the prophet Eliyahu. See Sanhedrin 97b, Yoma 19b and Berachos 29b. He was apparently a poor person; he and his son shared a pair of shoes between them. See Shabbos 112a. He was acquainted with Rav Huna of the third generation of *Amoraim*. See Berachos 5b for his explanation as to why Rav Huna's casks of wine soured and turned to vinegar. His brother, Rav Yosef Breih d'Rav Sala Chasida, is also mentioned in the Talmud. See Pesachim 73b.

SECTION VII

Rav Papa

1. See Gittin 6a and Kiddushin 73a.
2. See Pesachim 111b.
3. Gittin 90a; Megillah 25a; Kesubos 7a, and many other places in the Talmud.
4. Iggeres Rav Sherira Gaon, Levin edition, p. 89.
5. Ibid.
6. Shabbos 37b and see Rashi there.
7. Taanis 21b and see Rashi and Tosfos there.
8. Berachos 6a.
9. Shabbos 66a; Pesachim 107a; Kiddushin 44a, and other places in the Talmud.
10. Pesachim 105a.
11. Gittin 57b.
12. Yevamos 85a and see Rashi in Shabbos 145b.
13. Niddah 27a.
14. Pesachim 16a.
15. Chulin 33a.
16. See Meilah 3b and Yevamos 106a.
17. See Shabbos 93b; Pesachim 7a; Megillah 26b, and many other places in the Talmud.
18. See Bava Basra 130b; Horayos 10b; Kiddushin, 32b. However, Rava also apparently spoke to them sternly at times. See Gittin 73a. See Rashi there that they were already elderly and white-haired when they studied with Rava. See also Kesubos 85a where Rava addresses Rav Papa with the respectful term *Mar.*
19. Berachos 57a. See Rashi there.
20. Ibid.
21. See, for example, Bava Kama 7b and 89a; Eiruvin 12a; Shevuos 34b; Zevachim 15a, and many other places in the Talmud.
22. See Chulin 127a that when one deals with them one must "count his teeth" afterward.
23. Ibid.
24. Kesubos 106a.
25. Horayos 10b.
26. Ibid.; see also Gittin 73a.
27. See Bava Metzia 65a and Rashi there; also see Pesachim 113a.
28. See Pesachim 89b and Taanis 24b. Rav Papa mocked himself and his eating habits. See Pesachim 49a. He was an expert in food tastes. See Bava Basra 91b.
29. Pesachim 111a and see Rashbam there.
30. Rav Papa was called *sudni* – the malt liquor person. See Berachos 44b and Rashi there. Rashi in Menachos 71a states that the word was also used as a synonym for describing a Torah scholar. See Pesachim 113a where Rav Papa attributes his wealth to the *sheichar* business. Rav Papa's *sheichar* was of very high quality. See Bava Metzia 65a.
31. See Pesachim 107a that it was considered the "wine" of that land. Rav Papa himself valued *sheichar* as superior to wine. See Shabbos 140b.
32. Gittin 73b.
33. Bava Kama 104b.
34. For example, see Kesubos 97a.
35. He was one of the premier scholars among the *Amoraim* of the fifth generation

in Babylonia. He served as the head of the yeshivah in Nehardea, and in his later years, he became the head of the great yeshivah in Sura (for a period of five years) after the death of Rav Ashi. See Beitzah 22a. He was sometimes addressed by the title "*Mar*." See Menachos 37b. He opposed the Zoroastrian astrologers of Persia who invaded and controlled Babylonia for a period of time, and was eventually arrested and executed by Izigidur, the ruler of Persia. See Sanhedrin 39a.

36. He was a well-known scholar and later also served as the *Reish Galusa*/Exilarch of the Jewish community in Babylonia from the years 402-410 CE. He was the main colleague of Ameimar in Nehardea and was also a colleague of Rav Kahana IV, the head of the yeshivah in Pum Nahara. Mar Zutra II lived a century later, and died in the Land of Israel. The Mar Zutra who is mentioned in the Talmud many times is invariably Mar Zutra I.

37. As mentioned earlier, there were four main yeshivos operating in Babylonia after the death of Rava. Aside from Nehardea, the others were in Narash, Pumbedisa and Pum Nahara.

38. See Chulin 8b and 112a among many other places in the Talmud.

39. See Niddah 33b and Moed Katan 17a.

40. Sanhedrin 100a.

41. Ibid.

42. Shabbos 139a.

43. See Taanis 9a and 24b; Bava Basra 10a (according to the text of the Bach there); Rosh Hashanah 17a. See also Eiruvin 26a where the then Exilarch (*Reish Galusa*) harshly criticized a halachic ruling of Rav Papa that affected the city and location of the Exilarch.

44. Taanis 9b.

45. Bava Basra 10a.

46. Ibid.

47. Berachos 6b. We are all witness to the banalities often stated at such times despite the good intent of well-wishers.

48. Shabbos 32a.

49. Bava Metzia 28b.

50. Pesachim 49a. See also Chulin 132a.

51. Kesubos 85a. See also Berachos 45b.

52. Horayos 12b.

53. Kesubos 39b.

54. Kesubos 52b.

55. Iggeres Rav Sherira Gaon, Levin edition, p. 89.

56. Rosh Hashanah 17a.

57. As mentioned earlier, there were five people called Rav Kahana mentioned in the Talmud. Rav Kahana I was a colleague/student of Rav in the first generation of the Babylonian *Amoraim*. The second Rav Kahana was a student of Rav who flourished in the second generation of the Babylonian *Amoraim*. The third Rav Kahana was the student of Rabah bar Nachmani in the fourth generation of *Amoraim*. The fourth Rav Kahana is this Rav Kahana, who was the head of the yeshivah in Pum Nahara and was the main mentor of Rav Ashi, the chief editor of the Talmud in the fifth generation of *Amoraim*. The fifth Rav Kahana was the colleague/student of Rav Ashi and he was one of the leading scholars of the sixth generation of the Babylonian *Amoraim*.

58. Shabbos 10a.

59. For example, Succah 7a and 22a; Yevamos 106b.

60. Chulin 53b.
61. Yevamos 18a; Bava Metzia 73b.

SECTION VIII

Rav Ashi and Ravina

1. Gittin 59a.
2. Kiddushin 72b and see Hagahos Ranshburg there.
3. Meilah 3b; Rambam, Introduction to *Mishneh Torah*.
4. Menachos 102a. See Rashi and Rabeinu Gershom there.
5. Avodah Zarah 40a; Shabbos 37b.
6. Kiddushin 72b. See also footnote 58 below.
7. Sanhedrin 28a. Ulla II was an *Amora* of the last generation of *Amoraim* of the Land of Israel See Yerushalmi, Shabbos, chapter 13, section 5; Shekalim, chapter 1, section 1. He immigrated to Babylonia in the generation of Rava. As the persecutions of the Jews in the Land of Israel increased in the fourth century CE, many of the scholars of the Land of Israel escaped to Babylonia, Ullah II among them. He established a yeshivah of his own in Babylonia and was well regarded by Rava and the other Babylonian scholars. See Sanhedrin 63b; Shabbos 31b; Kiddushin 31a. He was a colleague of Rava in Babylonia. See Chulin 131b. He appears many times in the Talmud as Rav Ulla. His sons, Rava, see Shabbos 31b, Ravina, see Beitzah 3b, Rabi Banaah, see Pesachim 54a, were all noted Torah scholars. Ulla II should not be confused with Ulla I, Ulla bar Yishmael, who was also from the Land of Israel and went to study in Babylonia. Ulla I lived in the third generation of the *Amoraim* of Babylonia and was a colleague of Rav Yehudah bar Yechezkel, Rav Nachman and Rav Chisda. See Chulin 94a; Berachos 51b and 58b.
8. Rosh Hashanah 29b; Chulin 77a and 82a. Rav Papi was one of the earliest students of Rava. See Shabbos 93a; Pesachim 7a; Yevamos 75b. He was very highly regarded by the scholars of Babylonia. See, for example, Kesubos 7a and Moed Katan 19b. His colleagues included Rav Bibi bar Abayei, see Bava Metzia 109a; Yevamos 75b, and Rav Kahana IV. See Sotah 45a; Bava Basra 133a.
9. Zevachim 29a. Rav Masna I was an *Amora* of the third generation, a student of Rav and Mar Shmuel. This Rav Masna II was a colleague of Abayei and Rava in the fourth generation of *Amoraim*. (See Kesubos 35b; Shabbos 2b.)
10. Chulin 139b; Bava Basra 25b; Avodah Zarah 38b. Rav Chanina was also one of the *Amoraim* who fled the Land of Israel for the relative safety of Babylonia in the fourth century.
11. See Kiddushin 72b; see also Avodah Zarah 19a.
12. Menachos 37b; Bava Kama 70a; Beitzah 22a, and other places in the Talmud. Ameimar was a student of Rav Papa. See Chulin 8b. He was proud to be from Nehardea and mentioned this fact a number of times in his statements in the Talmud. See Bava Basra 31a and Bava Metzia 16b and 35a. Ameimar was respected and beloved by the community of Nehardea. See Beitzah 25b. He and Rav Ashi were on friendly terms and visited with each other often. See Berachos 26a. They participated together in deciding rabbinical court cases. See Kesubos 63b. He was one of the leading figures in his generation of scholars.
13. Pesachim 107a.
14. Yevamos 92b.

15. Gittin 40a; Rosh Hashanah 31b; Chulin 53b; Bava Basra 13b, and many other places in the Talmud.
16. Berachos 39a and 42a; Bava Basra 22b.
17. Bava Basra 76b; Bava Kama 24b; Bava Metzia 35a; Zevachim 106b, and very numerous other places in the Talmud.
18. Shabbos 10a; Berachos 39b, and other places in the Talmud.
19. Gittin 52b.
20. Bava Kama 95b.
21. See Shabbos 11a.
22. Yevamos 101b.
23. Kesubos 4a.
24. Shabbos 11a; Bava Basra 3b. See there in Bava Basra 3b that Rav Ashi actually slept in the unfinished building while it was being constructed in order that his presence would somehow speed up its construction and completion. See Rashi there.
25. See Sanhedrin 110a.
26. Bava Metzia 86a.
27. See Yevamos 21a and Moed Katan 5a.
28. See Shteinman, *Be'er HaTalmud* (Tel Aviv: Masada Press, 1967), volume 4, p. 180.
29. Ibid. Shteinman, p. 178.
30. Gittin 59a; Moed Katan 12b; Nedarim 62b; Pesachim 30b. There in Pesachim, Rav Ashi relates that he always bought new knives for Pesach instead of purging the year-round knives to make them suitable for Pesach use because he could afford to do so. See also Berachos 31a, that Rav Ashi purposely broke a goblet of white glass (very rare and expensive in those days) in order to diminish the levity at the wedding feast of his son. Tosfos there mentions that this is the origin of our custom to break a glass at a wedding ceremony. However, see also Megillah 6b that Rav Ashi hired merrymakers to celebrate his son's wedding feast. The great men of the Talmud were always able to strike the correct balance in life.
31. Beitzah 29a. However, see Dikdukei Sofrim there that the correct text should read Rami bar Abba. See also Chulin 111a that also states that Rav Ashi's father-in-law was Rami bar Abba.
32. A very famous scholar and much later in life, the successor to his father as the head of the yeshiva of Sura/Masa Machsiya. More regarding him in the next section of this book. See Chulin 86b and Rashi there. He signed his name as Tavyumei. See Bava Basra 12b.
33. Kesubos 33b.
34. Kesubos 69a and see Rashi there.
35. Moed Katan 28a.
36. Moed Katan 25b. The eulogy that Rav Ashi was told by the eulogizer that he would say at Rav Ashi's funeral would be, "If the flame has consumed the great cedars, then what hope is there for the wall pegs? If the leviathan has been caught by the harpoon, what hope is there for the small fish? If the great stream has dried up, then what hope is there for the small gatherings of water?" Bar Avin, who was present at the conversation, suggested a more respectful eulogy: "Weep you mourners, but not for the one who is lost to life – for his soul departs to serenity and rest and leaves us to sighs and sadness."
37. Ravina's given name was Avina. Ravina was a contraction of Rav Avina. See *Aruch HaShalem*, in the section on Abayei, where Rav Sherira Gaon is quoted as teaching that it was common practice among the Babylonian scholars to use contractions for titles and given names, such as Rachva for Rav Achva, or

Rafram for Rav Afram.

38. Yoma 86a and see Rashi there.
39. Bava Kama 119a. See there his discussion regarding the question of the acceptance of rich gifts for charity from the women of Mechoza.
40. Moed Katan 10; Bava Metzia 73b.
41. Bava Basra 5a; Bava Metzia 109a.
42. See Shteinman, volume 5, p. 252, quoting *Sefer HaKrisus* attributed to Rabeinu Shimshon of Kinun, who in turn quotes a tradition of Rav Sherira Gaon that Ravina died in 422 CE, five years before the death of Rav Ashi. See Moed Katan 25b according to the text of Rabeinu Chananel there regarding Rav Ashi's statement on the day of the death of his colleague, Ravina.
43. Kesubos 8a. See also Eiruvin 65a and Berachos 31a. See further in the text about this holy person.
44. Bava Metzia 104b.
45. See Avodah Zarah 50b where he describes his father as not being a *nagar* – a euphemism for a Torah sage who can unlock difficulties and construct answers to questions. In his modesty, Ravina did not consider himself to be a *nagar*.
46. Eiruvin 65a; Berachos 17a.
47. Bava Basra 16b; Berachos 20b; Eiruvin 85b; Bava Kama 14a, and many other places in the Talmud.
48. Gittin 73a; Shevuos 18a.
49. See Pesachim 105a-b; Horayos 9a; Gittin 32b.
50. See Sanhedrin 69a and Bava Metzia 74b for his discussions with Rav Huna and Rav Papa, the leading students and successors of Rava.
51. Zevachim 106b. However, as noted in the text, Rav Ashi's main mentor was Rav Kahana IV, an elder student of Rava, while Ravina was a younger disciple of Rava himself.
52. Shevuos 4b.
53. Eiruvin 63a and see Rashi there.
54. See for instance, Zevachim 2b; Sanhedrin 29b; Bava Metzia 61b; Moed Katan 24b, and many other places in the Talmud where Ravina is found visiting different locations in Babylonia.
55. Bava Metzia 86a.
56. Ibid.
57. Moed Katan 25b.
58. After the death of Rav Nachman bar Yitzchak, the *Rosh Yeshivah* in Pumbedisa was Rav Chama, from 357 to 378 CE. After his death, Rav Zvid became the head of the yeshivah, passing away in 385 CE. As mentioned above, Rav Ashi studied for a period of time with Rav Zvid, who himself was a student of Rava and of Abayei. See Bava Kama 5a, 21b and 27b as well as Berachos 46b and Sotah 32b, among many other places in the Talmud where Rav Zvid transmits teachings of Rava and Abayei. See also Iggeres Rav Sherira Gaon, Levin edition, p. 90, regarding Rav Zvid. He came to a tragic death at the hands of servants of the Exilarch. See Avodah Zarah 38b.
59. He succeeded Rav Zvid as the head of the yeshivah in Pumbedisa and served in that post for three years, passing away in 388 CE. There is another *Amora* mentioned in the Talmud also by the name of Rav Dimi. Therefore, this Rav Dimi is always referred to with the name of the city where he originally resided – Nehardea. See Avodah Zarah 11b where both Rav Dimi and Rav Dimi of Nehardea are mentioned regarding a ruling in halachah. See Bava Basra 21a and 22a; Shabbos 127a; Menachos 37b; Niddah 46a, and many other places in the

Talmud regarding teachings of his and incidents of his life. See also *Iggeres Rav Sherira Gaon*, Levin edition, p. 90. See footnote 104 in the previous chapter on Rava for other information about this scholar whose life span stretched over a number of generations of *Amoraim*.

60. He succeeded Rav Dimi of Nehardea as head of the yeshivah in Pumbedisa, serving in that role for seven years until his passing in 395 CE. See *Iggeres Rav Sherira Gaon*, Levin edition, p. 90. See also Yitzchak Isaac Halevi, *Doros HaRishonim*, (Warsaw, 1896) volume 3, p. 43 onwards. See also Bava Kama 98b and many other places in the Talmud where he is mentioned in conjunction with Rav Ashi.

61. He succeeded Rafram I as the head of the yeshivah in Pumbedisa and served in that capacity for nineteen years until his death in 414 CE. Again, see *Iggeres Rav Sherira Gaon*, Levin edition, p. 90. He is a colleague of Rav Ashi and Ravina and not to be confused with Rav Kahana IV of Pum Nahara, who was the teacher and mentor of Rav Ashi.

62. He succeeded Rav Kahana V as the head of the yeshivah in Pumbedisa, passing away in 419 CE. He was an important colleague of Rav Ashi and Ravina and aided them greatly in the work of editing the Talmud. See Eiruvin 90b; Zevachim 11b; Kesubos 31b; Chulin 58a; Bechoros 11a and Gittin 36a, among other places in the Talmud. His statements in the Talmud are almost always in conjunction with discussions with Ravina or Rav Ashi. See Chulin 93b; Pesachim 103b; Yoma 25b; Succah 18a, Yevamos 11a as examples. He was the son of Rava and studied for a period of time with Abayei.

63. See Bava Kama 36a; Zevachim 91a; Kiddushin 21a, and other places in the Talmud.

64. Taanis 4a; Bechoros 55a; Shabbos 103b; Yoma 48a, and other places in the Talmud. He was a close colleague of Rav Ashi and participated in the work of editing the Talmud. The two previous *Amoraim* named Rav Abba were Rav Abba I – who was a student of Rav Huna and Rav Yehudah bar Yechezkel – and Rav Abba II, who was a colleague of Rava and Abayei. See Halevi, volume 2, page 156, note 30.

65. Always associated in the Talmud with Rav Ashi. See Eiruvin 48b; Kesubos 76a; Chulin 39b; Nedarim 35a and Bava Metzia 96a, among many other places in the Talmud. There is another *Amora* with a very similar name, Rav Acha bar d'Rav Ivya, who was a disciple of Rabi Yochanan and a member of the third generation of *Amoraim*.

66. See Yevamos 59b; Chulin 26b; Meilah 10a; Bava Basra 83a; Menachos 8a and Bava Kama 82a, among many other places in the Talmud.

67. See Yevamos 31b; Bava Metzia 109b and Chulin 43a. There is another *Amora*, with a similar name, Rav Acha bar d'Rav Yosef, a disciple of Rav Huna and Rav Chisda, and a member of the third generation of *Amoraim*. See Dikdukei Sofrim, Bava Metzia 87a. Rav Nachman bar Yitzchak was his nephew. See Shabbos 140a.

68. Kesubos 63b. See Gittin,19b where Rav Gamda discusses a tradition in halachah with Rava himself. See also Nedarim 50a about a wondrous occurrence that happened to him.

69. Shabbos 109a; Chulin 53a; Avodah Zarah 69a. He was a student of Rav Kahana IV of Pum Nahara and many of his statements in the Talmud are recollections of the teachings of Rav Kahana IV.

70. Bava Metzia 61b; Gittin 77a; Kiddushin 6a, and many other places in the Talmud. He also was a student of Rav Kahana IV of Pum Nahara. See Bava Basra 171b and Avodah Zarah 59a.

71. Shabbos 82a and 155b. He was a colleague of Rav Kahana IV. See Kiddushin 81b and Niddah 66b.
72. He was a disciple of Avimei of Hagrunya, who was a student of Rava. See Bava Metzia 77b; Kesubos 109b; and Makkos 13b. His statements in the Talmud are also almost always associated with his discussions with Rav Ashi. See Bava Metzia 80a and 97a as well as Bava Kama 90a. He had a close personal relationship with Rav Ashi. See Sotah 46b.
73. See Berachos 3b, 44b, and 55b; Bava Metzia 22a and Pesachim 103b. Mar Zutra visited with Rav Ashi often. See, for example, Berachos 26a and 46b. Mar Zutra I was an *Amora* at the time of Mar Shmuel, almost two centuries earlier than Mar Zutra II.
74. See Zevachim 19b; Bava Basra 55a and Gittin 19b.

SECTION IX

Final Generation of Amoraim

1. See Yevamos 75b; Yoma 81b.
2. He ruled the yeshivah for five years, from 427 to 432 CE. See Iggeres Rav Sherira Gaon, Levin edition, p. 94.
3. See Eiruvin 8a; Pesachim 117b and Succah 13b.
4. See Eiruvin 93b; Gittin 15b, and other places in the Talmud.
5. More about him later in this chapter.
6. This Rav Huna is not to be confused with Rav Huna, the disciple of Rav or with Huna bar Nosson, the Exilarch of the time of Rav Ashi and Ravina the First. Regarding Mreimar's discussions with Ravina bar Rav Huna in the Talmud, see Beitzah 20a; Shabbos 81b and 86b; Pesachim 117b; Chulin 132a, and many other places in the Talmud.
7. Yitzchak Isaac Halevi, *Doros HaRishonim*, (Warsaw, 1896), volume 2, p. 588 forward and also in volume 3, p. 13.
8. See for example, Nedarim 60b and 90a
9. Iggeres Rav Sherira Gaon, Levin edition, p. 95.
10. Rav Idi bar Avin I was a student of Rav Chisda and a member of the fourth generation of Babylonian *Amoraim*. Rav Idi bar Avin II, who is the subject of this footnote, was a colleague of Rav Ashi and a bridge person between the sixth and seventh generations of the Babylonian *Amoraim*.
11. Iggeres Rav Sherira Gaon, Levin edition, p. 94-95.
12. I know that all of this is somewhat confusing, but please bear with me in this. This Rav Nachman is not to be confused with Rav Nachman bar Yaakov of the earlier generations of *Amoraim* or with Rav Nachman bar Yitzchak, also of an earlier generation. In the Talmud, Rav Nachman bar Rav Huna is referred to as Rav Nachman alone, without mention of his father's name. See Kiddushin 6b and Kesubos 7a, among many other places in the Talmud. See also Halevi, volume 3, p. 46. He was the brother of Ravina the Latter.
13. Iggeres Rav Sherira Gaon, Levin edition, p. 95.
14. Ibid.
15. Unlike Mreimar, Rav Idi bar Avin and Rav Nachman bar Huna – who were older than Mar bar Rav Ashi and were colleagues of his father – Rav Acha M'difti was of the same age as Mar bar Rav Ashi and was only a student of Rav Ashi. See

Berachos 45b and Rashi there. Mar bar Rav Ashi was invited by the rabbis to attend the nominating session, apparently to confirm Rav Acha M'difti for the leadership role. In his great modesty, Mar bar Rav Ashi attended this meeting for that purpose, though the position had been predicted to fall to him and he felt that it was due him. The rabbis in attendance, now somehow recognizing Mar bar Rav Ashi's greatness in Torah and exemplary character, changed their previous proposed plan and awarded the position as head of the Sura yeshivah to him. See Bava Basra 12b.

16. Bava Basra 12b.
17. Nedarim 81a.
18. Iggeres Rav Sherira Gaon, Levin edition, p. 95.
19. See Eiruvin 102b; Chulin 76b, 97b and 98a.
20. Kiddushin 31b.
21. Shabbos 119a. He stated that, "they [the Torah scholars] are as my own flesh and blood."
22. Bava Basra 12b; Iggeres Rav Sherira Gaon, Levin edition, p. 85.
23. Gittin 7a.
24. Iggeres Rav Sherira Gaon, Levin edition, p. 95.
25. Ibid.
26. Eiruvin 65a.
27. Berachos 39b.
28. Yevamos 22a.
29. Berachos 31a.
30. Ibid.
31. Pesachim 68b.
32. Eliezer Shteinman, *Be'er HaTalmud* (Tel Aviv: Masada Press, 1967), volume 4, p.183, quoting from *Seder HaDoros*.
33. Berachos 17a.
34. Berachos 54a.
35. Iggeres Rav Sherira Gaon, Levin edition, p. 95.
36. Ibid.
37. Shabbos 95a; Succah 32a; Bava Basra 64a and Bava Kama 119a.
38. Iggeres Rav Sherira Gaon, Levin edition, p. 95.
39. See Halevi, volume 3, p. 7 onwards, correcting our text in the Iggeres Rav Sherira Gaon. This is also the date given in the *Sefer Kabbalah* to Rabbi Avraham ben David.
40. Berachos 39b and Menachos 68b.
41. Chulin 132a.
42. Nedarim 60b and 90a.
43. Iggeres Rav Sherira Gaon, Levin edition, p. 95.
44. Ibid., pp. 69-70.
45. Later scholars and commentators to the Talmud have identified certain small portions of the actual Talmud, such as the first folio of Kiddushin, as being the work of the *Rabanan Savoraim*.
46. See Yevamos 59b; Chulin 64b; Meilah 10a; Bava Basra 83a; Menachos 8a; Beitzah 23a.
47. Iggeres Rav Sherira Gaon, Levin edition, pp. 95-97.
48. Ibid.
49. Rav Rechmei I was a student of Abayei. See Nazir 13a and Pesachim 39a according to the text of the ancient Munich manuscript of Pesachim. He died under strange and tragic circumstances on Yom Kippur eve. See Kesubos 62b.

Rav Rechumei III was a member of the first generation of *Rabanan Savoraim*. He is mentioned in the Talmud at Eiruvin 11a and 71b. See the gloss of the Bach (Rabbi Yoel Sirkis) there at Eiruvin 71b.

50. Zevachim 77a; Chulin 89a; Yoma 78a..
51. Iggeres Rav Sherira Gaon, Levin edition, pp. 95-97.
52. Zevachim 16a; Bava Metzia 42b; Chulin 47b.
53. Naftal, *HaTalmud V'yotzrav, Doros HaAmoraim*, (Tel Aviv: Yavneh Publishing House, 1972), volume 5, p. 283.
54. Iggeres Rav Sherira Gaon, Levin edition, p. 97. According to his reckoning, the *Rabanan Savoraim* completed their work about the year 500 CE. See Naftal, volume 5, p. 284.
55. Iggeres Rav Sherira Gaon, Levin edition, p. 97.
56. Ibid., pp. 69-70.
57. Ibid.

Glossary

Abuha D'Shmuel – the father of Mar Shmuel

Acharonim – the latter rabbinic scholars dating from the sixteenth century onwards

Acheirim – others

Acher – Rabi Elisha ben Avuyah – the "other" one – the apostate

Achnaee – a snake

Achsanya – an inn; a home

Aggadah – legend, metaphor, the non-halachic aspect and discipline of the Oral Law

Aggadic – referring to *aggadah*

Aleph – the first letter of the Hebrew alphabet.

Amidah – the basic eighteen (nineteen) blessing prayer recited thrice daily in Jewish prayer services

Amoraim – the scholars and authors of the Talmud

Apikores, Apikorsim – a non-believer, a rebel against Judaism's tenets and observances

Arvis – the evening/night prayer services

Oso hayom – that particular day, the day that Rabi Elazar ben Azaryah became the Nasi

Av beis din – the chief judge of a rabbinic court. In the times of the Sanhedrin, he was the assistant to the *Nasi*, who was the titular head of the Sanhedrin.

Avi Hamishna – literally, the "father" of the Mishnah. It was used in reference to *Rabi Oshiya*, the scholar most expert regarding the Mishnah

Avinu Malkeinu – a penitential prayer recited on fast days and the Ten Days of Repentance

Avos D'Rabi Nosson – an expanded form of the Mishnah tractate of Avos as developed in the yeshiva of Rabi Nosson in late Mishnaic times

Ayin Hara – the evil eye

Bas Kol – an "echo" from heaven, a spiritual message from heaven

Batei Din – Jewish rabbinic courts

Beis Din – a Jewish rabbinic court

Beis HaBechirah – a synonym for the Temple in Jerusalem; a commentary to the Talmud by Rabbi Menachem HaMeiri of fourteenth-century Provence

Be'er HaTalmud – a four volume work by Eliezer Shteinman on the men of the Talmud

Beis HaVaad – literally, the meeting place of the scholars

Bikurim – the offering in the Temple of the first fruits of the yearly crop

Birkas HaMazon – the prayers that constitute grace after meals

Birchas HaMinin – the additional nineteenth blessing added to the Amidah. It is aimed to exclude proselytizing Jewish Christians from participating in Jewish prayer services and society

Bo Bayom – on that particular day
Breisa, Breisos – Talmudic comments and addenda to the Mishnah

C   *Chacham* – literally, a wise man. Also used as a rabbinic title.
Chatas – a sin offering in the Temple
Chaver – a Torah scholar; a friend
Chazara – a review session of the Talmudic lesson of the day
Cherem – a ban, to ostracize, excommunication
Ches – the eighth letter of the Hebrew alphabet
Chevra Kadisha – the holy society, a Jewish burial society
Chidush – a new original interpretation or explanation in Torah studies
Chilul Hashem – behavior that denigrates God's Name and Torah and Jews in the eyes
    of the public
Chulin – a tractate of Mishnah/Talmud; something which is not holy

D   *Darkei Noam* – ways of pleasantness. It is one of the basic values of Torah and Judaism.
Diaspora – the Jewish people scattered throughout the Exile in the world
Derech Eretz Zuta – a tractate of halacha and aggadah of immediate post-Talmudic times
Devarim – the fifth of the Five Books of Moses
Doros HaRishonim – a seminal Jewish history book written in the latter part of the
    nineteenth century by Yitzhak Isaac Halevi

E   *Eeseeyim* – Essenes, a sect of Jews that existed in Mishnaic times
Ein mazal l'Yisrael – literally Israel is not governed by any stars or constellations; it
    has also come to mean that Israel has no predetermined fortune; in the popular
    vernacular it is used to indicate that the Jewish people do not always have good
    luck
Eiruv – literally, a mixing; an halachic construct that joins different property positions
    as far as Sabbath and holiday requirements are concerned
Ells – a measure of distance
Eshkolos – *Shehakol Bo* – the combination of all positive qualities and talents in one
    person

G   *Gavrah Rabah* – a great person
Gavra Rabah U'mitla – a great man who limps
Gematria – the science of determining the numerical value of the letters of the
    Hebrew alphabet
Gemilus chasadim – acts of loving kindness and charity towards other human beings
Geonim – the rabbinic scholars and rulers of Jewish Babylonia from the seventh to the
    eleventh centuries
Giyura – a convert to Judaism

H   *Haggadah shel Pesach* – the book of the service of the Pesach seder
Halacha – Jewish Torah law and practice
Halacha l'Moshe miSinai – Jewish law and practice as received by Moses on Sinai,
    though not specifically mentioned or indicated in the text of the Torah itself
Halachos – specific Jewish Torah laws and practices
HaTalmud V'yotzrav – a multi-volume work by Avraham Naftal describing the history
    of the writing of the Mishnah and Talmud and sketching the lives of the scholars
    of that time
Hatzalah Poorta – a small salvation

Hilchos Melachim – the final section of Mishneh Torah authored by Rabbi Moshe ben Maimon

Iggeres Rav Sherira Gaon – a concise history of the Jewish people written by one of the leading scholars of tenth-century Babylonia

Kabbalah – the secret, hidden, spiritual, mystical interpretation of Torah and texts

Kabbalistic – relating to Kabbalah

Kapdan – someone who is exacting, a disciplinarian

Kareis – literally, "cut off." It refers to a heavenly punishment for sins by a shortened life span.

Kesubah – the marriage contract between husband and wife detailing their obligations towards one another

Kidah – a form of bowing or prostrating one's self

Kiddush Hashem – behavior that sanctifies God's Name in the eyes of the public

Kodashim b'chutz – eating or slaughtering "holy" food from the sacrifices outside of the required Temple precincts

Kineret – the Sea of Galilee

Kinos – lamentations, dirges, prayers of sadness and mourning

Kodashim – the fifth series of the Mishnah dealing with laws of the Temple service and of kashrus

Kohein, kohanim – a member or members the priestly clan of Israel descended patrilineally from Aharon

Kohein Gadol – the great kohein, the High Priest of Israel

Koheles – the book of Ecclesiastes

Koreich – the "sandwich" of matzo, bitter herbs and the Paschal Lamb (in Temple times) eaten as part of the Pesach seder service

Knesses HaGedolah – the Great Assembly of 120 scholars convened and established at the time of Ezra and the beginning of the Second Temple times

Kusim – the Samaritans in Second Temple times. The word was later was used as a generic term for any and all non-Jews.

L'tarbus raah – joining a bad society, following a bad culture

Maasecha Yekarvucha, Umaasecha Yerachakucha – your actions and behavior will bring you closer to the scholars of Israel or they will distance you from them.

Maharsha – Rabbi Shmuel Eidelis, a sixteenth-century Polish commentator to the Talmud

Maror – bitter herbs eaten as part of the Pesach seder service

Matzoh – the unleavened grain "bread" that is eaten by Jews on Pesach

Mavo LaTalmud – literally, The Introduction to the Talmud. A scholarly work written by Rabbi Shmuel Hanagid of eighth-century Spain.

Mechadedei Tfei – sharper, more creative, more brilliant

Mechkarim B'Toldos Yisrael – a book of essays on matters of Jewish history

Megillos – literally, scrolls, manuscripts

Mesorah – literally, tradition. It is used especially regarding the punctuation and cantillation of the words of the Torah.

Middos – literally "measures." It is the name of a tractate in Mishnah. It also refers to human character traits.

Mincha – the afternoon prayer service

Minim – the early Christians; a synonym for Jewish apostates

Misah Yafah – a good death

Mishnah, Mishnayos – a section of Oral Law teachings as written and edited by Rabi Yehudah HaNasi of second/third-century Galilee. The Mishnah is the basis for the Talmud.

Mishnah Rishona – the earliest forms of the Mishnah produced before the time of Rabi Yehudah HaNasi.

Mishnahso Kav V'Naki – his statements in the Mishnah are few in number but are of high quality

Mishneh Torah – the encyclopedic fourteen volume compilation of Rabbi Moshe ben Maimon (Rambam) of twelfth-century Spain, Morocco and Egypt

Mitzvos – literally commandments. The 613 obligations of Jews as prescribed by the Torah.

Mitzpeh Eisan – a commentary to Talmud by a nineteenth-century scholar, Rabbi Avraham Eisan

Moed – the second series of the Mishnah dealing with Sabbath and holidays

Mufla Sheb'sanhedrin – the most noted scholar sitting on the Sanhedrin

Musaf – the additional morning prayer on the New Moon, Sabbath and holidays

Mussar – ethics; chastisement

N   *Nasi* – literally, prince, leader, president. The head of the Sanhedrin was the Nasi.

Nashim – the third series of the Mishnah dealing with domestic relations and vows

Nazir – a tractate of the Mishnah/Talmud; a person who has accepted Nazarite vows

Negaim – a volume of the Mishnah concerning the laws of purity regarding dermatological and other "plagues"

Nesi'im – the plural of nasi

Netzivin – a town in Babylonia, the home of Rabi Yehudah ben Bseira

Nezikin – the fourth series of the Mishnah dealing with matters of commerce, law, courts and torts

O   *Oholos* – a volume of the Mishnah concerning the laws of purity and impurity regarding the presence of a corpse or its limbs in an enclosed area

P   *Pardes* – literally, an orchard. It is a term euphemistically used to describe the place where one enters into deeply spiritual and metaphysical inquiry and thought.

Perush HaRambam l'Mishnah – the commentary of Maimonides to Mishnah

Perushim – the Pharisees; the group that composed the Tannaim of the Mishnah

Pnei Moshe – a commentary to Talmud Yerushalmi by Rabbi Moshe Margoliyus of seventeenth-century Amsterdam and later of Lithuania

Pruzbul – a legalism created by Hillel to enable creditors to preserve their loans after the Sabbatical year passed

Pulmos Shel Kitos - the wars and persecution inflicted on the Jews by Kitos (Quietos) a Roman general

R   *Rishonim* – the great rabbinic scholars of the Medieval Era

Rosh Yeshiva – the head of the yeshiva

Ruach HaKodesh – holy spirit, Divine inspiration

S   *Stam Mishnah* – a Mishnah which has no attribution as to its author

Shochet – a ritual slaughterer of poultry and animals

Seder – one of the six orders of the Mishnah; the Pesach service and meal of the first night of the holiday

Seder Eliyahu Zuta – a minor tractate supplementing the Talmud from post-Talmudic times

Selichos – penitential prayers

Semichah – rabbinic ordination

Shacharis – the morning prayer service

Shechinah – the Divine Presence and Spirit

Shechitah – the ritual method of slaughtering animals and birds

Sh'Ein Tocho K'Varo – insincerity, hypocrisy

Shemittah – the sabbatical year occurring once every seven years

Sheyarei Knesses HaGedolah – the last surviving members of the Men of the Great Assembly constituted by Ezra

Shisha Sidrei Mishnah – the six orders of the Mishnah that comprises its entire content

Shma Yisrael – Hear O Israel. It is the basic declaration of the Judaic faith and testifies to God's oneness, unity and uniqueness It is recited twice daily by Jews in their prayer services.

Shmad – forced conversion, extermination

Shmoneh Esrei – literally, eighteen. It is the name commonly used for the standing part of the three prayer services of the day. It contains eighteen blessings, hence its name. A nineteenth blessing was added in Mishnaic times but the name "eighteen" remained in popular use.

Simchas Beis HaShoevah – the celebration in Jerusalem on *Succos* in honor of the drawing of the water for the libation of the water on the altar of the Temple

Stam Mishnah Rabi Meir – a Mishnah that has no author attributed to it in its text is from Rabi Meir

Succah – the booth in which Jews reside during the festival of *Succos*

Succos – the plural of succah

Taharos – the sixth series of the Mishnah dealing with the laws of ritual purity   T

Tahor – Hebrew word for "pure"

Takanos - rabbinic ordinances

Takanos Usha – the decrees and decisions of the Sanhedrin when it met in Usha

Tanna Hu uPalig - he is a Tanna and therefore can disagree with the opinion of the Mishnah

Tannaim – the scholars of the Mishnah

Targum or *Tirgum* – the translation of the Torah into a non-Hebrew language, usually Aramaic or Greek

Tefillin – phylacteries

Teshuva – repentance

Tikun haolam – perfecting the world

Tosefta – a collection of breisos that complement the Talmud arranged in a separate work

Tzaddik – a most righteous, holy person

Tzedokim – the Sadducees

Tzipor – bird

Uktzin – the final tractate of the Mishnah   U

Vatran – someone who gives up on one's rights easily, a forgiving person   V

Vayikrah Rabah – the section of Midrash Rabah dealing with Vayikra/Leviticus

World to Come – spiritual afterlife after physical death; the world after the messianic era   W

Y   *Yalkut Shimoni* – an anthology of aggadic interpretations of the Torah by the medieval
        sage, Rabbi Shimon Hadarshan
        Yalkut Shimoni Tehillim – the Yalkut Shimoni to Psalms
        Yatza L'Tarbus Raah – literally, went out to a bad environment or culture. It became
        an accepted euphuism for apostasy as well.
        Yesh Omrim – there are those who say
        Yesod HaMishnah v'Arichasa – a seminal work on the origins of the Mishnah by Rabbi
        Reuven Margoliyus, a noted twentieth-century scholar
        Yetzer Hara – the evil inclination within humans

Z   *Zecher L'Mikdash* – a reminder of the Temple and its rituals and procedures
        Zechus – a merit
        Zeir – Hebrew for "small" or "little"
        Zeraim – the first series of the Mishnah dealing with agricultural issues
        Zohar - the basic book of kabbalistic thought attributed to Rabi Shimon ben Yochai of
        third-century Land of Israel
        Zugos – literally, pairs. The early Tannaim until Hillel and Shammai were paired
        together in their studies and teachings and positions in the Sanhedrin.

Index

A

Abayei *105, 106, 108, 109, 110, 120, 129, 135, 136, 137, 138, 139, 140, 142, 143, 144, 146, 147, 148, 153, 154, 209, 212, 215, 218, 220, 221, 222, 223, 226, 227, 230, 231, 232, 233, 235*
Abba bar Abba *29, 30, 40, 191*
Abba bar Acha Karsala *21*
Abba Kohein Bardala *66, 67*
Abba Mar *156*
Abba Suraah *156*
Abuha d'Shmuel *29, 40*
Acher *63, 241*
Aggadata D'bei Rav *38*
Aleinu *37*
Ameimar *153, 155, 161, 165, 166, 227, 229, 230*
Amgushei *35*
Antoninus *34*
Artban *34*
Artchan *34*
Avimei *78, 80, 88, 89, 99, 142, 148, 206, 220, 234*
Ayvu *21, 38, 39*

B

Bar Kapara *30, 66, 67, 201*
Bar Kochba *4, 13*
Bas Kol *241*
Beis Shearim *22*
Ben Azai *24, 138, 185*
Ben Bahg Bahg *12*
Bnei Brak *190*
Breisa *29*

C

Chaverim *35, 36*
Cherem *242*

chevraya d'bei Rav *84*
Chezkiyah *67*
Choma *138, 220*
Chova *87*
Christianity *4, 13, 129, 138*
Christians *79, 126, 129, 137, 138, 177, 203, 241, 243*

D

dina d'malchusa dina *44*

E

Egypt *70, 244*

G

Galilee *187, 243, 244*
Great Assembly *4, 6, 13, 38, 243, 245*

H

halachah l'Moshe mi'Sinai *11*
Herod *76*
High Priest *135, 217, 243*
Hillel *VII, 6, 130, 166, 193, 244, 246*
Hillel II *130*
Huna bar Nosson *161, 166, 234*
Hutzal *26, 27, 33, 34, 43, 95, 186, 188*

I

Ilfa *58, 198*
Isur *47, 194*

K

Karna *21, 26, 27, 32, 40, 42, 186, 192*
Kaylil *135, 212*
Knesses HaGedolah *38, 243, 245*

M

Mar bar Rav Ashi *161, 163, 172, 173, 174, 175, 234, 235*
Mar breih d'Ravina *165, 174, 175*
Mar Kashisha *88, 92, 208*
Mar Shmuel *21, 26, 27, 28, 29, 30, 31, 32, 33, 35, 36, 37, 40, 41, 42, 43, 44, 45, 46, 47, 48, 49, 50, 51, 55, 56, 62, 76, 84, 89, 95, 96, 97, 99, 114, 143, 186, 188, 189, 191, 192, 193, 194, 195, 196, 197, 200, 204, 206, 209, 210, 211, 212, 215, 216, 227, 230, 234, 241*
Marta *148, 226*
Mar Ukva *30, 89, 92, 210*
Mar Yenuka *88, 92, 208*
Mar Zutra I *47, 153, 155, 229, 234*
Masa Machsiya *35, 96, 149, 162, 163, 165, 171, 173, 175, 189, 231*

Mechilta *38*
Mechoza *142, 146, 147, 149, 153, 154, 223, 227, 232*
Mreimar *165, 171, 176, 234*

N

Narash *149, 153, 154, 155, 156, 161, 229*
Nasi *25, 34, 69, 70, 130, 241, 244*
Nehardea *26, 29, 30, 31, 32, 33, 34, 35, 40, 41, 42, 43, 50, 58, 62, 84, 89, 96, 135, 149, 155, 157, 161, 165, 188, 189, 191, 197, 211, 215, 227, 229, 230, 232, 233*
Netzivin *34, 40, 191, 244*

O

Odenath *50, 51*

P

Palmyra *50, 51*
Papa bar Netzer *50*
Papunaya *120*
Parthian Empire *34, 35, 44, 50*
Pumbedisa *90, 93, 96, 97, 98, 105, 106, 107, 108, 109, 110, 112, 120, 125, 136, 138, 140, 142, 143, 146, 147, 148, 149, 153, 154, 161, 176, 204, 207, 211, 213, 220, 226, 227, 229, 232, 233*
Pum Nahara *149, 156, 157, 162, 229, 233*

Q

Queen Ifra Hurmiz *143*

R

Rabah bar Nachmani *107, 118*
Rabah bar Rav Huna *84, 87, 99, 142, 144*
rabanan d'kisri *76*
rabanan nechusei *137, 211*
Raban Gamliel *VIII, 23, 25, 185*
Rabi Abahu *78, 79, 80, 81, 125, 128, 129, 191, 198, 203, 206, 220*
Rabi Abba *125, 126, 127, 128, 166, 219*
Rabi Affeis *31, 66, 67*
Rabi Akiva *VII, VIII, 24, 112*
Rabi Chanina bar Chama *31, 40, 66, 67, 192*
Rabi Chanina of Tzipori *161*
Rabi Chiya *VIII, 21, 22, 23, 24, 25, 28, 29, 33, 55, 57, 67, 68, 78, 80, 87, 107, 184, 185, 192, 201*
Rabi Chizkiyah *78, 80*
Rabi Elazar ben Pedas *55, 76, 108, 114, 115, 125, 126, 216*
Rabi Hoshiyahu *67, 125, 197*
Rabi Meir *VIII, 183, 185, 193, 197, 200, 245*
Rabi Nosson *241*
Rabi Pinchas *78, 80*
Rabi Shemen ben Abba *40, 47*

Rabi Shimon ben Lakish 28, 55, 56, 60, 63, 66, 67, 68, 69, 70, 71, 72, 73, 76, 78, 81, 115, 116, 125, 128, 199, 200, 201, 219

Rabi Tachlifa 78, 79

Rabi Yanai 55, 57, 66, 68

Rabi Yehoshua ben Levi 67, 71

Rabi Yehudah ben Chanina 67

Rabi Yehudah HaNasi VIII, 21, 22, 23, 38, 40, 55, 66, 95, 143, 163, 184, 200, 210, 244

Rabi Yehudah Nesia 25

Rabi Yirmiyahu 78, 80, 204

Rabi Yishmael 33

Rabi Yitzchak ben Avdimi 22, 184

Rabi Yitzchak Nafcha 125, 127, 128

Rabi Yochanan 28, 29, 55, 56, 57, 58, 59, 60, 61, 62, 63, 64, 65, 66, 67, 68, 69, 70, 71, 72, 76, 78, 80, 81, 89, 99, 105, 106, 107, 108, 115, 118, 125, 127, 128, 146, 184, 197, 198, 199, 200, 201, 211, 212, 216, 217, 220, 233

Rabi Yonah 78, 80

Rabi Yossi 78

Rabi Zeira 78, 105, 110, 114, 115, 116, 117, 212, 215

Rafram I 161, 165, 233

Rafram II 176

Rami bar Chama 88, 92, 142, 161

Rami bar Yechezkel 95, 97

Rava 21, 29, 39, 40, 84, 87, 88, 89, 92, 95, 105, 107, 109, 110, 120, 128, 135, 138, 142, 143, 144, 145, 146, 147, 148, 149, 153, 154, 156, 161, 165, 175, 176, 185, 186, 194, 206, 208, 209, 210, 215, 218, 221, 222, 223, 224, 225, 226, 227, 228, 229, 230, 232, 233, 234

Rava bar Rabah 107

Rava bar Rav Acha 84, 87, 226

Rav Acha 84, 87, 88, 99, 110, 119, 120, 129, 142, 148, 149, 153, 154, 161, 165, 166, 172, 176, 226, 233, 234, 235

Rav Acha bar Adah 119

Rav Acha bar Rav Huna 84, 87

Rav Acha bar Yaakov 120, 153, 154

Rav Acha breih d'Ravah 166

Rav Acha breih d'Rav Ika 120

Rav Achaei m'bei Chatim and Rav Ravai m'Rov 177

Rav Acha M'difti 172, 234, 235

Rav Achdvoi bar Ami 120

Rav Achi 27, 33

Rav Ada bar Ahava 99, 105, 142, 209, 226

Rav Ada Sava 47

Rav Affeis 57

Rav Ami 55, 63, 66, 78, 80, 105, 107, 114, 118, 125, 126, 127, 128, 186, 197, 205, 213, 218, 219, 220, 226

Rav Ashi 149, 153, 157, 161, 162, 163, 164, 165, 166, 171, 172, 173, 174, 175, 186, 194, 229, 230, 231, 232, 233, 234, 235

Rav Assi 26, 27, 28, 29, 33, 43, 55, 66, 78, 80, 95, 105, 107, 114, 115, 120, 125, 126, 127, 128, 186, 204, 205, 213, 218, 219, 220

Rav Assi I 26, 27, 28, 29, 33, 43, 95, 186

Rav Bibi bar Abayei 135, 138, 218, 230

Rav Chama bar Gurya 88, 89

Rav Chanan bar Nosson *227*

Rav Chanan of Nehardea *166*

Rav Chanina bar Chama *21, 55, 57, 210*

Rav Chilkiyah *226*

Rav Chisda *21, 29, 39, 84, 86, 87, 88, 89, 90, 91, 92, 93, 95, 96, 98, 99, 105, 106, 107, 110, 118, 119, 121, 135, 136, 142, 143, 146, 183, 190, 197, 206, 207, 208, 209, 210, 211, 213, 223, 226, 230, 233, 234*

Rav Chiya *21, 22, 29, 30, 40, 66, 84, 99, 135, 136, 204*

Rav Chiya bar Ada *66*

Rav Dimi *99, 110, 113, 135, 137, 148, 161, 165, 166, 215, 226, 227, 232, 233*

Rav Gamda *166, 233*

Rav Geviha m'bei Ksil *165, 176*

Rav Gidel *21, 29, 225, 226*

Rav Hamnuna *42, 84, 95, 110, 114, 119, 148, 153, 154, 214, 216, 217*

Rav Hamnuna II *95, 110, 119, 153, 154*

Rav Hillel *166*

Rav Hoshiya *30*

Rav Huna *21, 28, 35, 37, 40, 42, 43, 84, 85, 86, 87, 88, 89, 90, 95, 96, 99, 105, 106, 108, 110, 114, 118, 119, 120, 121, 125, 126, 142, 144, 153, 154, 155, 156, 157, 161, 165, 171, 172, 176, 186, 192, 197, 204, 205, 209, 210, 211, 214, 218, 227, 232, 233, 234*

Rav Huna bar Chiya *95, 105, 108*

Rav Idi bar Avin *120, 153, 154, 161, 165, 171, 234*

Ravin *95, 120, 135, 137, 142, 148, 222*

Ravina *142, 161, 162, 163, 165, 166, 171, 174, 175, 176, 209, 227, 230, 231, 232, 233, 234*

Ravina the First *171, 174, 175, 176, 234*

Ravina the Latter *171, 175, 176, 234*

Rav Kahana I *28, 186, 210, 229*

Rav Kahana IV *142, 153, 156, 157, 161, 162, 186, 227, 229, 230, 232, 233*

Rav Kahana V *161, 165, 186, 233*

Rav Levi ben Sissas *30*

Rav Mari *40, 47, 88, 92, 194*

Rav Masna *30, 114, 161, 216, 230*

Rav Mesharshiya *142, 146*

Rav Mordechai *165*

Rav Nachman bar Rav Huna *161, 165, 171, 172, 234*

Rav Nachman bar Yaakov *88, 95, 105, 106, 110, 120, 142, 204, 207, 225, 234*

Rav Nachman bar Yitzchak *142, 153, 154, 156, 161, 165, 174, 226, 232, 233, 234*

Rav Oshiya *38, 95, 105, 118, 119, 129, 197, 217*

Rav Papa *95, 99, 120, 135, 142, 153, 154, 155, 156, 161, 209, 228, 229, 230, 232*

Rav Papi *161, 230*

Rav Pinchas *88, 92*

Rav Rechumei II *165, 176*

Rav Safra *128, 129, 135, 137*

Rav Sama breih d'Rav Ashi *161, 163*

Rav Sheishes *88, 95, 105, 106, 120, 135, 136, 142, 174, 211, 212, 213, 218, 226*

Rav Shmuel bar Rav Yitzchak *118*

Rav Shmuel bar Sheila *36*

Rav Yaakov bar Acha *120*

Rav Yechezkel *95*

Rav Yehudah bar Yechezkel *28, 37, 40, 42, 84, 88, 90, 95, 97, 105, 106, 110, 114, 118, 119, 121, 126, 135, 136, 142, 186, 204, 210, 211, 212, 216, 217, 218, 230, 233*
Rav Yeymar *161*
Rav Yonah *225, 226*
Rav Yosef *84, 88, 95, 97, 105, 106, 107, 108, 110, 111, 112, 113, 114, 120, 121, 135, 136, 137, 138, 139, 142, 143, 146, 176, 177, 209, 212, 214, 215, 218, 221, 226, 227, 233*
Rav Yosef bar Ravah *146*
Rav Yosef Breih d'Rav Sala Chasida *227*
Rav Zeira *78, 80*
Rav Zvid *135, 148, 157, 161, 165, 227, 232*
Reish Galusa *32, 39, 89, 119, 143, 186, 210, 229*
Rosh Yeshivah *84, 87, 90, 204, 207, 232*
Ruach HaKodesh *244*

S

Sadducees *245*
Sanhedrin *22, 23, 130, 183, 184, 185, 186, 187, 188, 189, 190, 192, 194, 195, 196, 197, 198, 199, 200, 201, 202, 203, 204, 205, 206, 207, 208, 209, 211, 212, 213, 214, 215, 216, 217, 218, 219, 220, 221, 222, 224, 226, 227, 229, 230, 231, 232, 239, 241, 244, 245, 246*
Savoraim *7, 166, 176, 177, 180, 235, 236*
Second Temple *4, 13, 97, 115, 243*
semichah *23, 24, 41, 80, 115, 125, 126, 192*
Shachnatzvu *154*
Shammai *VII, 6, 246*
Sheila bar Avina *28*
Shevor Malka *36, 46, 49, 50*
Shimi *21, 38, 39, 129, 135, 138, 191*
sidra *26, 27, 32, 34, 41, 42, 189*
Sifra D'bei Rav *38*
Sifrei D'bei Rav *38*
Stam Mishnah *244, 245*
Sura *21, 30, 34, 35, 36, 42, 43, 50, 58, 84, 85, 86, 87, 88, 89, 90, 93, 95, 96, 98, 106, 107, 110, 142, 149, 160, 162, 171, 172, 173, 174, 175, 188, 189, 204, 209, 213, 229, 231, 235*

T

Tachlifa *78, 79, 88, 92, 99, 129*
Tadmor *50*
Takanos *245*
Tavyumei *174, 231*
tekiasa d'bei Rav *37, 191*
Tiberias *22, 24, 28, 29, 56, 58, 66, 68, 76, 78, 79, 81, 107, 108, 114, 115, 116, 117, 118, 119, 124, 125, 126, 134, 137, 138, 146, 174, 186, 191, 211, 216, 218*
Tosefta D'bei Rav *38*
Tzedokim *245*
Tzipori *22, 161, 197*

U

Ukva *21, 30, 39, 88, 89, 92, 210*
Ulla *99, 114, 161, 215, 216, 230*
Ulla bar Yishmael *114, 215, 216, 230*

Y

yarchei kallah *35, 85, 109, 154, 189*
Yavneh *184, 192, 197, 200, 207, 208, 212, 214, 221, 223, 236*

Z

Zavdi *120, 227*
Zeirei I *29, 187, 215*
Zoroastrian sect *35*

About the Author

Rabbi Berel Wein, the founder and director of The Destiny Foundation since 1996, has, for over 20 years, been identified with the popularization of Jewish history through worldwide lectures, his more than 600 audiotapes, books, seminars, educational tours and, most recently, dramatic and documentary films.

Rabbi Wein is a graduate of the Hebrew Theological College and Roosevelt College in Chicago. He received his Juris Doctor Degree from De Paul University Law School and a Doctor of Hebrew Letters from Hebrew Theological College.

Rabbi Wein was a practicing lawyer for a number of years and in 1964 assumed the pulpit of the Beth Israel Congregation in Miami Beach, Florida, where he remained until 1972. In 1973 he became the Rabbi of Congregation Bais Torah in Suffern, New York and remained in that position for 24 years. He was then appointed Executive Vice President of the Union of Orthodox Organizations of America and was Rabbinic Administrator of the Kashrus Division for five years after that.

In 1977 he founded Yeshiva Shaarei Torah in Suffern, New York and remained its Rosh Hayeshiva until 1997. Rabbi Wein's book of halachic essays, *Chikrei Halacha* was published by Mosad Harav Kook in 1976 and *Eyunim B'm'sechtoth Hatalmud* was published in 1989.

Rabbi Wein has authored four Jewish history books – *Triumph of*

Survival, The Story of the Jews in the Modern Era; Herald of Destiny, the Medieval Era; Echoes of Glory, the Classical Era and *Faith and Fate, The Story of the Jews in the Twentieth Century* – all of which have received popular and critical acclaim.

Rabbi Wein authors and edits a monthly newsletter – *The Wein Press* – a source of information and inspiration on topics of Jewish interest. He also pens a weekly column for *The Jerusalem Post.*

Currently, the Destiny Foundation is in the process of translating Rabbi Wein's riveting accounts of Jewish history into a series of films on Jewish personalities – the first, entitled *Rashi–A Light After The Dark Ages,* was released in 2000, and *Rambam–The Story of Maimonides* had its premiere in New York, in November 2004. Currently in production, the Destiny Foundation is preparing a 10-part documentary series, based on Rabbi Wein's history of the Jews in the twentieth century, *Faith & Fate.*

Rabbi Wein, a member of the Illinois Bar Association, received the Educator of the Year Award from the Covenant Foundation in 1993. Most recently, Rabbi Wein received the Torah Prize Award from Machon Harav Frank in Jerusalem for his achievements in teaching Torah and spreading Judaism throughout the world. Rabbi Wein and his wife now make their home in Jerusalem.

Photo Credits

Page XVI   Collection of the Israel Antiquities Authority,
© The Israel Museum, Jerusalem
Caption information from Steven Fine, "Rehov Synagogue Mosaic Floor,"
Printing the Talmud: From Bomberg to Schottenstein, Yeshiva University
Museum, The Center for Jewish History, New York, 2005.

Page 2   © The Library of the Jewish Theological Seminary

Page 5   © The Library of the Jewish Theological Seminary

Page 6   © The Library of the Jewish Theological Seminary

Page 7   © The Library of the Jewish Theological Seminary

Page 13   © The Israel Museum, Jerusalem

Page 20   © Bible Land Pictures Photo Archive

Page 22   © Reconstruction by Dr. Leen Ritmeyer

Page 26   © Beth Hatefutsoth, Photo Archive, Tel Aviv

Page 33   © Bible Land Pictures Photo Archive

Page 49   © Bible Land Pictures Photo Archive

Page 54   © Bible Land Pictures Photo Archive

Page 56   © The Israel Museum, Jerusalem

Page 62-63 © Bible Land Pictures Photo Archive

Page 68-69 © Bible Land Pictures Photo Archive

Page 70   © Bible Land Pictures Photo Archive